D1106462

WITHDRAWN

This book is a gift of

# THE FRIENDS
# OF THE
# MORAGA LIBRARY

Moraga Branch, Contra Costa County Library

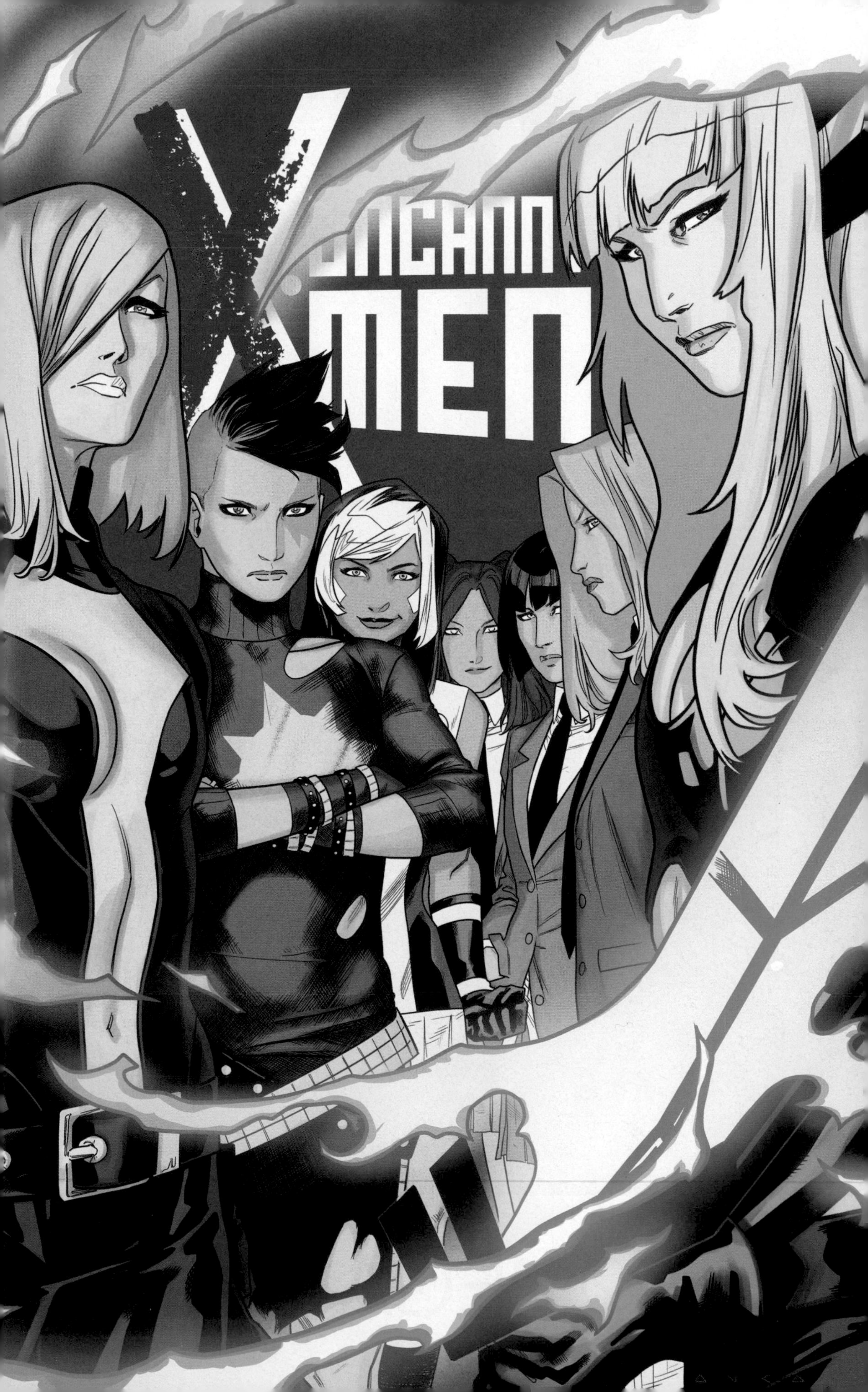
UNCANN
MEN

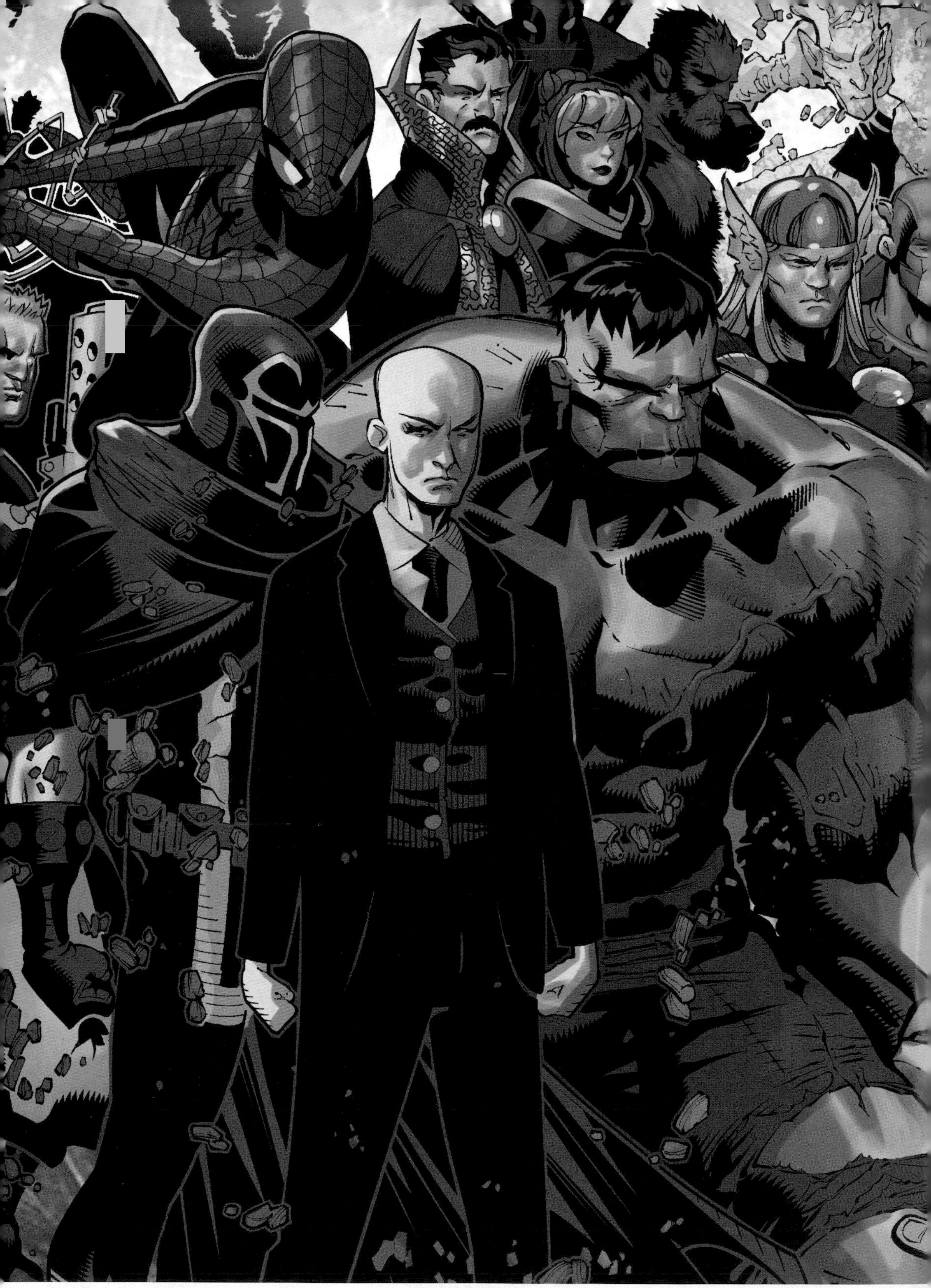

# THE OMEGA MUTANT

**CYCLOPS**
SCOTT SUMMERS

**EMMA FROST**

# UNCANNY X-MEN

**TRIAGE**
CHRISTOPHER MUSE

**TEMPUS**
EVA BELL

**MAGNETO**
ERIK LEHNSHERR

**MAGIK**
ILLYANA RASPUTIN

FABIO MEDIA

BENJAMIN DEEDS

BRIAN MICHAEL
## BENDIS
WRITER

CHRIS
## BACHALO
PENCILER, #27 & #29-31

KRIS
## ANKA
ART/COLORS, #26 & #28

MARC
## DEERING

WAYNE
## FAUCHER

MARK
## IRWIN

JAIME
## MENDOZA

VICTOR
## OLAZABA

TIM
## TOWNSEND

AL
## VEY

INKERS, #27 & #29-31

CHRIS
## BACHALO

RAIN
## BEREDO

ANTONIO
## FABELA

JOSE
## VILLARRUBIA

COLORISTS, #27 & #29-31

COVER ART: **CHRIS BACHALO & TIM TOWNSEND** (#26-27, #29, #31) AND **KRIS ANKA** (#28, #30)
LETTERER: **VC'S JOE CARAMAGNA**   ASSISTANT EDITOR: **XANDER JAROWEY**   EDITOR: **MIKE MARTS**

X-MEN CREATED BY **STAN LEE & JACK KIRBY**

COLLECTION EDITOR: **JENNIFER GRÜNWALD**  ASSOCIATE MANAGING EDITOR: **ALEX STARBUCK**
EDITOR, SPECIAL PROJECTS: **MARK D. BEAZLEY**  SENIOR EDITOR, SPECIAL PROJECTS: **JEFF YOUNGQUIST**
SVP PRINT, SALES & MARKETING: **DAVID GABRIEL**  BOOK DESIGNER: **RODOLFO MURAGUCHI**

EDITOR IN CHIEF: **AXEL ALONSO**  CHIEF CREATIVE OFFICER: **JOE QUESADA**
PUBLISHER: **DAN BUCKLEY**  EXECUTIVE PRODUCER: **ALAN FINE**

CANNY X-MEN VOL. 5: THE OMEGA MUTANT. Contains material originally published in magazine form as UNCANNY X-MEN #26-31. First printing 2015. ISBN# 978-0-7851-5490-7. Published by MARVEL WORLDWIDE,
., a subsidiary of MARVEL ENTERTAINMENT, LLC. OFFICE OF PUBLICATION: 135 West 50th Street, New York, NY 10020. Copyright © 2014 and 2015 Marvel Characters, Inc. All rights reserved. All characters featured
his issue and the distinctive names and likenesses thereof, and all related indicia are trademarks of Marvel Characters, Inc. No similarity between any of the names, characters, persons, and/or institutions in this
gazine with those of any living or dead person or institution is intended, and any such similarity which may exist is purely coincidental. **Printed in the U.S.A.** ALAN FINE, EVP - Office of the President, Marvel Worldwide,
, and EVP & CMO Marvel Characters B.V.; DAN BUCKLEY, Publisher & President - Print, Animation & Digital Divisions; JOE QUESADA, Chief Creative Officer; TOM BREVOORT, SVP of Publishing; DAVID BOGART, SVP of
erations & Procurement, Publishing; C.B. CEBULSKI, SVP of Creator & Content Development; DAVID GABRIEL, SVP Print, Sales & Marketing; JIM O'KEEFE, VP of Operations & Logistics; DAN CARR, Executive Director
Publishing Technology; SUSAN CRESPI, Editorial Operations Manager; ALEX MORALES, Publishing Operations Manager; STAN LEE, Chairman Emeritus. For information regarding advertising in Marvel Comics or on
rvel.com, please contact Niza Disla, Director of Marvel Partnerships, at ndisla@marvel.com. For Marvel subscription inquiries, please call 800-217-9158. **Manufactured between 1/23/2015 and 3/9/2015 by R.R.
NNELLEY, INC., SALEM, VA, USA.**

Born with genetic mutations that gave them abilities beyond those of normal humans, mutants are the next stage in evolution. As such, they are feared and hated by humanity. A group of mutants known as the X-Men fight for peaceful coexistence between mutants and humankind. But not all mutants see peaceful coexistence as a reality.

Cyclops is the public face of what he calls "the new mutant revolution." Vowing to protect the mutant race, he's begun to gather and train a new generation of young mutants.

Recently, She-Hulk arrived at the Jean Grey School for higher learning with a startling pacakage for the X-Men, the last will and testament of Charles Xavier! Appearing as a hologram, Xavier revealed that at the time of his death, he was married to Raven Darkholme, A.K.A. Mystique. When he first developed Cerebro, Xavier discovered a mutant, Matthew Malloy, whose abilities were so great and terrifying that he was forced to erase the young man's memory of his powers. With his death, the mental blocks that Xavier had been keeping in place have been weakening, leaving the X-Men with the task of finding and securing Matthew before the threat he poses becomes real. Little do they know that Matthew's re-emerging powers have already brought him to the attention of S.H.I.E.L.D.!

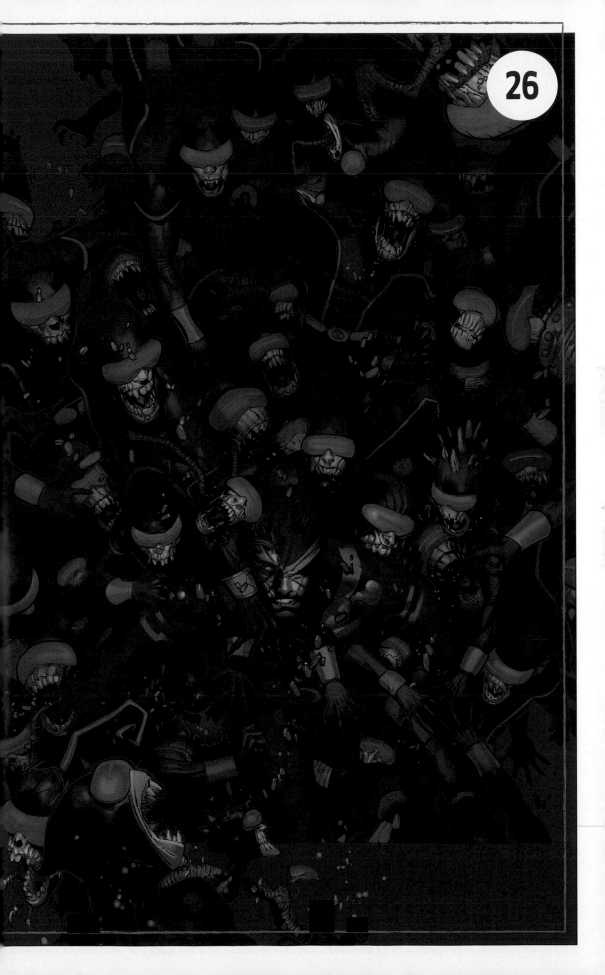

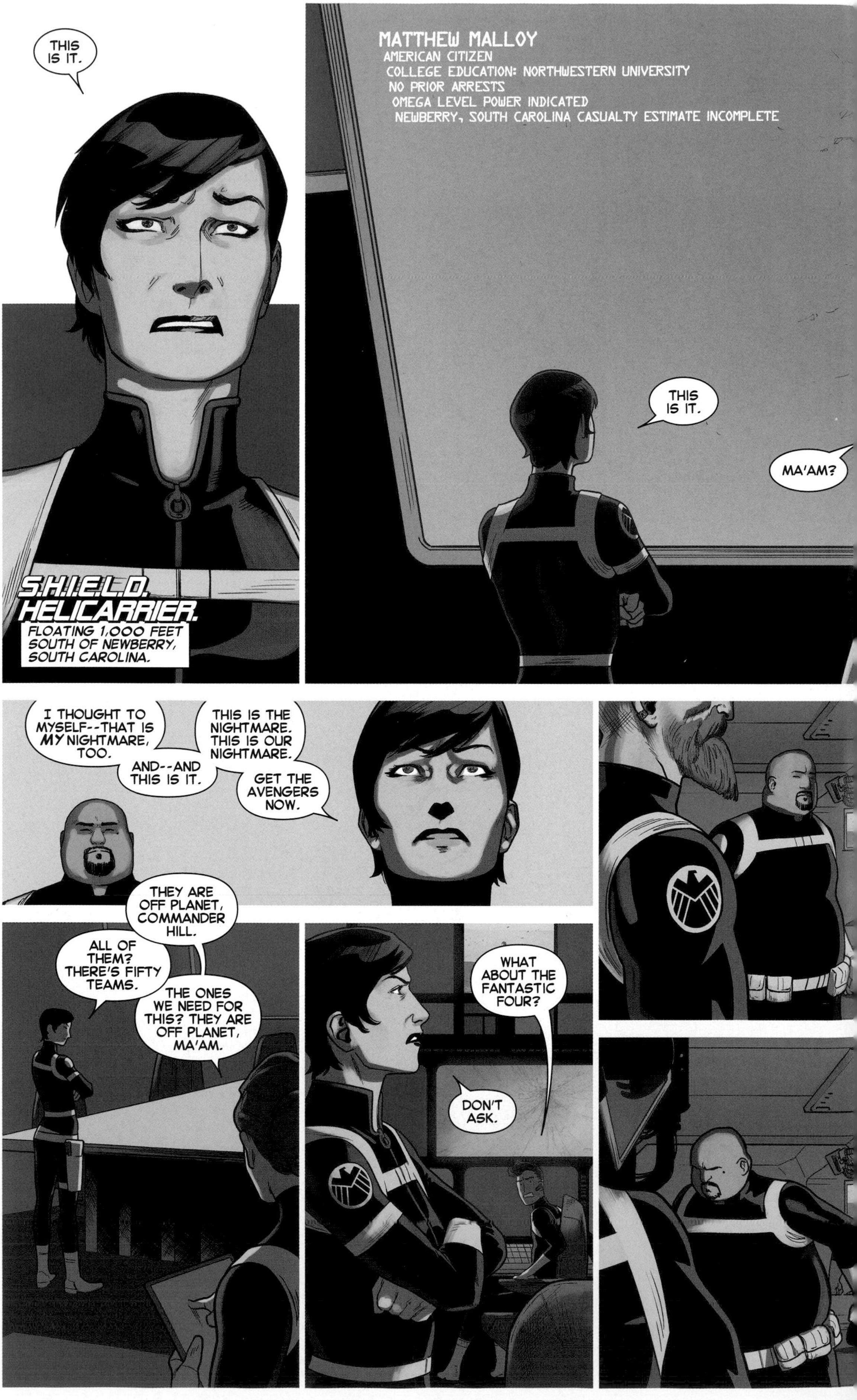
THIS IS IT.
MATTHEW MALLOY
AMERICAN CITIZEN
COLLEGE EDUCATION: NORTHWESTERN UNIVERSITY
NO PRIOR ARRESTS
OMEGA LEVEL POWER INDICATED
NEWBERRY, SOUTH CAROLINA CASUALTY ESTIMATE INCOMPLETE
S.H.I.E.L.D. HELICARRIER.
FLOATING 1,000 FEET SOUTH OF NEWBERRY, SOUTH CAROLINA.
THIS IS IT.
MA'AM?
I THOUGHT TO MYSELF--THAT IS MY NIGHTMARE, TOO.
AND--AND THIS IS IT.
THIS IS THE NIGHTMARE. THIS IS OUR NIGHTMARE.
GET THE AVENGERS NOW.
THEY ARE OFF PLANET, COMMANDER HILL.
ALL OF THEM? THERE'S FIFTY TEAMS.
THE ONES WE NEED FOR THIS? THEY ARE OFF PLANET, MA'AM.
WHAT ABOUT THE FANTASTIC FOUR?
DON'T ASK.

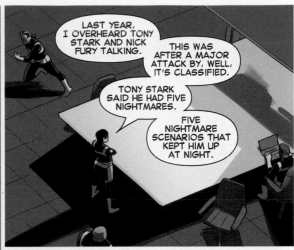

LAST YEAR, I OVERHEARD TONY STARK AND NICK FURY TALKING.

THIS WAS AFTER A MAJOR ATTACK BY, WELL, IT'S CLASSIFIED.

TONY STARK SAID HE HAD FIVE NIGHTMARES.

FIVE NIGHTMARE SCENARIOS THAT KEPT HIM UP AT NIGHT.

BEFORE HE COULD EVER SAY WHAT THEY WERE FURY SNARLED BACK AT HIM-- I ONLY GOT *ONE* NIGHTMARE.

MY NIGHTMARE IS THAT SOME GUY, JUST SOME GUY, WAKES UP ONE MORNING WITH THE POWER OF *GOD.*

HE DOESN'T KNOW HOW HE GOT IT, HE DOESN'T KNOW WHAT TO DO WITH IT, AND HE JUST $#%&$#% HICCUPS AND THOUSANDS OF PEOPLE $#%&$#% DIE.

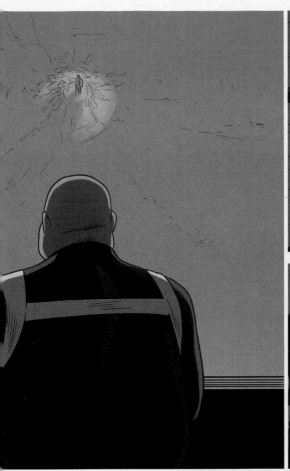

EVACUATE THE ENTIRE STATE OF SOUTH CAROLINA!

MA'AM?

YOU HEARD ME.

THERE IS AN OMEGA THREAT PROTOCOL!

FIRST STEP IS EVACUATION!

QUICKLY AND QUIETLY EMPTY THE ENTIRE STATE.

I DON'T CARE WHERE THEY GO OR WHERE YOU PUT THEM...

...NOBODY ELSE DIES TODAY.

"NO!"

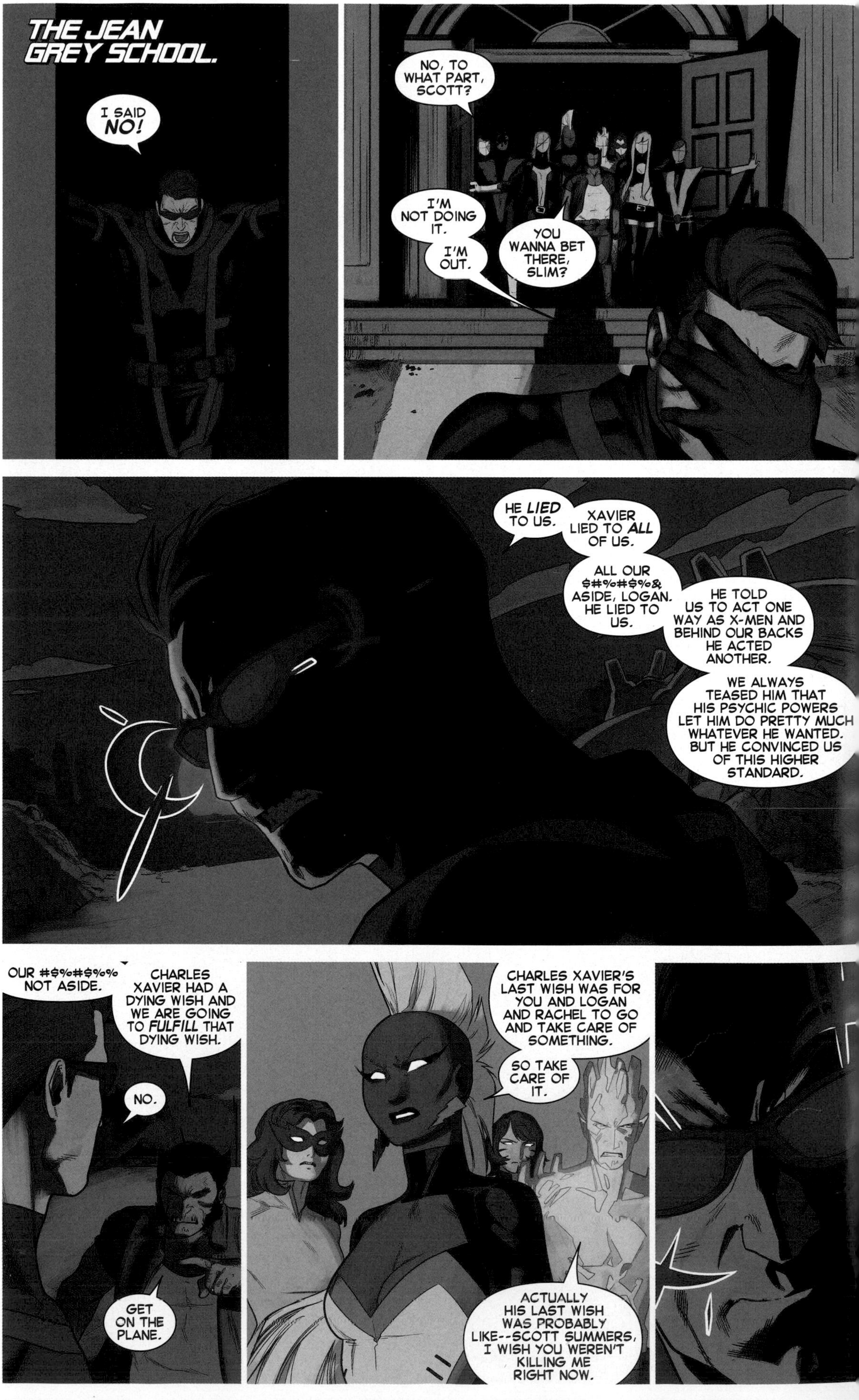

THE JEAN GREY SCHOOL.
I SAID NO!
NO, TO WHAT PART, SCOTT?
I'M NOT DOING IT.
I'M OUT.
YOU WANNA BET THERE, SLIM?
HE LIED TO US.
XAVIER LIED TO ALL OF US.
ALL OUR $#%#$%& ASIDE, LOGAN. HE LIED TO US.
HE TOLD US TO ACT ONE WAY AS X-MEN AND BEHIND OUR BACKS HE ACTED ANOTHER.
WE ALWAYS TEASED HIM THAT HIS PSYCHIC POWERS LET HIM DO PRETTY MUCH WHATEVER HE WANTED. BUT HE CONVINCED US OF THIS HIGHER STANDARD.
OUR #$%#$%% NOT ASIDE.
CHARLES XAVIER HAD A DYING WISH AND WE ARE GOING TO FULFILL THAT DYING WISH.
NO.
GET ON THE PLANE.
CHARLES XAVIER'S LAST WISH WAS FOR YOU AND LOGAN AND RACHEL TO GO AND TAKE CARE OF SOMETHING.
SO TAKE CARE OF IT.
ACTUALLY HIS LAST WISH WAS PROBABLY LIKE--SCOTT SUMMERS, I WISH YOU WEREN'T KILLING ME RIGHT NOW.

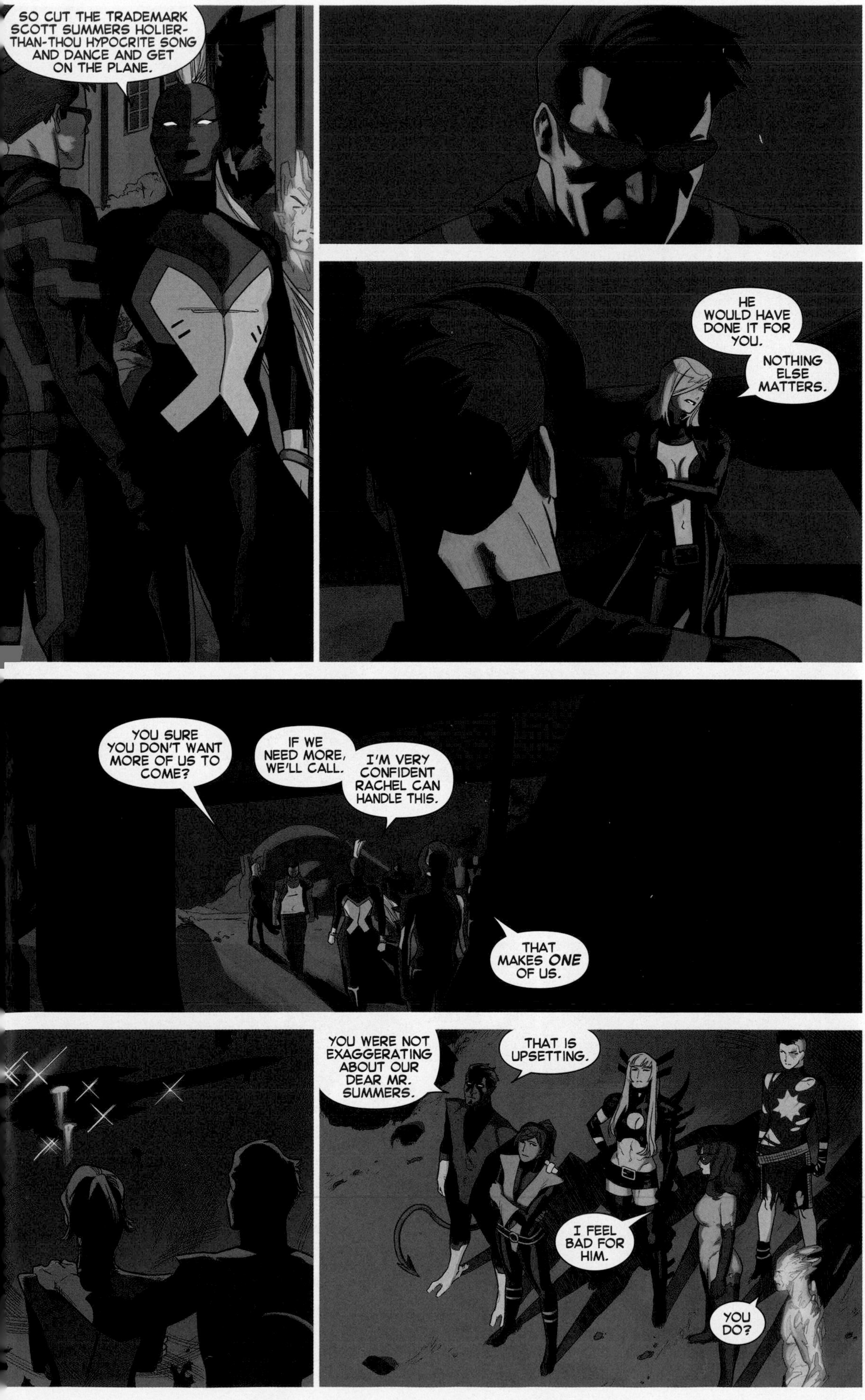
SO CUT THE TRADEMARK SCOTT SUMMERS HOLIER-THAN-THOU HYPOCRITE SONG AND DANCE AND GET ON THE PLANE.
HE WOULD HAVE DONE IT FOR YOU.
NOTHING ELSE MATTERS.
YOU SURE YOU DON'T WANT MORE OF US TO COME?
IF WE NEED MORE, WE'LL CALL.
I'M VERY CONFIDENT RACHEL CAN HANDLE THIS.
THAT MAKES ONE OF US.
YOU WERE NOT EXAGGERATING ABOUT OUR DEAR MR. SUMMERS.
THAT IS UPSETTING.
I FEEL BAD FOR HIM.
YOU DO?

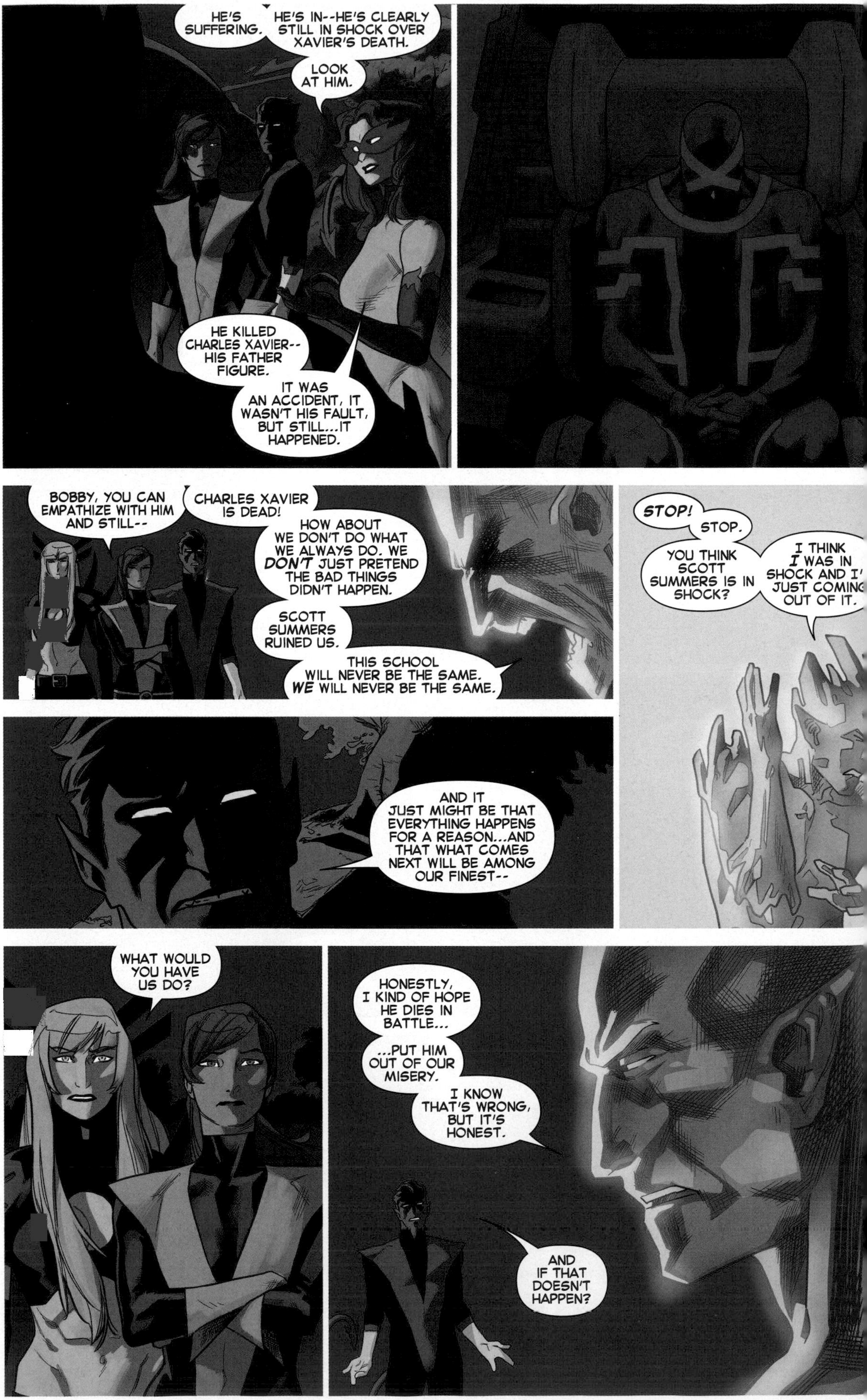
HE'S SUFFERING.
HE'S IN--HE'S CLEARLY STILL IN SHOCK OVER XAVIER'S DEATH.
LOOK AT HIM.
HE KILLED CHARLES XAVIER-- HIS FATHER FIGURE.
IT WAS AN ACCIDENT, IT WASN'T HIS FAULT, BUT STILL...IT HAPPENED.
BOBBY, YOU CAN EMPATHIZE WITH HIM AND STILL--
CHARLES XAVIER IS DEAD!
HOW ABOUT WE DON'T DO WHAT WE ALWAYS DO. WE *DON'T* JUST PRETEND THE BAD THINGS DIDN'T HAPPEN.
SCOTT SUMMERS RUINED US.
THIS SCHOOL WILL NEVER BE THE SAME. *WE* WILL NEVER BE THE SAME.
AND IT JUST MIGHT BE THAT EVERYTHING HAPPENS FOR A REASON...AND THAT WHAT COMES NEXT WILL BE AMONG OUR FINEST--
*STOP!*
STOP.
YOU THINK SCOTT SUMMERS IS IN SHOCK?
I THINK *I* WAS IN SHOCK AND I' JUST COMING OUT OF IT.
WHAT WOULD YOU HAVE US DO?
HONESTLY, I KIND OF HOPE HE DIES IN BATTLE...
...PUT HIM OUT OF OUR MISERY.
I KNOW THAT'S WRONG, BUT IT'S HONEST.
AND IF THAT DOESN'T HAPPEN?

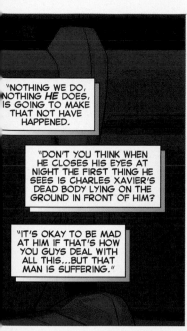

"NOTHING WE DO, NOTHING *HE* DOES, IS GOING TO MAKE THAT NOT HAVE HAPPENED.

"DON'T YOU THINK WHEN HE CLOSES HIS EYES AT NIGHT THE FIRST THING HE SEES IS CHARLES XAVIER'S DEAD BODY LYING ON THE GROUND IN FRONT OF HIM?

"IT'S OKAY TO BE MAD AT HIM IF THAT'S HOW YOU GUYS DEAL WITH ALL THIS...BUT THAT MAN IS SUFFERING."

DON'T YOU THINK HE--

PLEASE, ANGELICA, DON'T!

DON'T MAKE ME SYMPATHIZE WITH SCOTT SUMMERS' PLIGHT.

DON'T MAKE ME FEEL BAD FOR HIM!

MAYBE IT'S LOOKING AT XAVIER'S HOLOGRAM TODAY OR HEARING HIS CRAZINESS THAT HE MARRIED MYSTIQUE.

BUT I'M ANGRY!

I'M REALLY, REALLY ANGRY THAT SCOTT SUMMERS MURDERED THE MAN WHO GAVE ME THIS LIFE!

GAVE MY ENTIRE LIFE PURPOSE!

I'M ANGRY!

AND I'M GETTING ANGRIER BY THE SECOND!

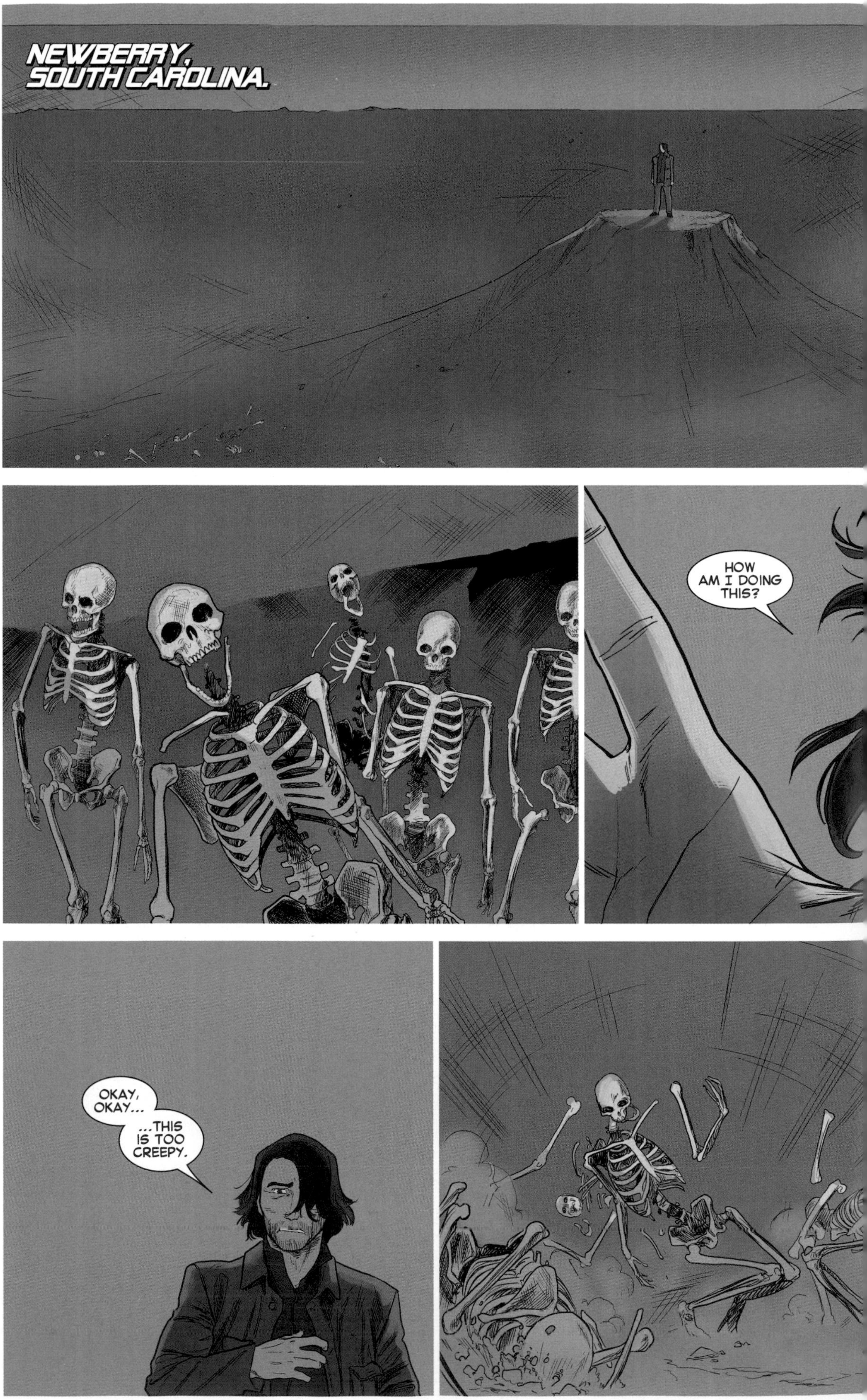
NEWBERRY, SOUTH CAROLINA.
HOW AM I DOING THIS?
OKAY, OKAY...
...THIS IS TOO CREEPY.

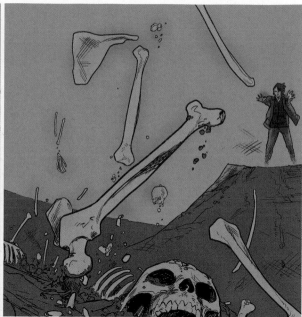

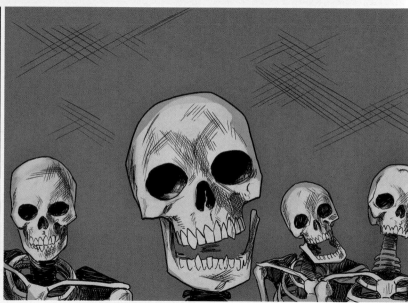

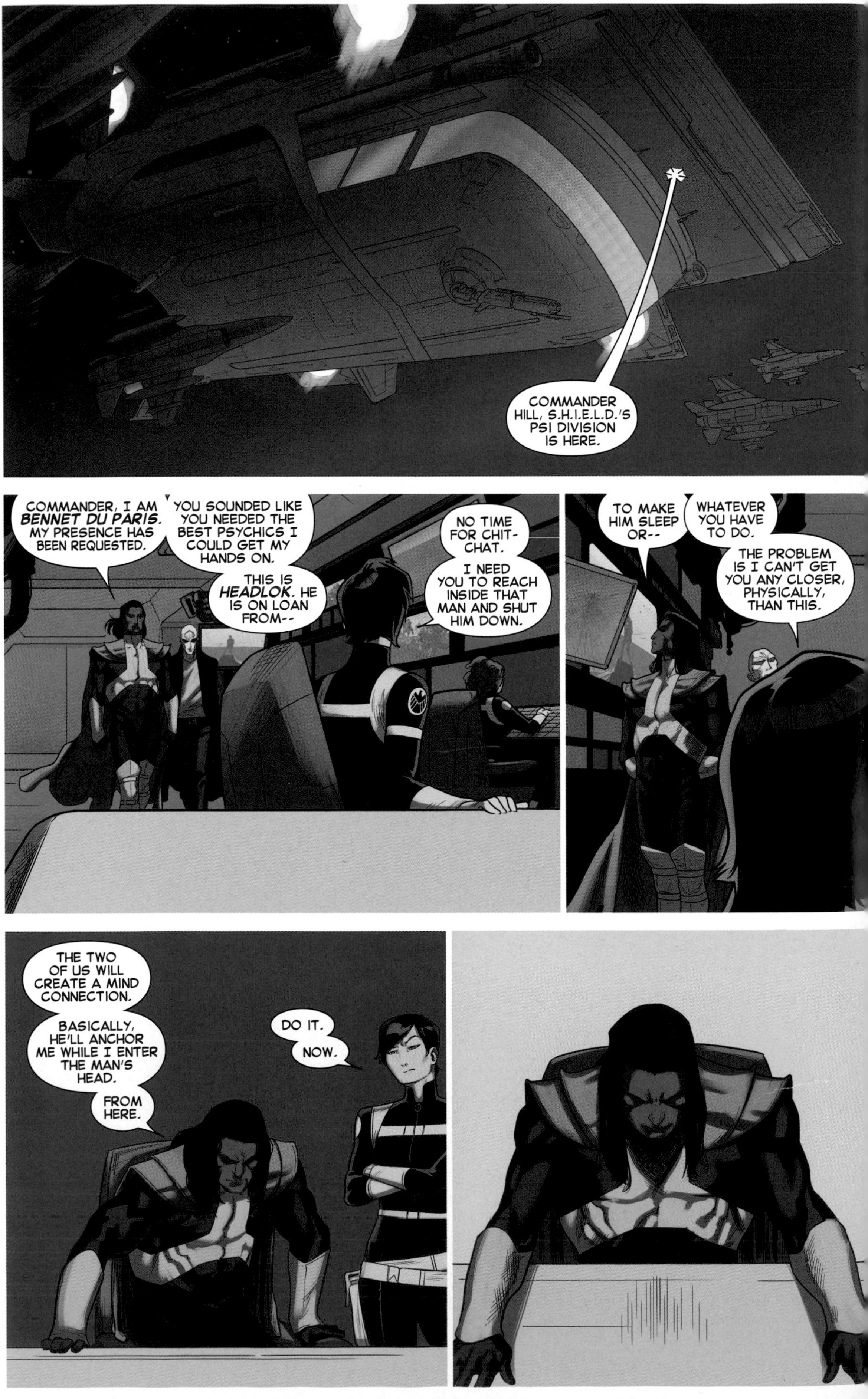
COMMANDER HILL, S.H.I.E.L.D.'S PSI DIVISION IS HERE.
COMMANDER, I AM BENNET DU PARIS. MY PRESENCE HAS BEEN REQUESTED.
YOU SOUNDED LIKE YOU NEEDED THE BEST PSYCHICS I COULD GET MY HANDS ON.
THIS IS HEADLOK. HE IS ON LOAN FROM--
NO TIME FOR CHIT-CHAT.
I NEED YOU TO REACH INSIDE THAT MAN AND SHUT HIM DOWN.
TO MAKE HIM SLEEP OR--
WHATEVER YOU HAVE TO DO.
THE PROBLEM IS I CAN'T GET YOU ANY CLOSER, PHYSICALLY, THAN THIS.
THE TWO OF US WILL CREATE A MIND CONNECTION.
BASICALLY, HE'LL ANCHOR ME WHILE I ENTER THE MAN'S HEAD.
FROM HERE.
DO IT.
NOW.

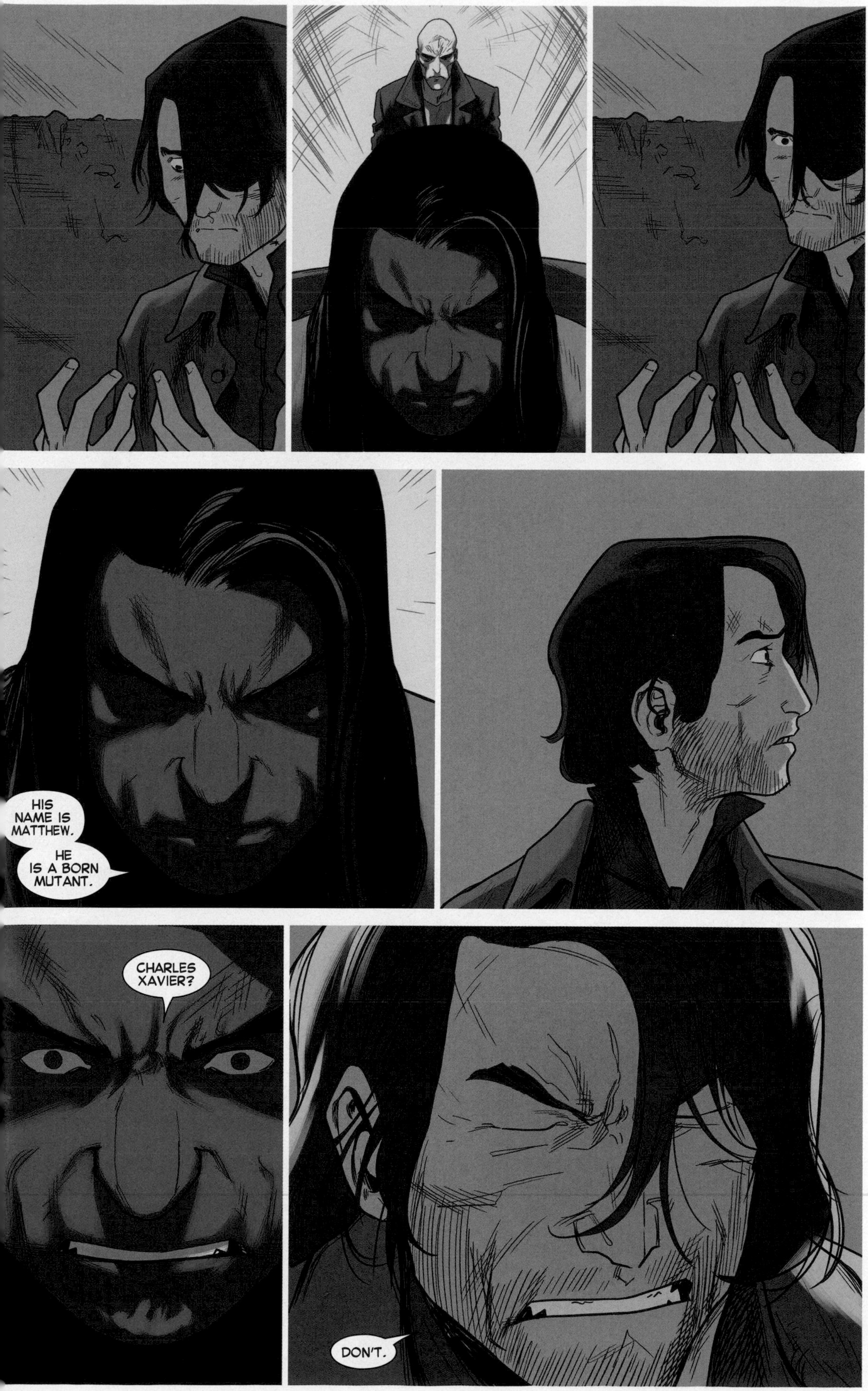
HIS NAME IS MATTHEW.
HE IS A BORN MUTANT.
CHARLES XAVIER?
DON'T.

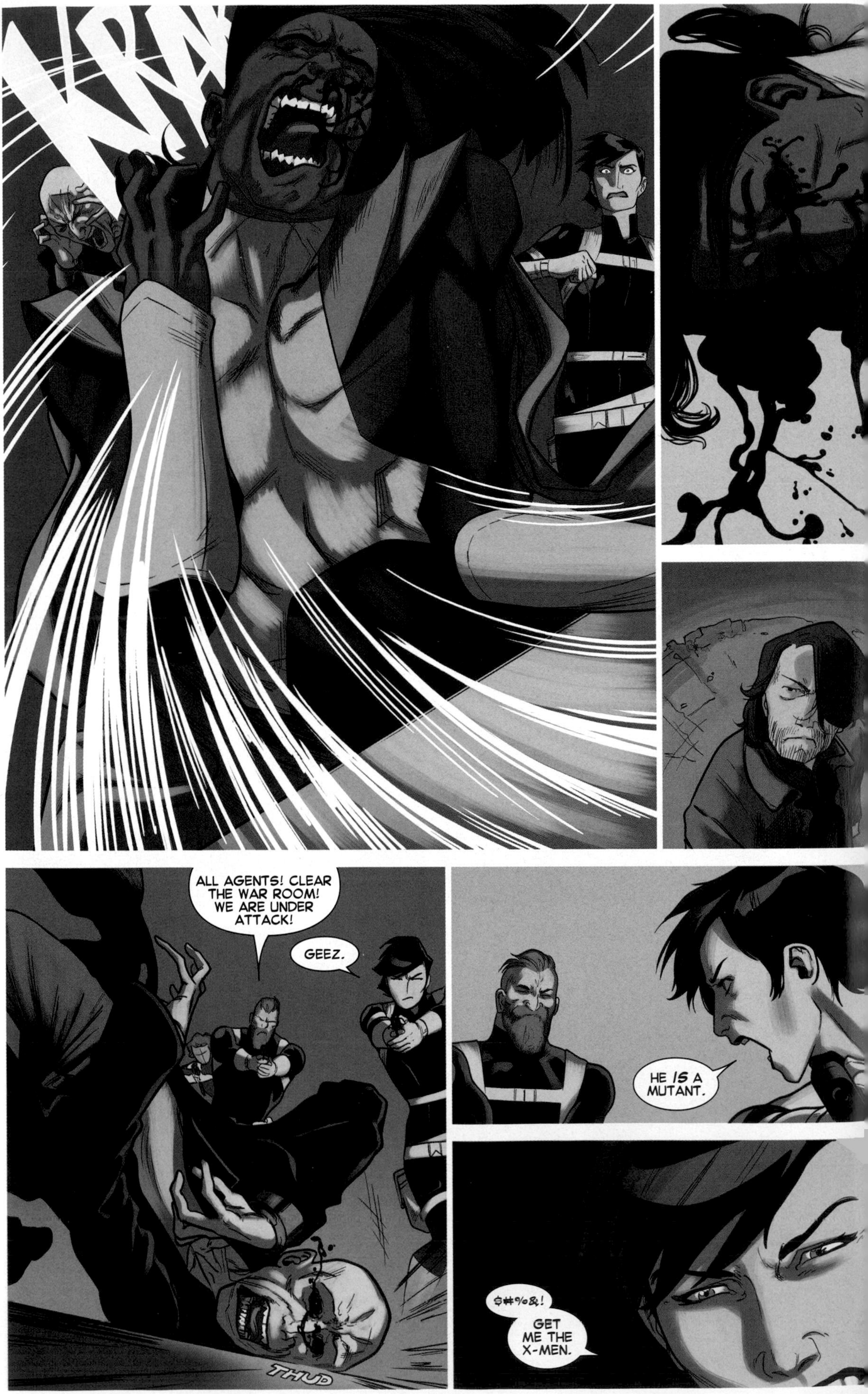
ALL AGENTS! CLEAR THE WAR ROOM! WE ARE UNDER ATTACK!
GEEZ.
THUD
HE *IS* A MUTANT.
$#%&!
GET ME THE X-MEN.

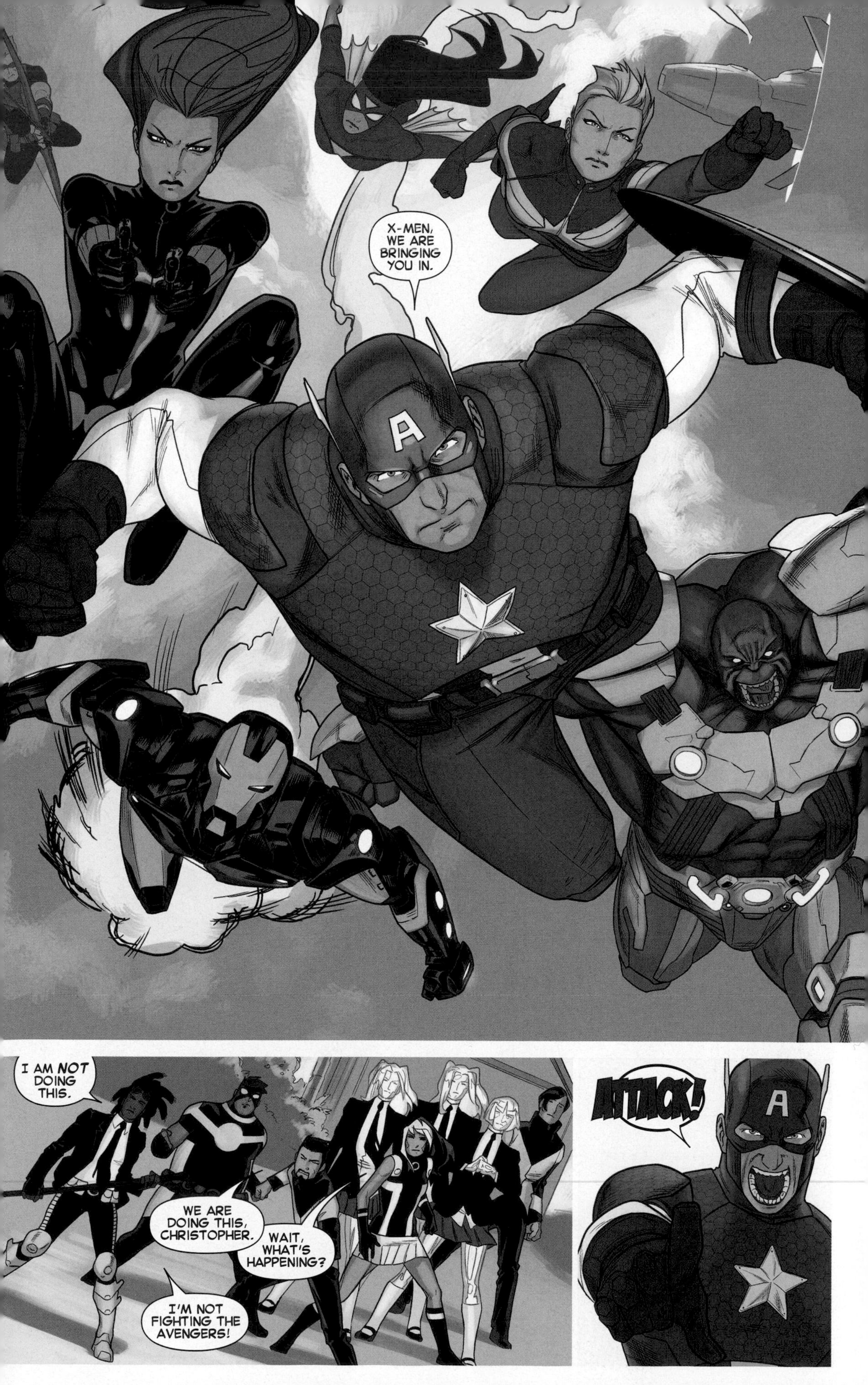
X-MEN, WE ARE BRINGING YOU IN.
I AM *NOT* DOING THIS.
WE ARE DOING THIS, CHRISTOPHER.
WAIT, WHAT'S HAPPENING?
I'M NOT FIGHTING THE AVENGERS!
ATTACK!

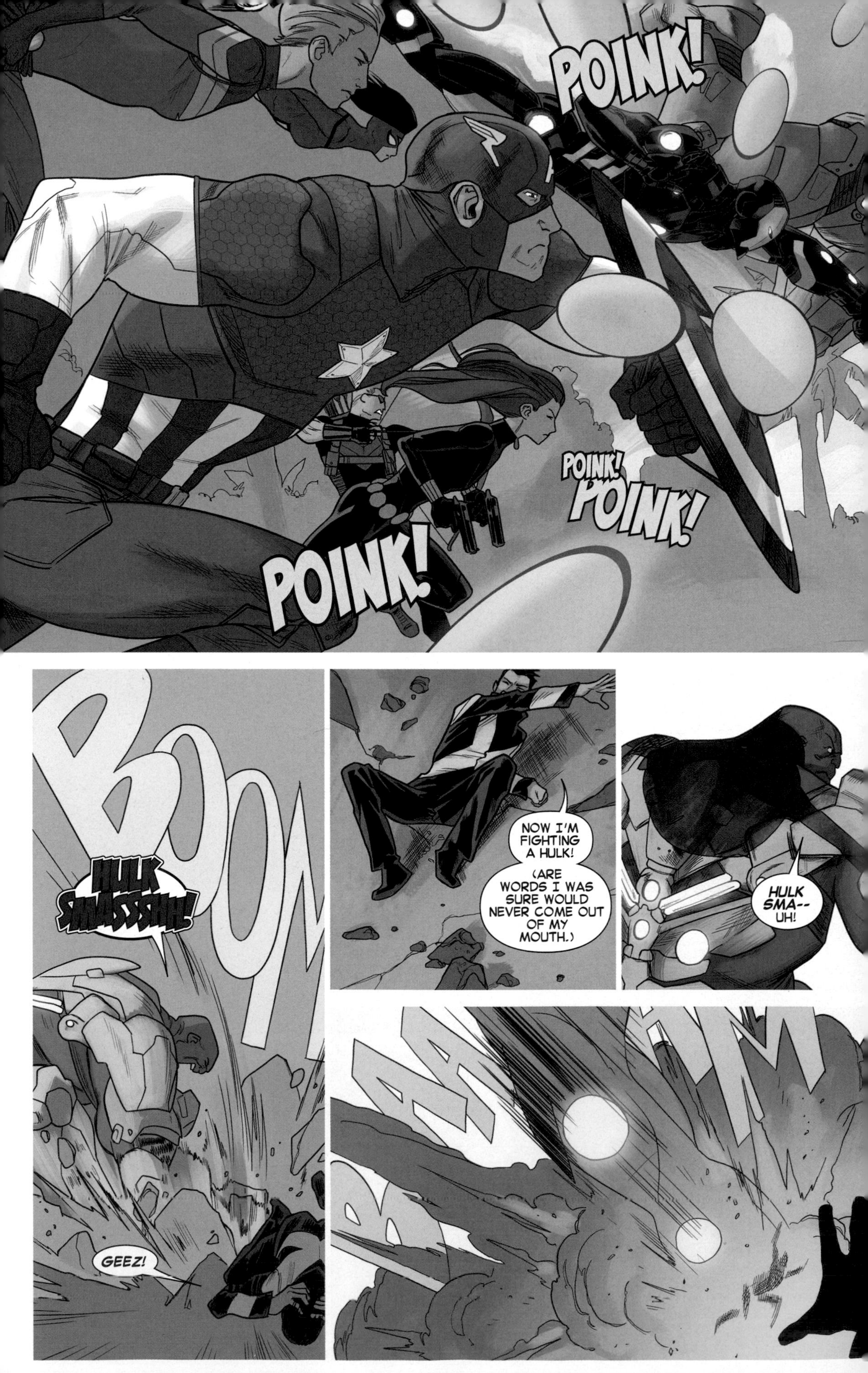
POINK!
POINK!
POINK!
POINK!
HULK SMASSSHH!
GEEZ!
NOW I'M FIGHTING A HULK!
(ARE WORDS I WAS SURE WOULD NEVER COME OUT OF MY MOUTH.)
HULK SMA-- UH!

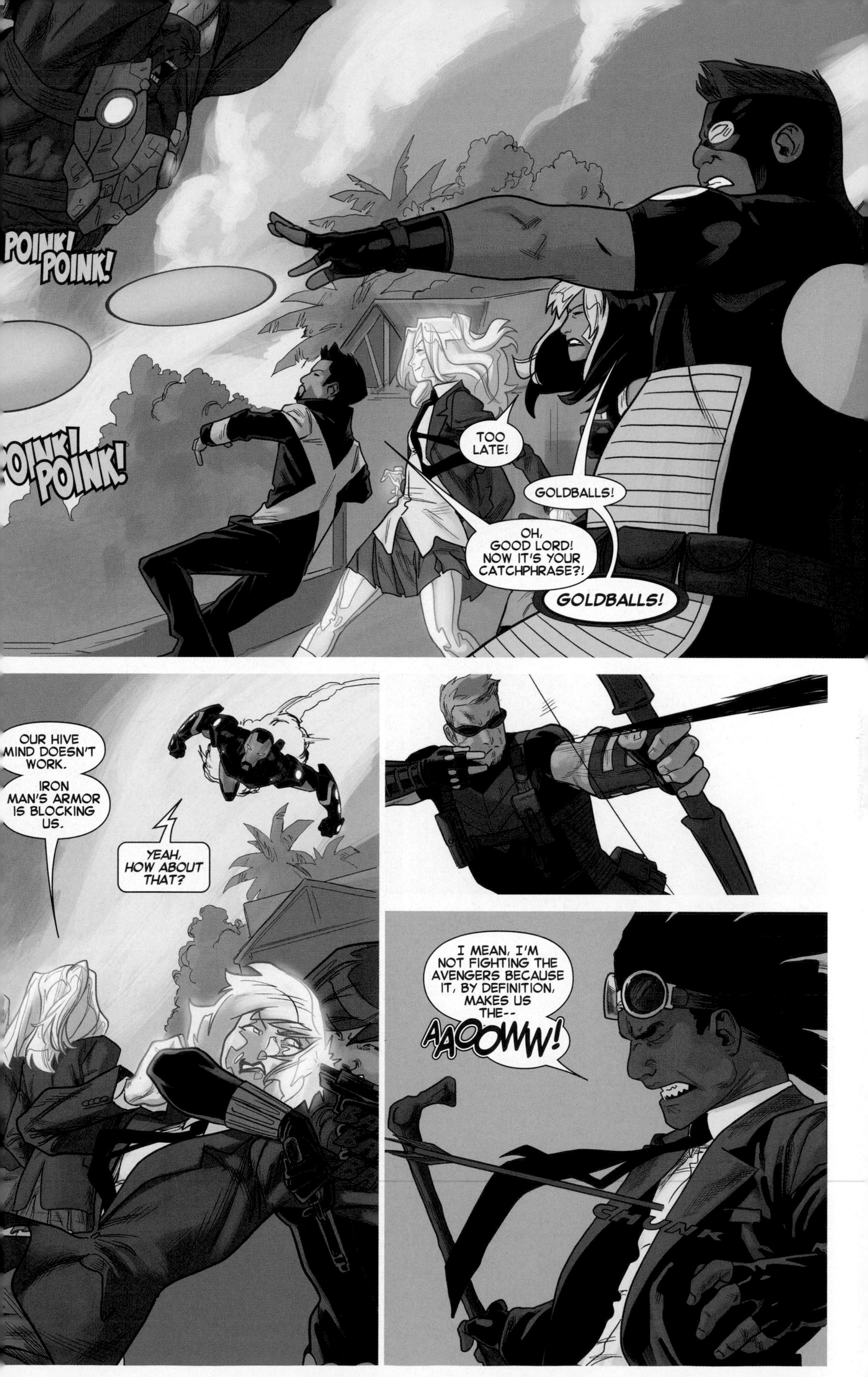
POINK! POINK!
POINK! POINK!
TOO LATE!
GOLDBALLS!
OH, GOOD LORD! NOW IT'S YOUR CATCHPHRASE?!
GOLDBALLS!
OUR HIVE MIND DOESN'T WORK.
IRON MAN'S ARMOR IS BLOCKING US.
YEAH, HOW ABOUT THAT?
I MEAN, I'M NOT FIGHTING THE AVENGERS BECAUSE IT, BY DEFINITION, MAKES US THE--
AAOOWW!
CHUNK

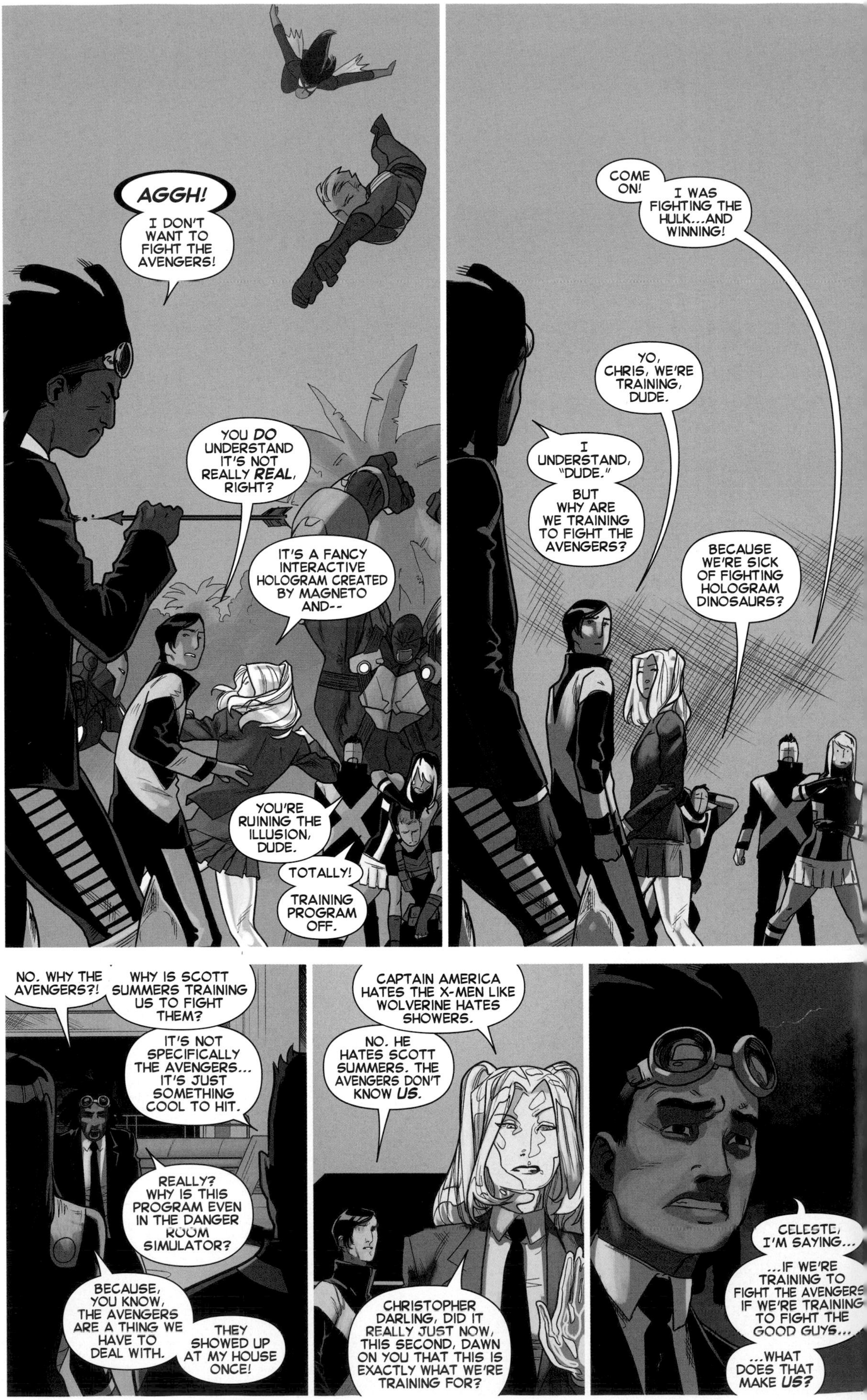
AGGH!
I DON'T WANT TO FIGHT THE AVENGERS!
YOU DO UNDERSTAND IT'S NOT REALLY REAL, RIGHT?
IT'S A FANCY INTERACTIVE HOLOGRAM CREATED BY MAGNETO AND--
YOU'RE RUINING THE ILLUSION, DUDE.
TOTALLY!
TRAINING PROGRAM OFF.
COME ON!
I WAS FIGHTING THE HULK...AND WINNING!
YO, CHRIS, WE'RE TRAINING, DUDE.
I UNDERSTAND, "DUDE."
BUT WHY ARE WE TRAINING TO FIGHT THE AVENGERS?
BECAUSE WE'RE SICK OF FIGHTING HOLOGRAM DINOSAURS?
NO. WHY THE AVENGERS?!
WHY IS SCOTT SUMMERS TRAINING US TO FIGHT THEM?
IT'S NOT SPECIFICALLY THE AVENGERS... IT'S JUST SOMETHING COOL TO HIT.
REALLY? WHY IS THIS PROGRAM EVEN IN THE DANGER ROOM SIMULATOR?
BECAUSE, YOU KNOW, THE AVENGERS ARE A THING WE HAVE TO DEAL WITH.
THEY SHOWED UP AT MY HOUSE ONCE!
CAPTAIN AMERICA HATES THE X-MEN LIKE WOLVERINE HATES SHOWERS.
NO. HE HATES SCOTT SUMMERS. THE AVENGERS DON'T KNOW US.
CHRISTOPHER DARLING, DID IT REALLY JUST NOW, THIS SECOND, DAWN ON YOU THAT THIS IS EXACTLY WHAT WE'RE TRAINING FOR?
CELESTE, I'M SAYING...
...IF WE'RE TRAINING TO FIGHT THE AVENGERS IF WE'RE TRAINING TO FIGHT THE GOOD GUYS...
...WHAT DOES THAT MAKE US?

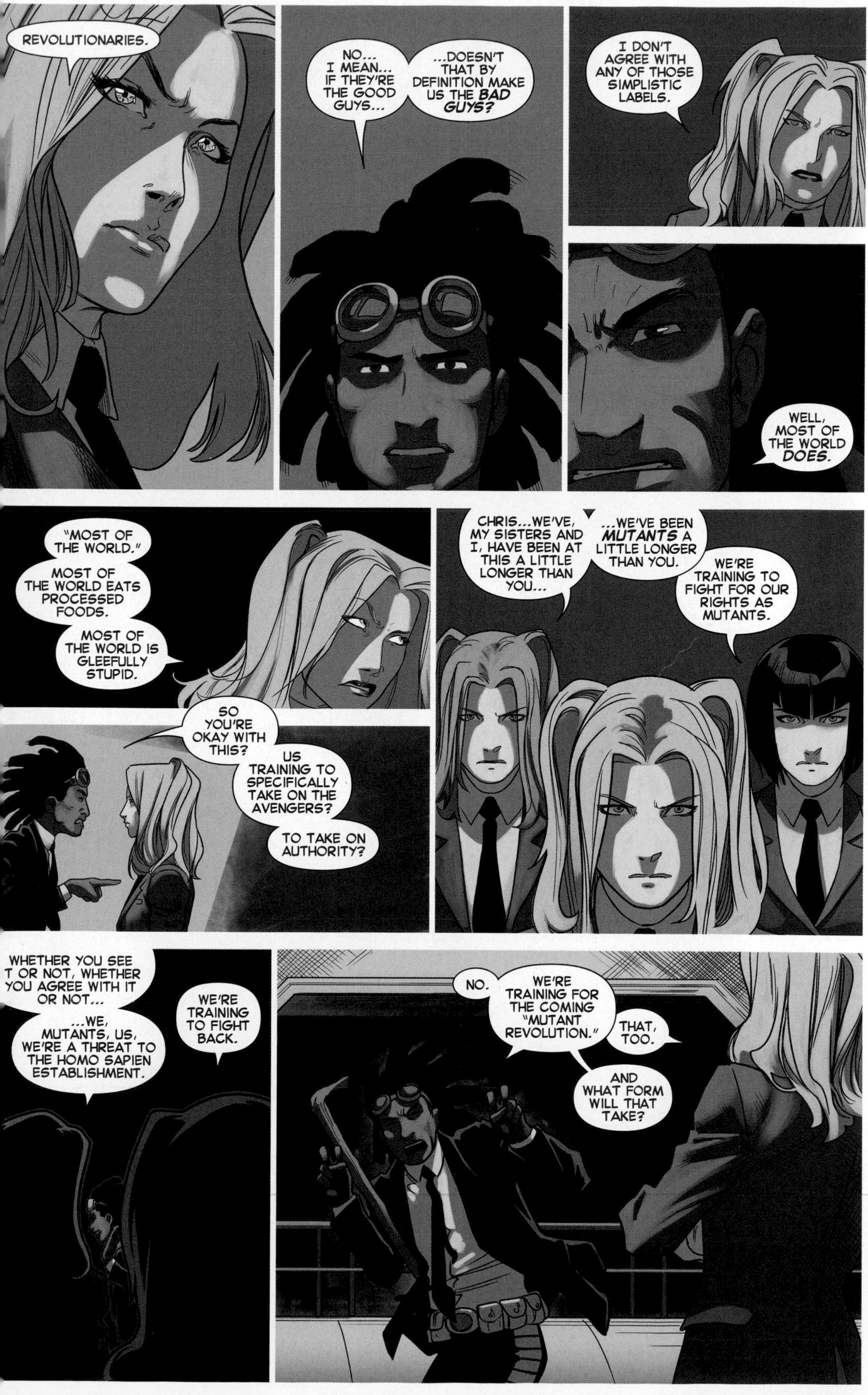

REVOLUTIONARIES.
NO... I MEAN... IF THEY'RE THE GOOD GUYS...
...DOESN'T THAT BY DEFINITION MAKE US THE *BAD GUYS?*
I DON'T AGREE WITH ANY OF THOSE SIMPLISTIC LABELS.
WELL, MOST OF THE WORLD *DOES.*
"MOST OF THE WORLD."
MOST OF THE WORLD EATS PROCESSED FOODS.
MOST OF THE WORLD IS GLEEFULLY STUPID.
SO YOU'RE OKAY WITH THIS?
US TRAINING TO SPECIFICALLY TAKE ON THE AVENGERS?
TO TAKE ON AUTHORITY?
CHRIS...WE'VE, MY SISTERS AND I, HAVE BEEN AT THIS A LITTLE LONGER THAN YOU...
...WE'VE BEEN *MUTANTS* A LITTLE LONGER THAN YOU.
WE'RE TRAINING TO FIGHT FOR OUR RIGHTS AS MUTANTS.
WHETHER YOU SEE T OR NOT, WHETHER YOU AGREE WITH IT OR NOT...
...WE, MUTANTS, US, WE'RE A THREAT TO THE HOMO SAPIEN ESTABLISHMENT.
WE'RE TRAINING TO FIGHT BACK.
NO.
WE'RE TRAINING FOR THE COMING "MUTANT REVOLUTION."
THAT, TOO.
AND WHAT FORM WILL THAT TAKE?

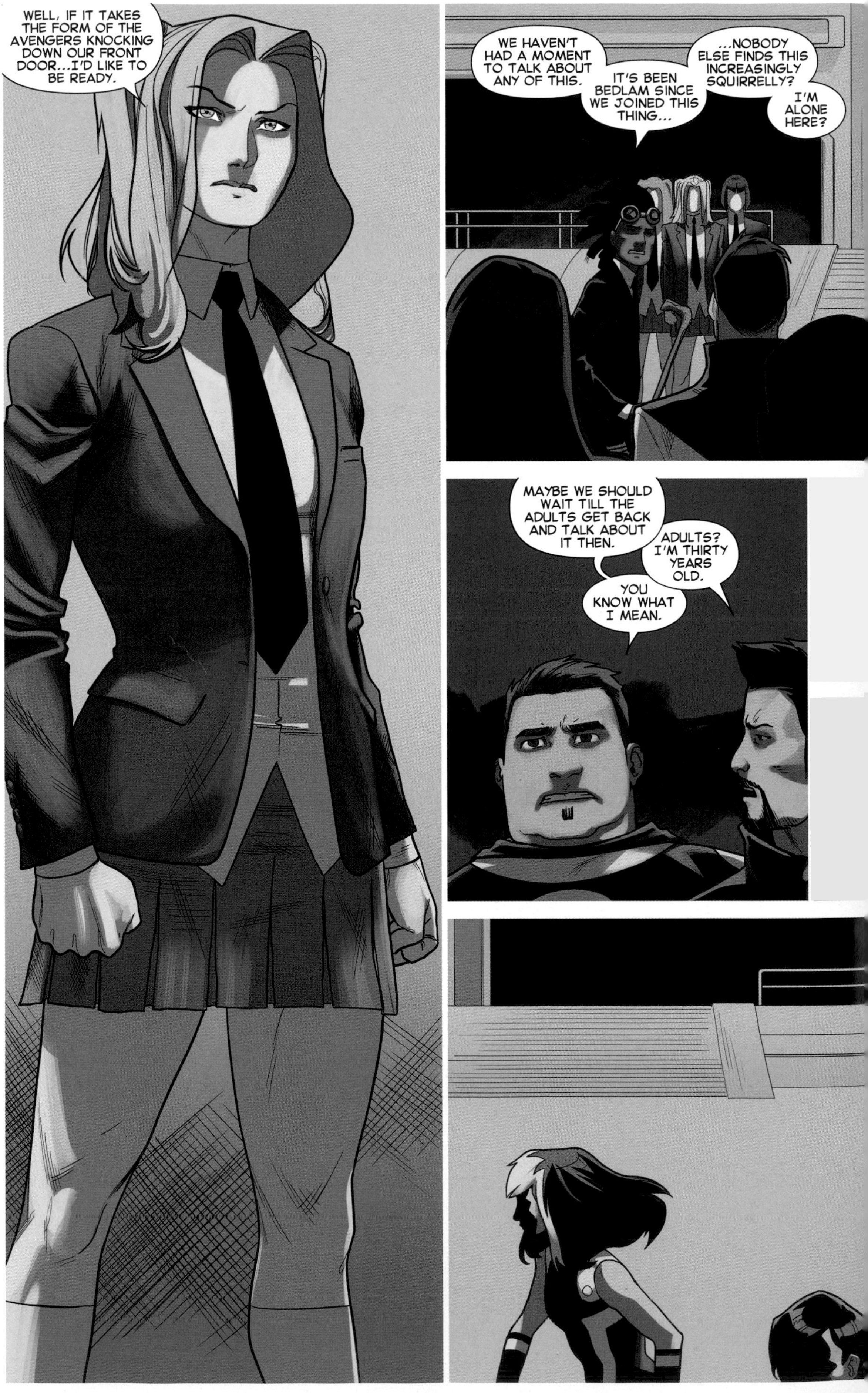
WELL, IF IT TAKES THE FORM OF THE AVENGERS KNOCKING DOWN OUR FRONT DOOR...I'D LIKE TO BE READY.
WE HAVEN'T HAD A MOMENT TO TALK ABOUT ANY OF THIS.
IT'S BEEN BEDLAM SINCE WE JOINED THIS THING...
...NOBODY ELSE FINDS THIS INCREASINGLY SQUIRRELLY?
I'M ALONE HERE?
MAYBE WE SHOULD WAIT TILL THE ADULTS GET BACK AND TALK ABOUT IT THEN.
ADULTS? I'M THIRTY YEARS OLD.
YOU KNOW WHAT I MEAN.

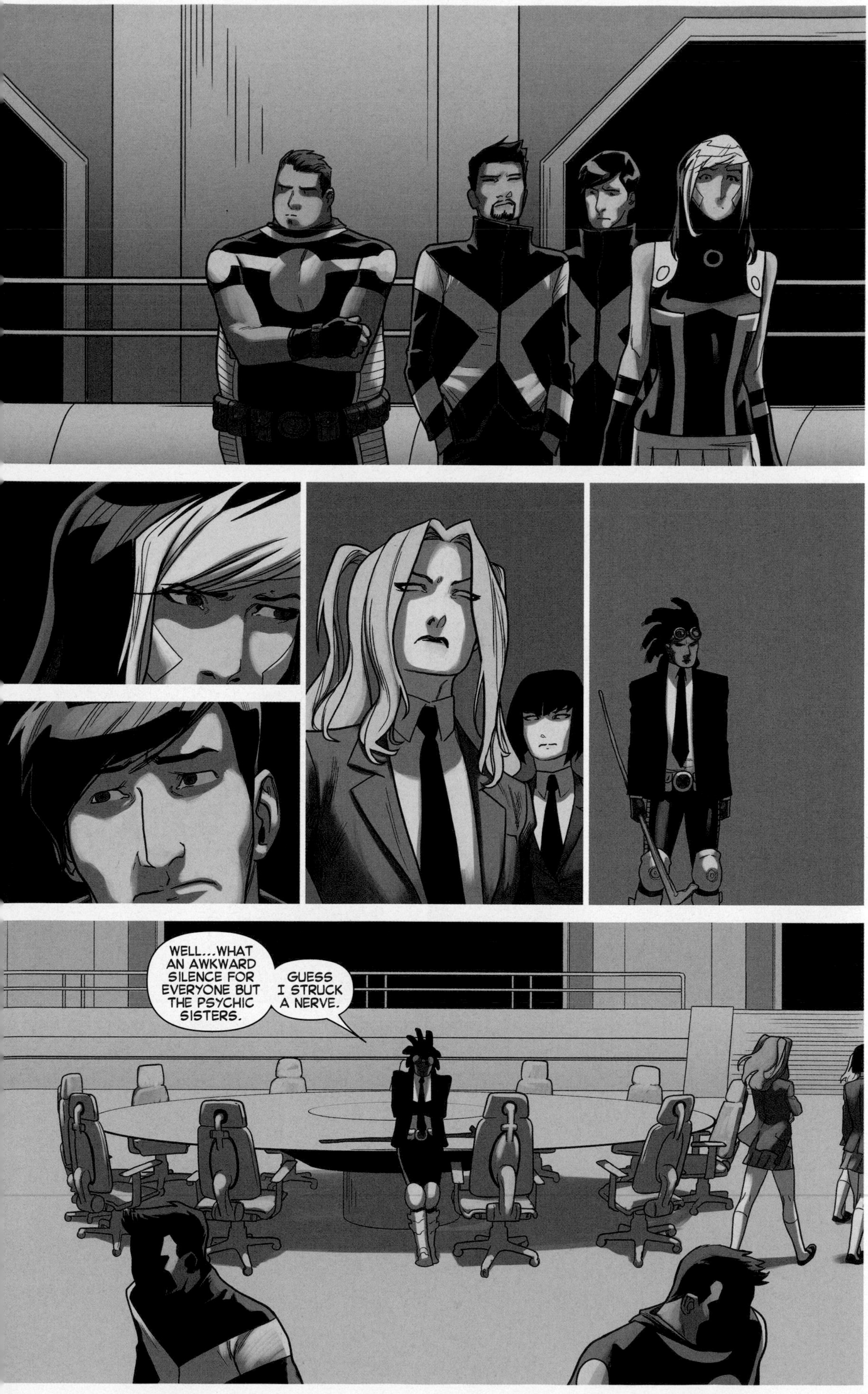
WELL...WHAT AN AWKWARD SILENCE FOR EVERYONE BUT THE PSYCHIC SISTERS.
GUESS I STRUCK A NERVE.

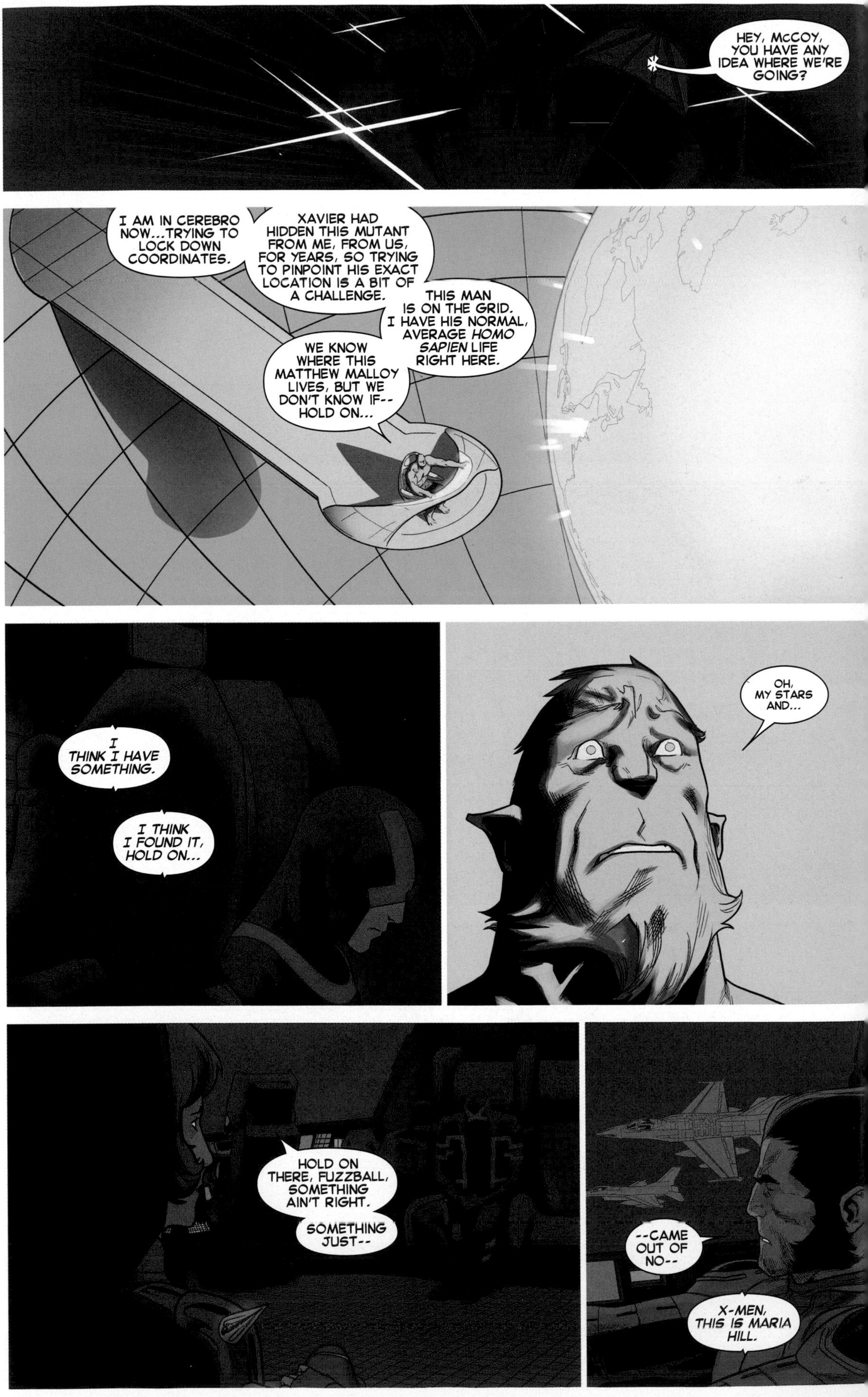
HEY, McCOY, YOU HAVE ANY IDEA WHERE WE'RE GOING?
I AM IN CEREBRO NOW...TRYING TO LOCK DOWN COORDINATES.
XAVIER HAD HIDDEN THIS MUTANT FROM ME, FROM US, FOR YEARS, SO TRYING TO PINPOINT HIS EXACT LOCATION IS A BIT OF A CHALLENGE.
THIS MAN IS ON THE GRID. I HAVE HIS NORMAL, AVERAGE HOMO SAPIEN LIFE RIGHT HERE.
WE KNOW WHERE THIS MATTHEW MALLOY LIVES, BUT WE DON'T KNOW IF-- HOLD ON...
I THINK I HAVE SOMETHING.
I THINK I FOUND IT, HOLD ON...
OH, MY STARS AND...
HOLD ON THERE, FUZZBALL, SOMETHING AIN'T RIGHT.
SOMETHING JUST--
--CAME OUT OF NO--
X-MEN, THIS IS MARIA HILL.

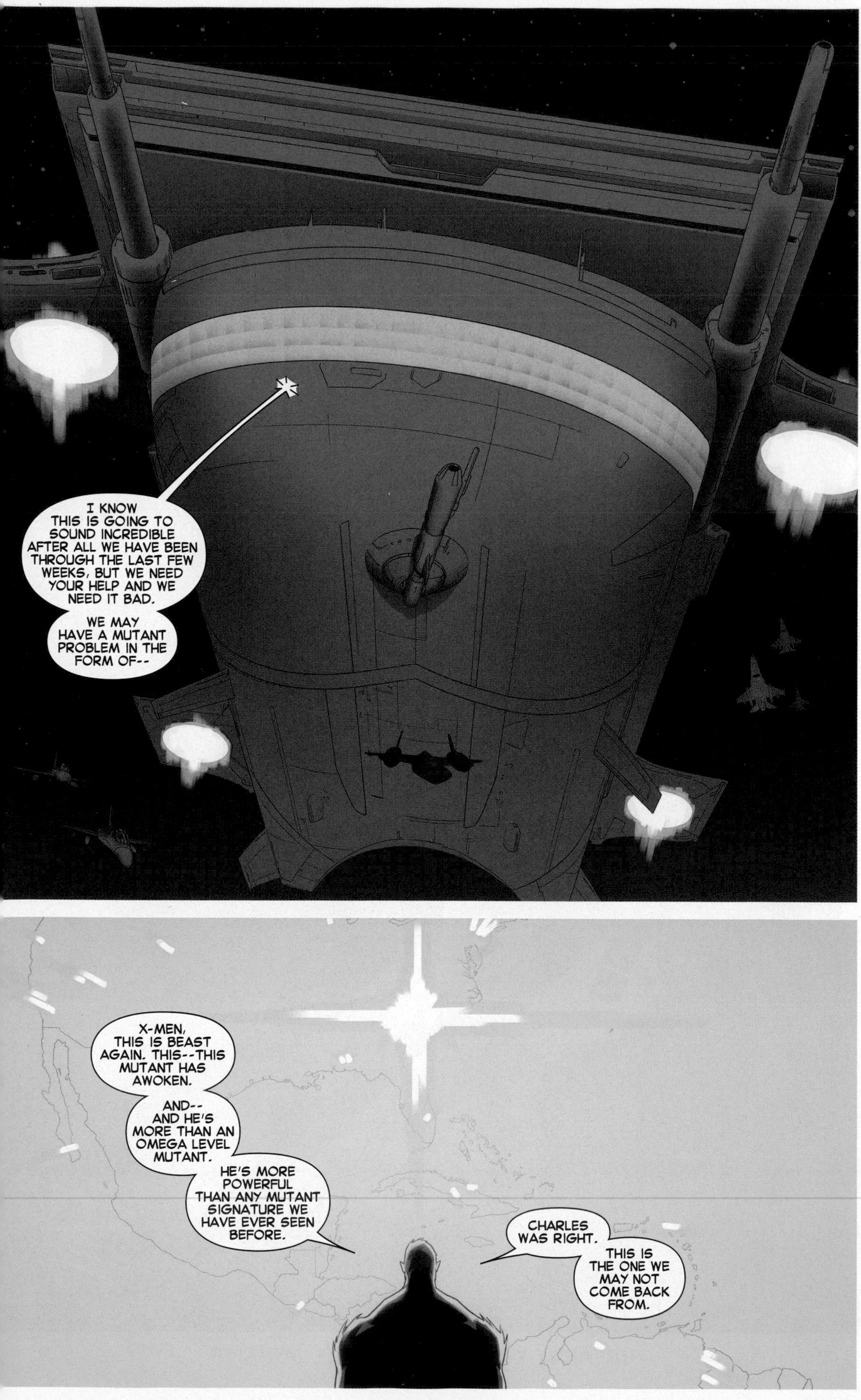

I KNOW THIS IS GOING TO SOUND INCREDIBLE AFTER ALL WE HAVE BEEN THROUGH THE LAST FEW WEEKS, BUT WE NEED YOUR HELP AND WE NEED IT BAD.
WE MAY HAVE A MUTANT PROBLEM IN THE FORM OF--
X-MEN, THIS IS BEAST AGAIN. THIS--THIS MUTANT HAS AWOKEN.
AND-- AND HE'S MORE THAN AN OMEGA LEVEL MUTANT.
HE'S MORE POWERFUL THAN ANY MUTANT SIGNATURE WE HAVE EVER SEEN BEFORE.
CHARLES WAS RIGHT.
THIS IS THE ONE WE MAY NOT COME BACK FROM.

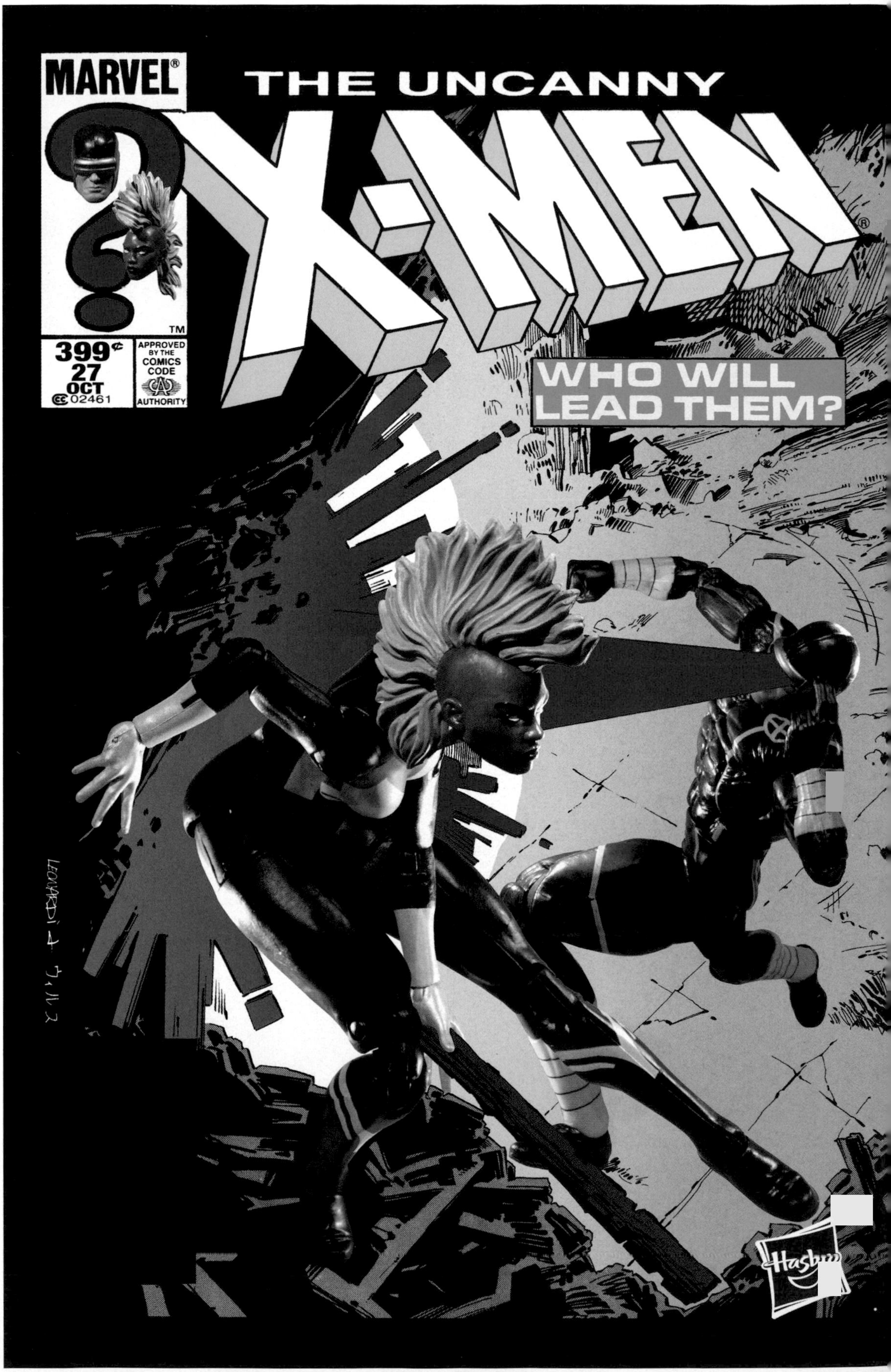
MARVEL®
THE UNCANNY
X-MEN®
TM
399¢
27
OCT
APPROVED BY THE COMICS CODE AUTHORITY
WHO WILL LEAD THEM?
Hasbro

**UNCANNY X-MEN #27** HASBRO VARIANT

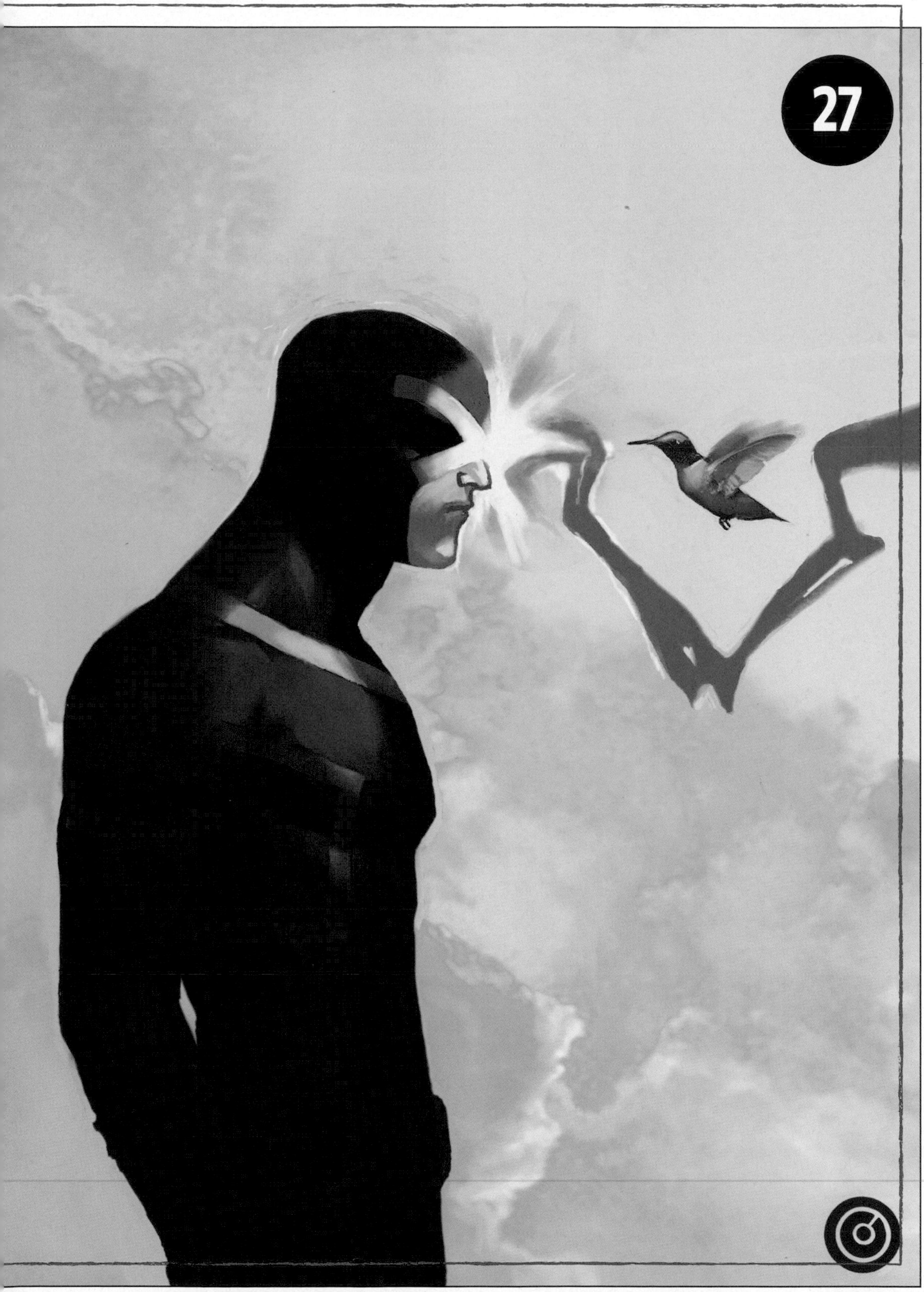
27

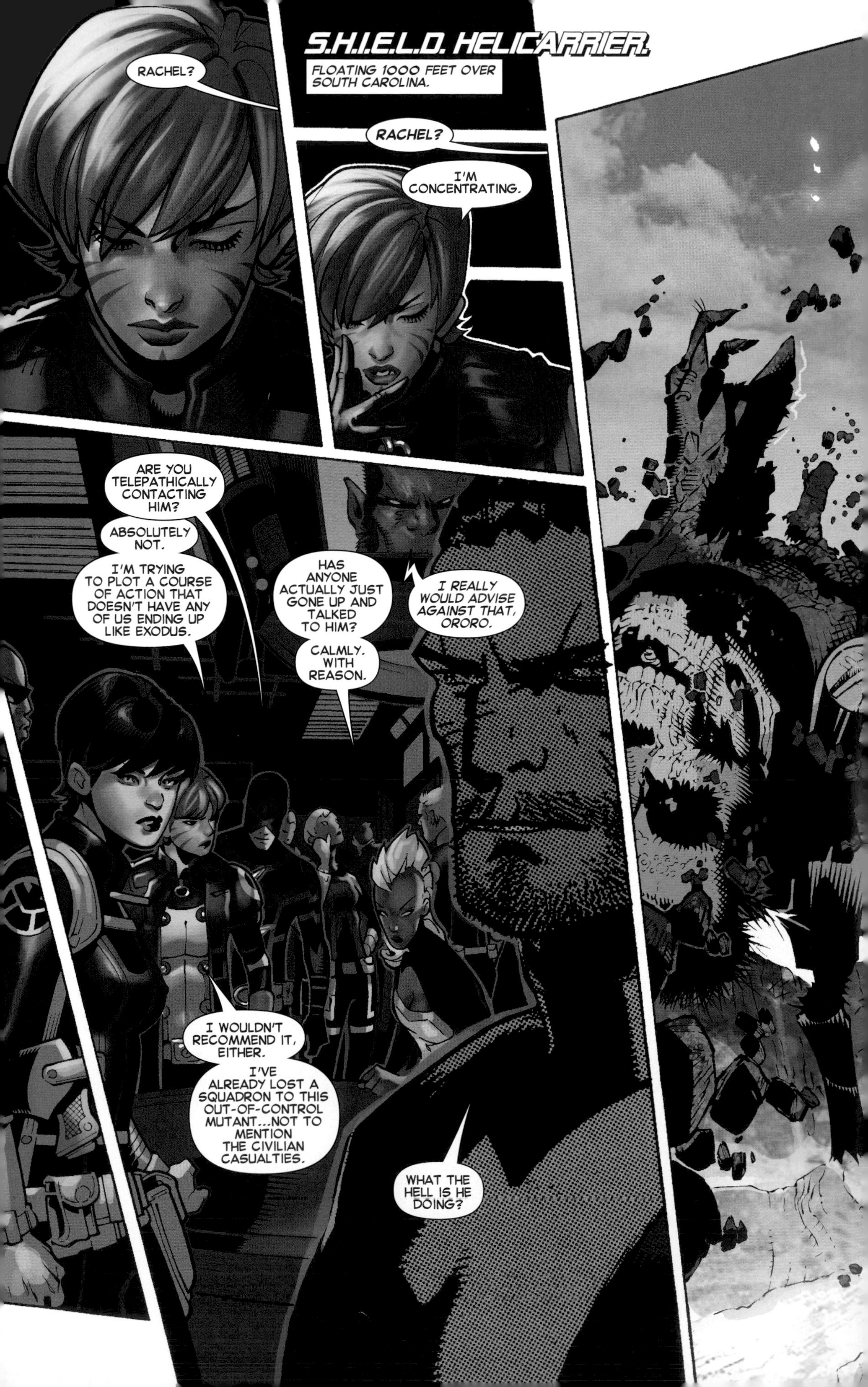
RACHEL?
S.H.I.E.L.D. HELICARRIER.
FLOATING 1000 FEET OVER SOUTH CAROLINA.
RACHEL?
I'M CONCENTRATING.
ARE YOU TELEPATHICALLY CONTACTING HIM?
ABSOLUTELY NOT.
I'M TRYING TO PLOT A COURSE OF ACTION THAT DOESN'T HAVE ANY OF US ENDING UP LIKE EXODUS.
HAS ANYONE ACTUALLY JUST GONE UP AND TALKED TO HIM?
CALMLY. WITH REASON.
I REALLY WOULD ADVISE AGAINST THAT, ORORO.
I WOULDN'T RECOMMEND IT, EITHER.
I'VE ALREADY LOST A SQUADRON TO THIS OUT-OF-CONTROL MUTANT...NOT TO MENTION THE CIVILIAN CASUALTIES.
WHAT THE HELL IS HE DOING?

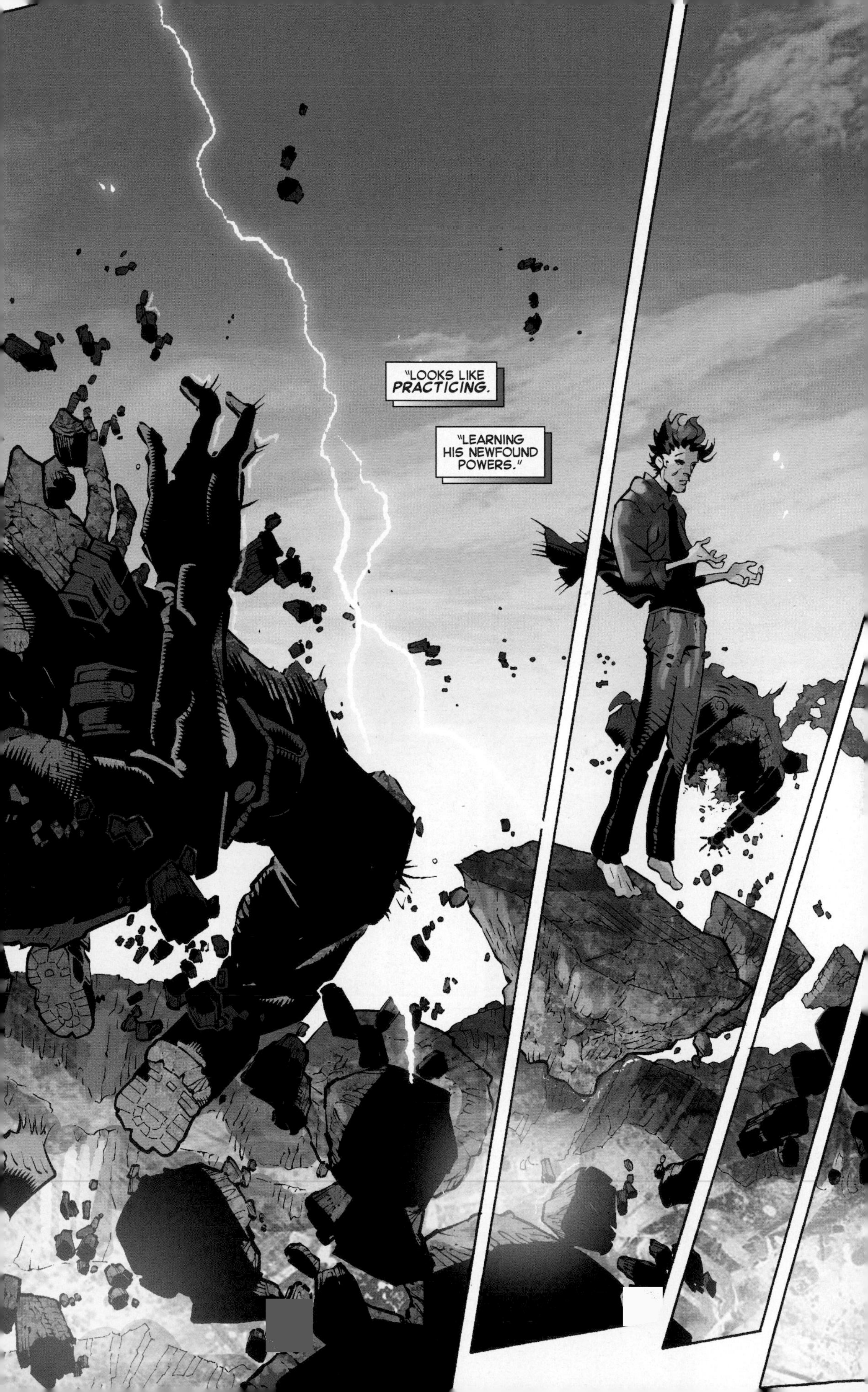
"LOOKS LIKE PRACTICING.
"LEARNING HIS NEWFOUND POWERS."

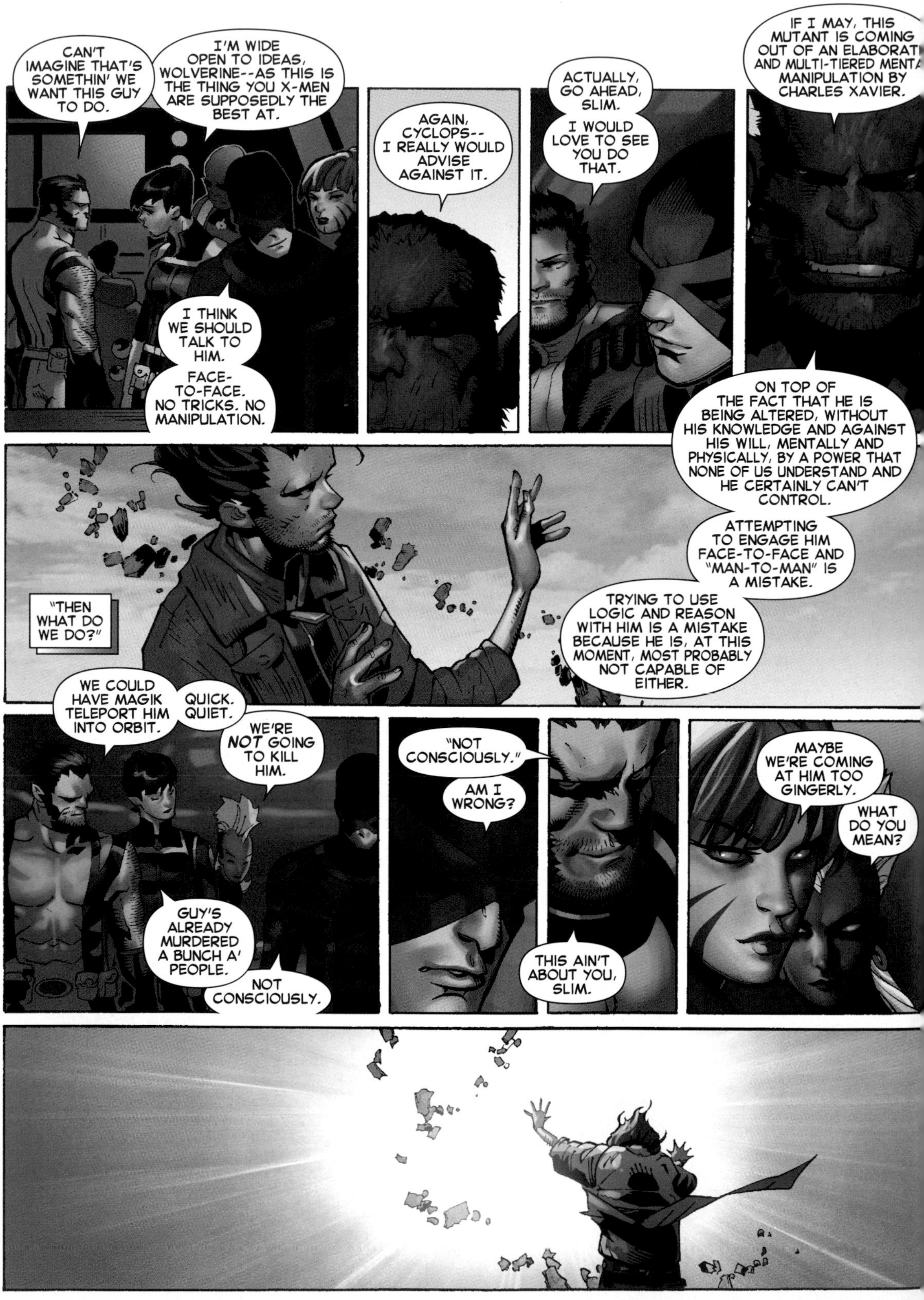
CAN'T IMAGINE THAT'S SOMETHIN' WE WANT THIS GUY TO DO.
I'M WIDE OPEN TO IDEAS, WOLVERINE--AS THIS IS THE THING YOU X-MEN ARE SUPPOSEDLY THE BEST AT.
I THINK WE SHOULD TALK TO HIM.
FACE-TO-FACE. NO TRICKS. NO MANIPULATION.
AGAIN, CYCLOPS-- I REALLY WOULD ADVISE AGAINST IT.
ACTUALLY, GO AHEAD, SLIM.
I WOULD LOVE TO SEE YOU DO THAT.
IF I MAY, THIS MUTANT IS COMING OUT OF AN ELABORAT AND MULTI-TIERED MENTA MANIPULATION BY CHARLES XAVIER.
ON TOP OF THE FACT THAT HE IS BEING ALTERED, WITHOUT HIS KNOWLEDGE AND AGAINST HIS WILL, MENTALLY AND PHYSICALLY, BY A POWER THAT NONE OF US UNDERSTAND AND HE CERTAINLY CAN'T CONTROL.
ATTEMPTING TO ENGAGE HIM FACE-TO-FACE AND "MAN-TO-MAN" IS A MISTAKE.
TRYING TO USE LOGIC AND REASON WITH HIM IS A MISTAKE BECAUSE HE IS, AT THIS MOMENT, MOST PROBABLY NOT CAPABLE OF EITHER.
"THEN WHAT DO WE DO?"
WE COULD HAVE MAGIK TELEPORT HIM INTO ORBIT.
QUICK. QUIET.
WE'RE *NOT* GOING TO KILL HIM.
GUY'S ALREADY MURDERED A BUNCH A' PEOPLE.
NOT CONSCIOUSLY.
"NOT CONSCIOUSLY."
AM I WRONG?
THIS AIN'T ABOUT YOU, SLIM.
MAYBE WE'RE COMING AT HIM TOO GINGERLY.
WHAT DO YOU MEAN?

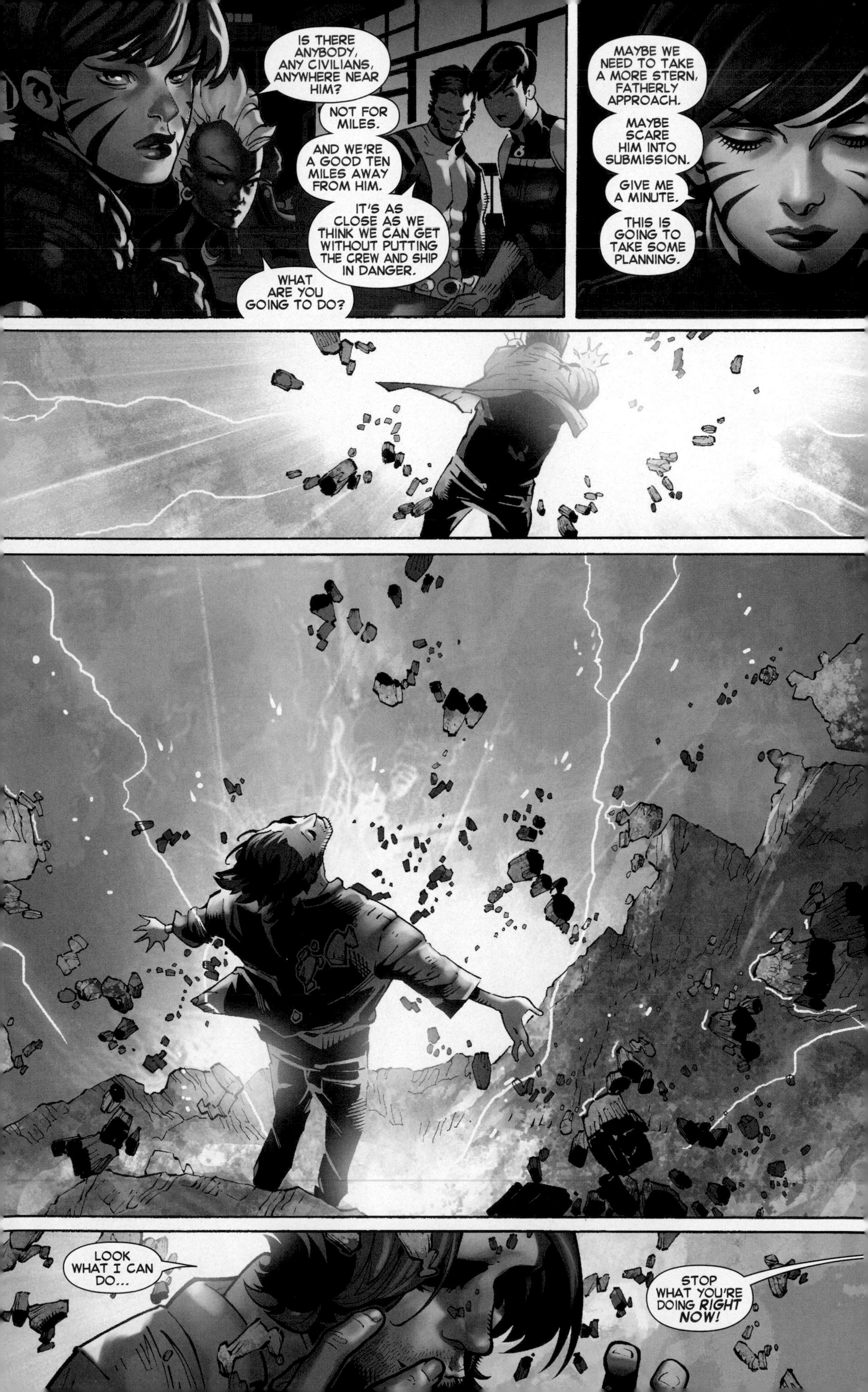
IS THERE ANYBODY, ANY CIVILIANS, ANYWHERE NEAR HIM?
NOT FOR MILES.
AND WE'RE A GOOD TEN MILES AWAY FROM HIM.
IT'S AS CLOSE AS WE THINK WE CAN GET WITHOUT PUTTING THE CREW AND SHIP IN DANGER.
WHAT ARE YOU GOING TO DO?
MAYBE WE NEED TO TAKE A MORE STERN, FATHERLY APPROACH.
MAYBE SCARE HIM INTO SUBMISSION.
GIVE ME A MINUTE.
THIS IS GOING TO TAKE SOME PLANNING.
LOOK WHAT I CAN DO...
STOP WHAT YOU'RE DOING *RIGHT NOW!*

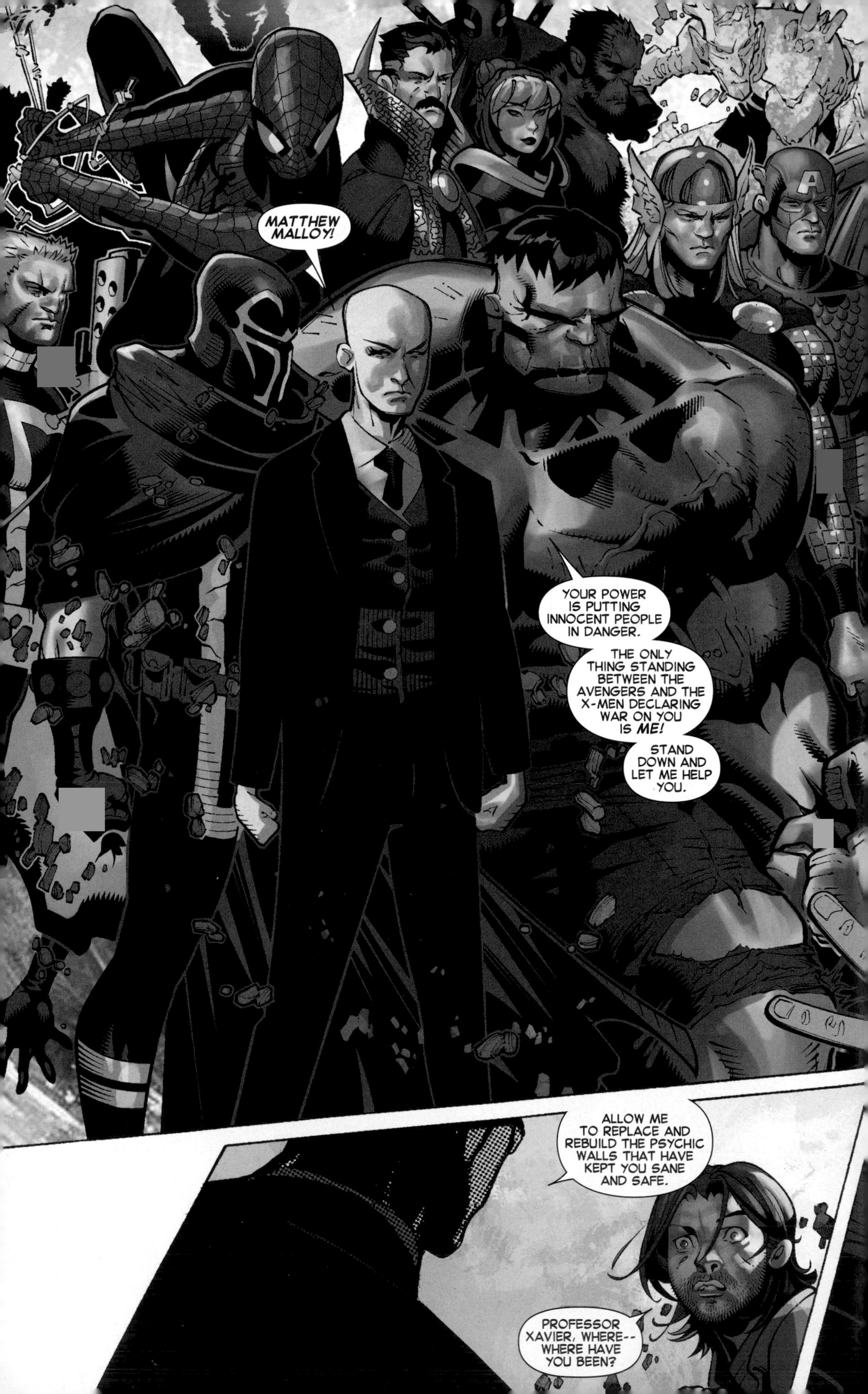
MATTHEW MALLOY!
YOUR POWER IS PUTTING INNOCENT PEOPLE IN DANGER.
THE ONLY THING STANDING BETWEEN THE AVENGERS AND THE X-MEN DECLARING WAR ON YOU IS *ME!*
STAND DOWN AND LET ME HELP YOU.
ALLOW ME TO REPLACE AND REBUILD THE PSYCHIC WALLS THAT HAVE KEPT YOU SANE AND SAFE.
PROFESSOR XAVIER, WHERE-- WHERE HAVE YOU BEEN?

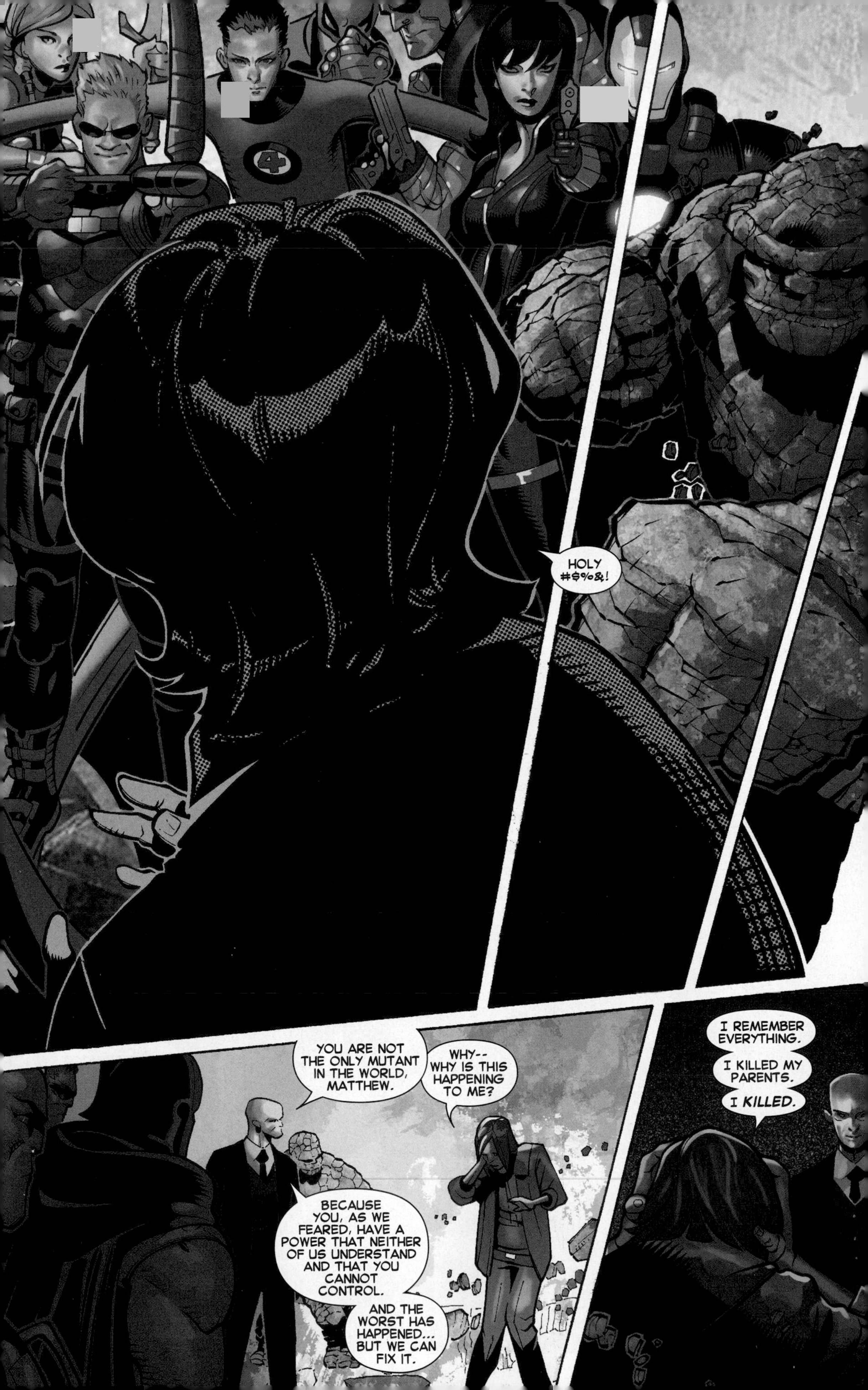
HOLY #$%&!
YOU ARE NOT THE ONLY MUTANT IN THE WORLD, MATTHEW.
WHY-- WHY IS THIS HAPPENING TO ME?
BECAUSE YOU, AS WE FEARED, HAVE A POWER THAT NEITHER OF US UNDERSTAND AND THAT YOU CANNOT CONTROL.
AND THE WORST HAS HAPPENED... BUT WE CAN FIX IT.
I REMEMBER EVERYTHING.
I KILLED MY PARENTS.
I *KILLED.*

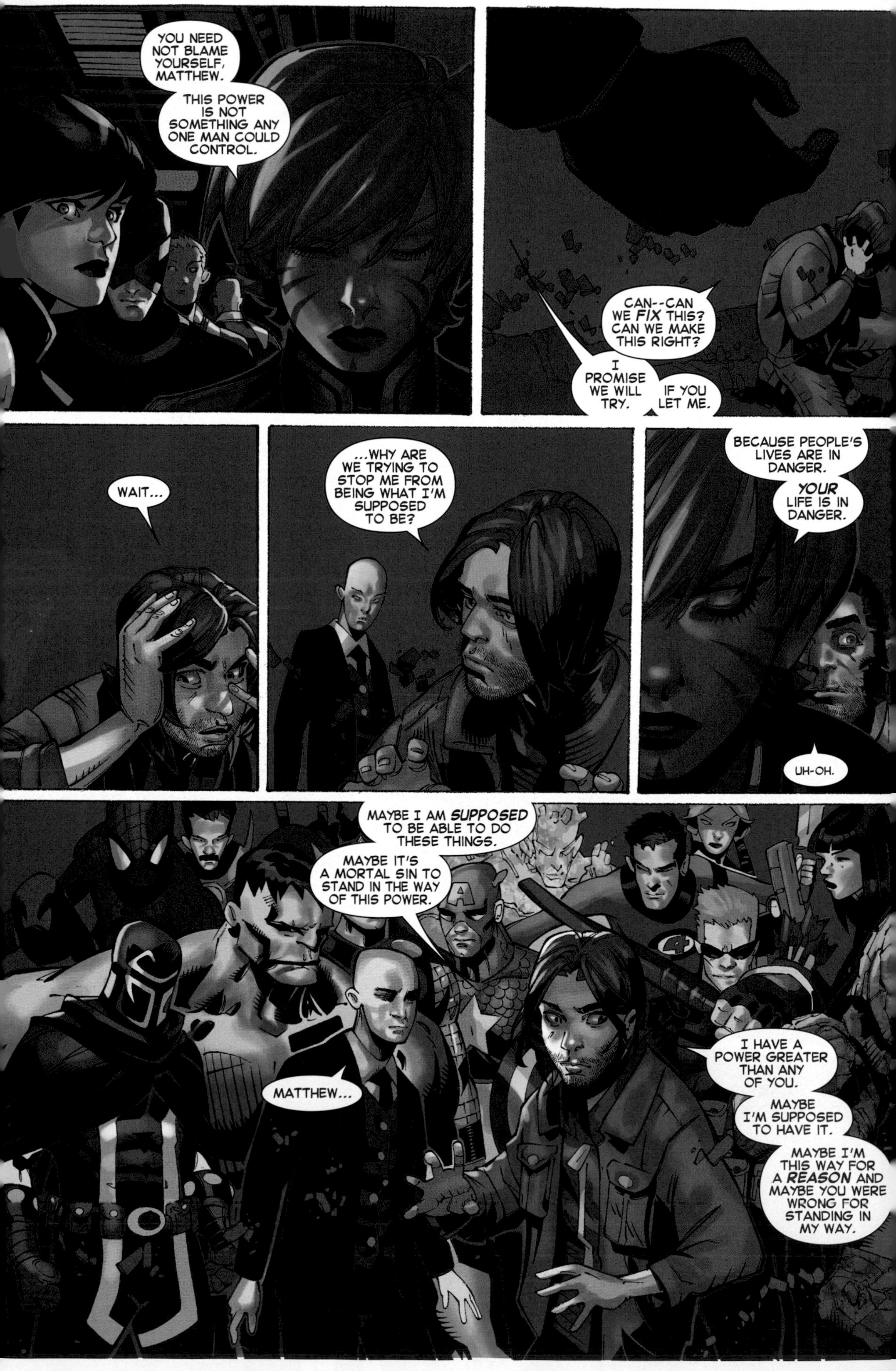
YOU NEED NOT BLAME YOURSELF, MATTHEW.
THIS POWER IS NOT SOMETHING ANY ONE MAN COULD CONTROL.
CAN--CAN WE FIX THIS? CAN WE MAKE THIS RIGHT?
I PROMISE WE WILL TRY.
IF YOU LET ME.
WAIT...
...WHY ARE WE TRYING TO STOP ME FROM BEING WHAT I'M SUPPOSED TO BE?
BECAUSE PEOPLE'S LIVES ARE IN DANGER.
YOUR LIFE IS IN DANGER.
UH-OH.
MAYBE I AM SUPPOSED TO BE ABLE TO DO THESE THINGS.
MAYBE IT'S A MORTAL SIN TO STAND IN THE WAY OF THIS POWER.
MATTHEW...
I HAVE A POWER GREATER THAN ANY OF YOU.
MAYBE I'M SUPPOSED TO HAVE IT.
MAYBE I'M THIS WAY FOR A REASON AND MAYBE YOU WERE WRONG FOR STANDING IN MY WAY.

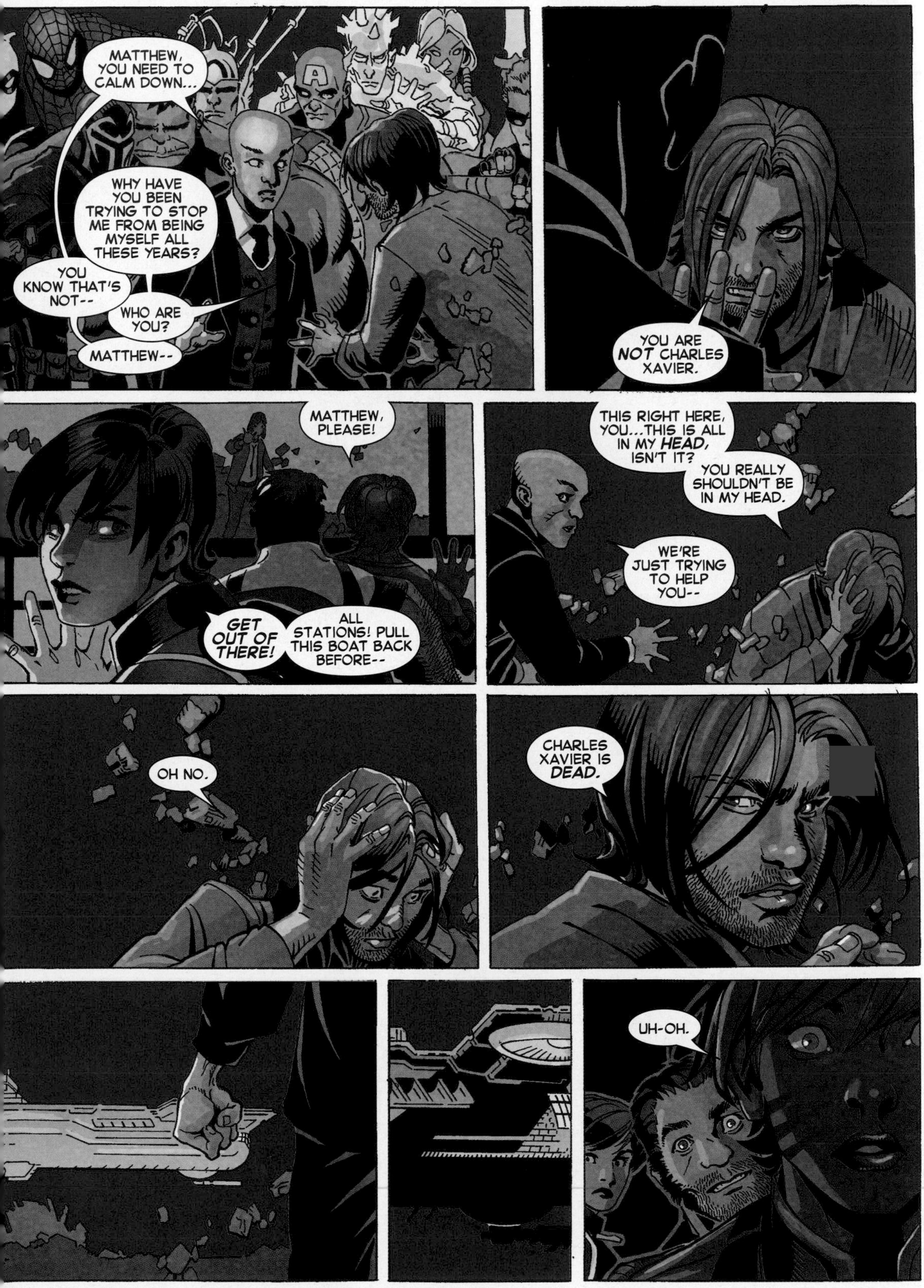
MATTHEW, YOU NEED TO CALM DOWN...
WHY HAVE YOU BEEN TRYING TO STOP ME FROM BEING MYSELF ALL THESE YEARS?
YOU KNOW THAT'S NOT--
WHO ARE YOU?
MATTHEW--
YOU ARE NOT CHARLES XAVIER.
MATTHEW, PLEASE!
GET OUT OF THERE!
ALL STATIONS! PULL THIS BOAT BACK BEFORE--
THIS RIGHT HERE, YOU...THIS IS ALL IN MY HEAD, ISN'T IT?
YOU REALLY SHOULDN'T BE IN MY HEAD.
WE'RE JUST TRYING TO HELP YOU--
OH NO.
CHARLES XAVIER IS DEAD.
UH-OH.

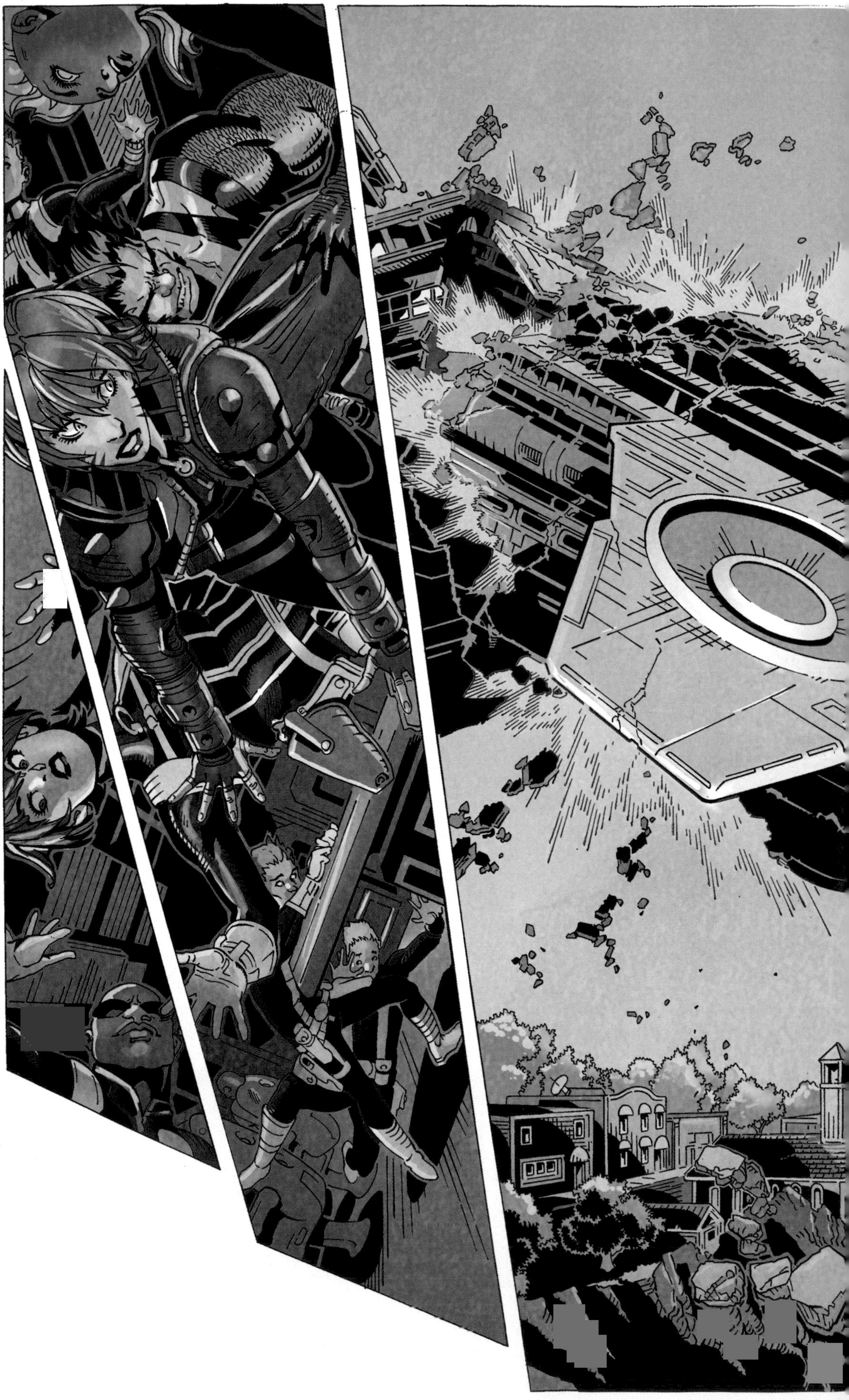

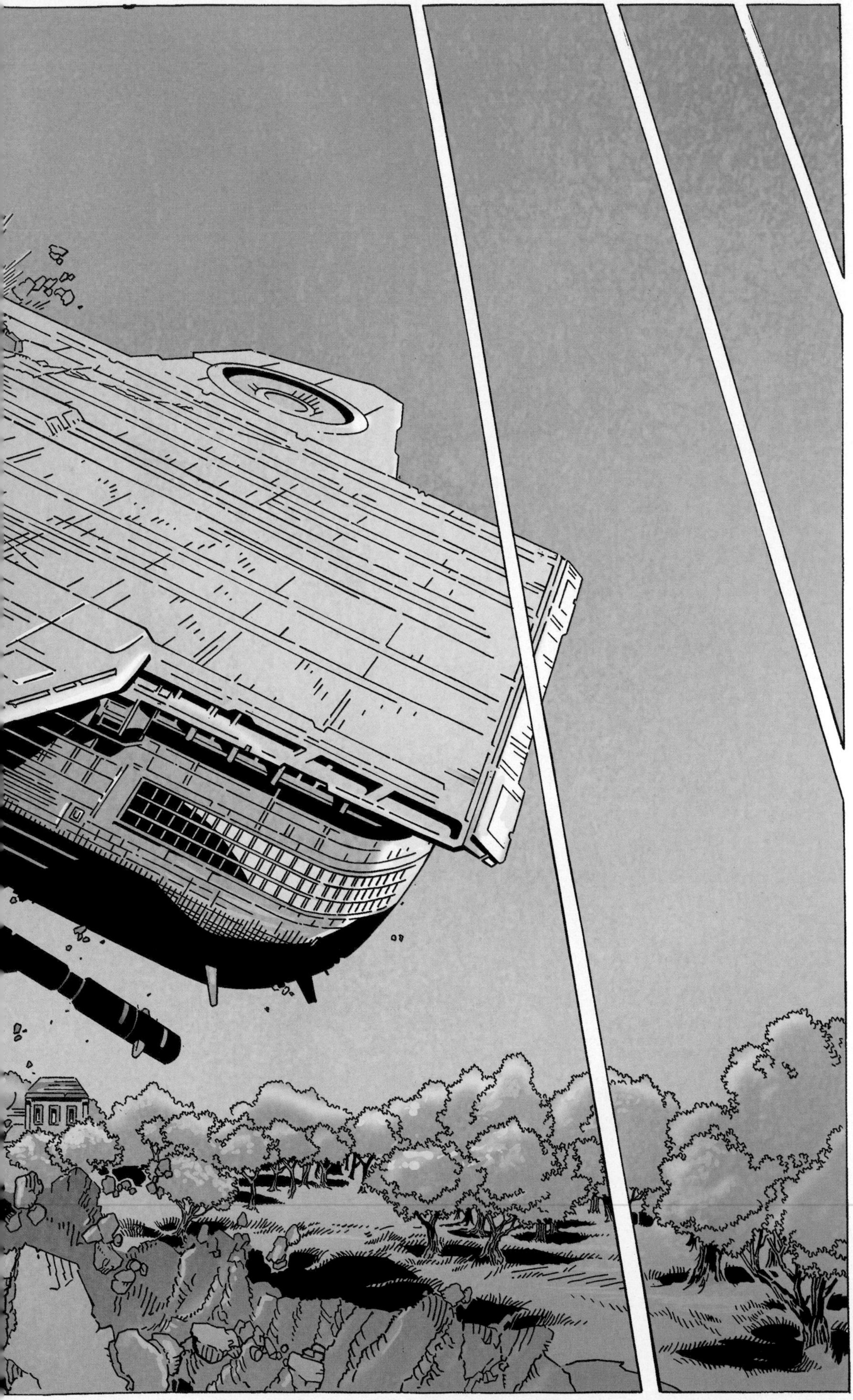

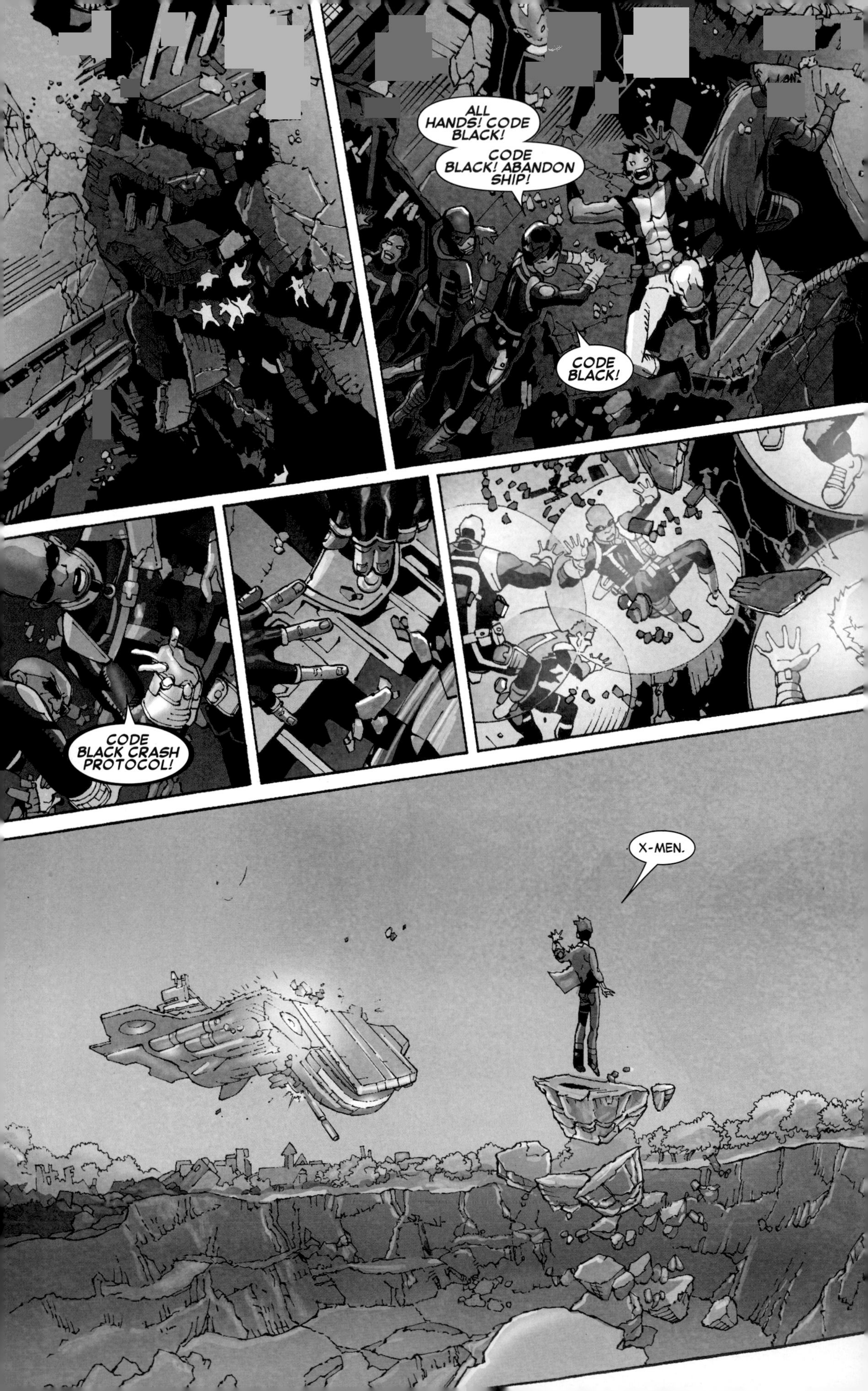
ALL HANDS! CODE BLACK!
CODE BLACK! ABANDON SHIP!
CODE BLACK!
CODE BLACK CRASH PROTOCOL!
X-MEN.

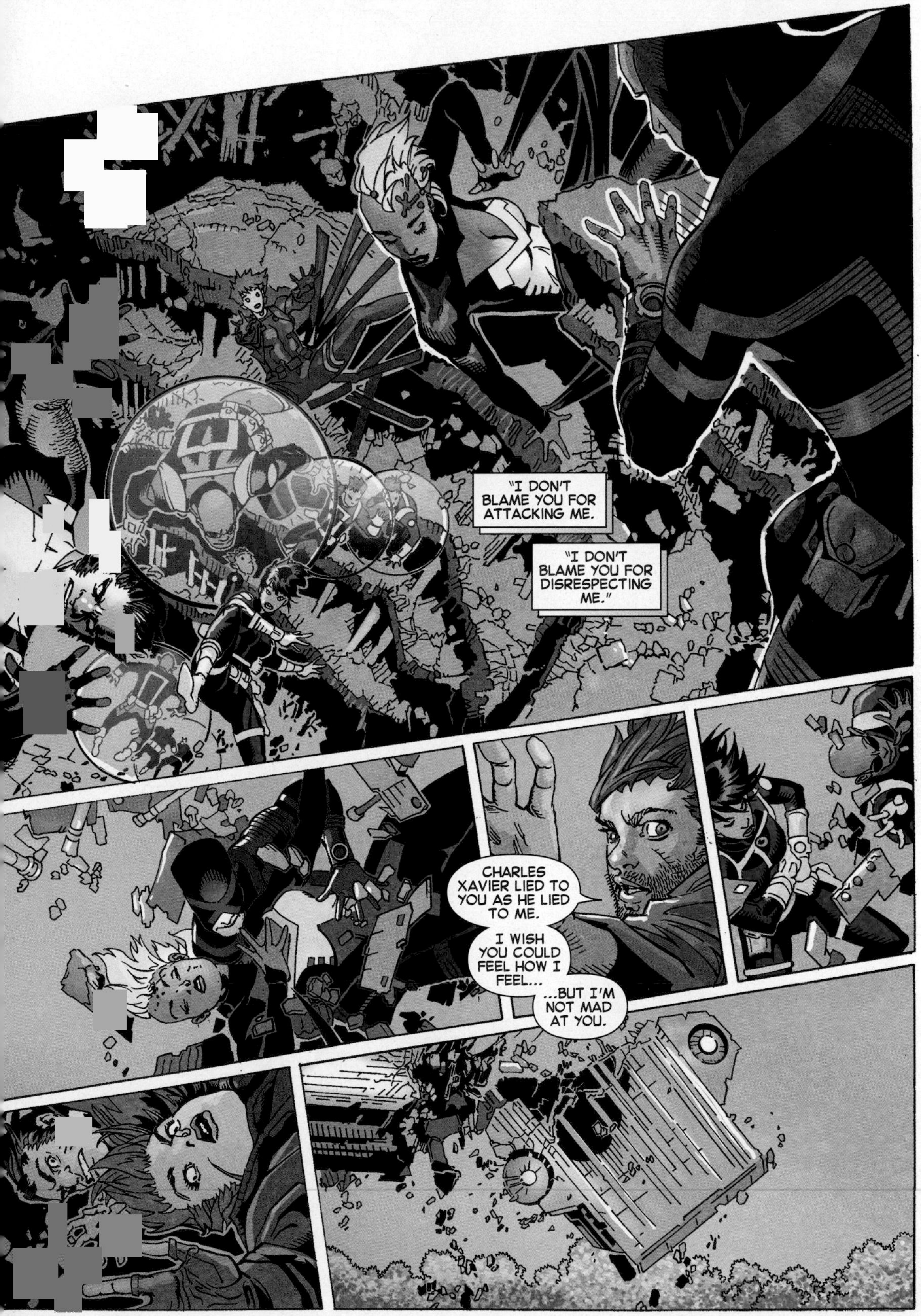
"I DON'T BLAME YOU FOR ATTACKING ME.
"I DON'T BLAME YOU FOR DISRESPECTING ME."
CHARLES XAVIER LIED TO YOU AS HE LIED TO ME.
I WISH YOU COULD FEEL HOW I FEEL...
...BUT I'M NOT MAD AT YOU.

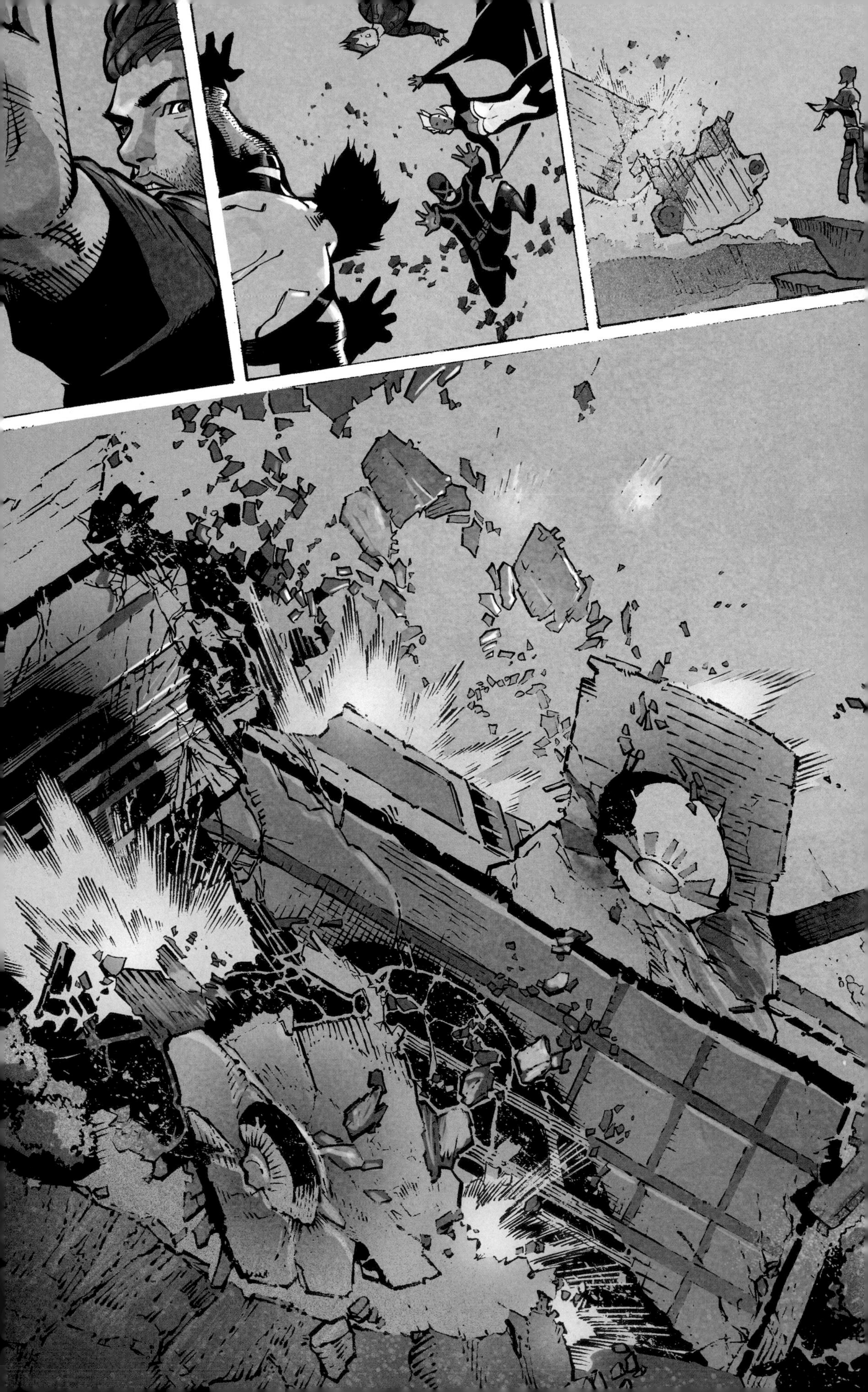

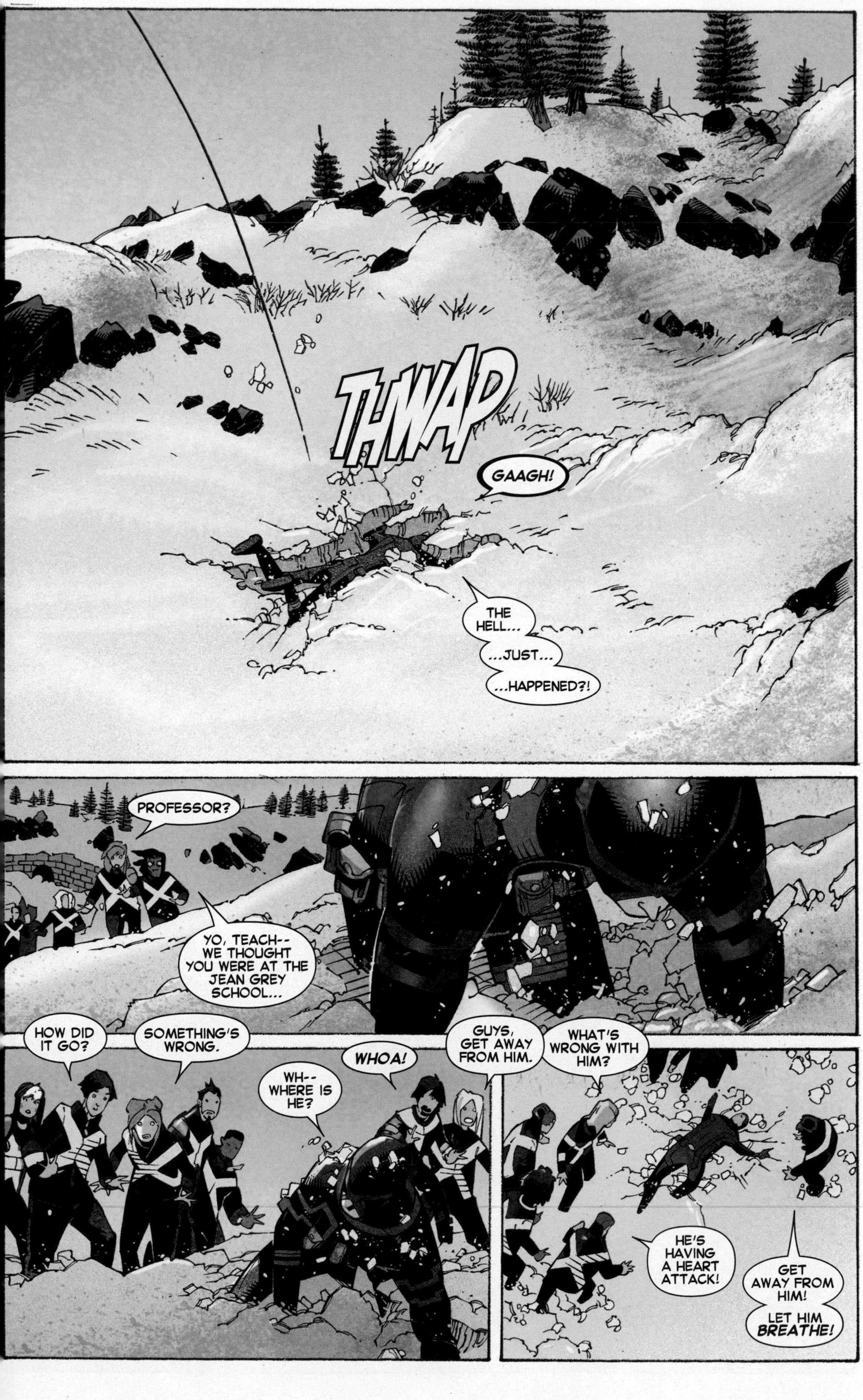
THWAP
GAAGH!
THE HELL...
...JUST...
...HAPPENED?!
PROFESSOR?
YO, TEACH-- WE THOUGHT YOU WERE AT THE JEAN GREY SCHOOL...
HOW DID IT GO?
SOMETHING'S WRONG.
WH-- WHERE IS HE?
WHOA!
GUYS, GET AWAY FROM HIM.
WHAT'S WRONG WITH HIM?
HE'S HAVING A HEART ATTACK!
GET AWAY FROM HIM!
LET HIM BREATHE!

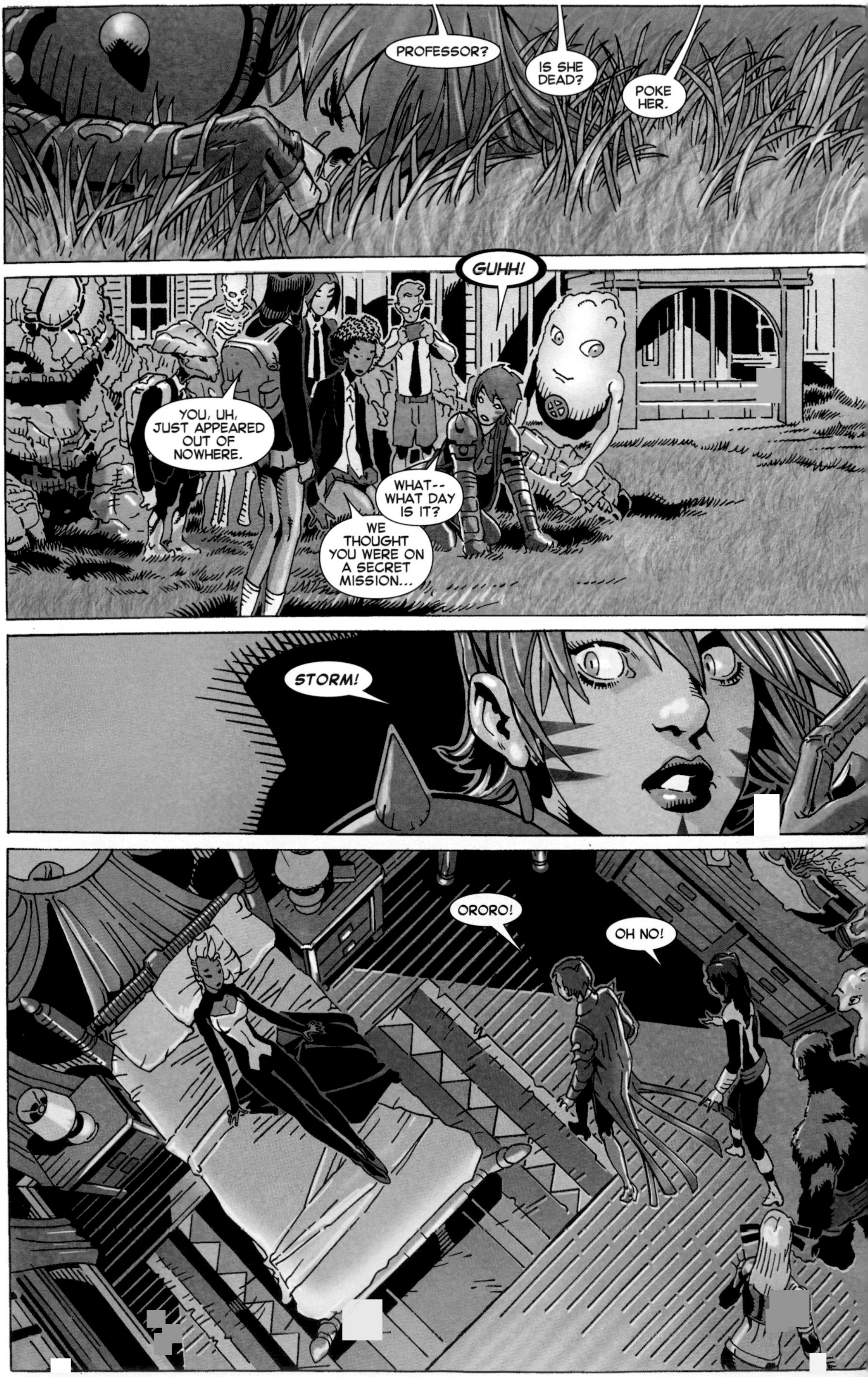
PROFESSOR?
IS SHE DEAD?
POKE HER.
GUHH!
YOU, UH, JUST APPEARED OUT OF NOWHERE.
WHAT-- WHAT DAY IS IT?
WE THOUGHT YOU WERE ON A SECRET MISSION...
STORM!
ORORO!
OH NO!

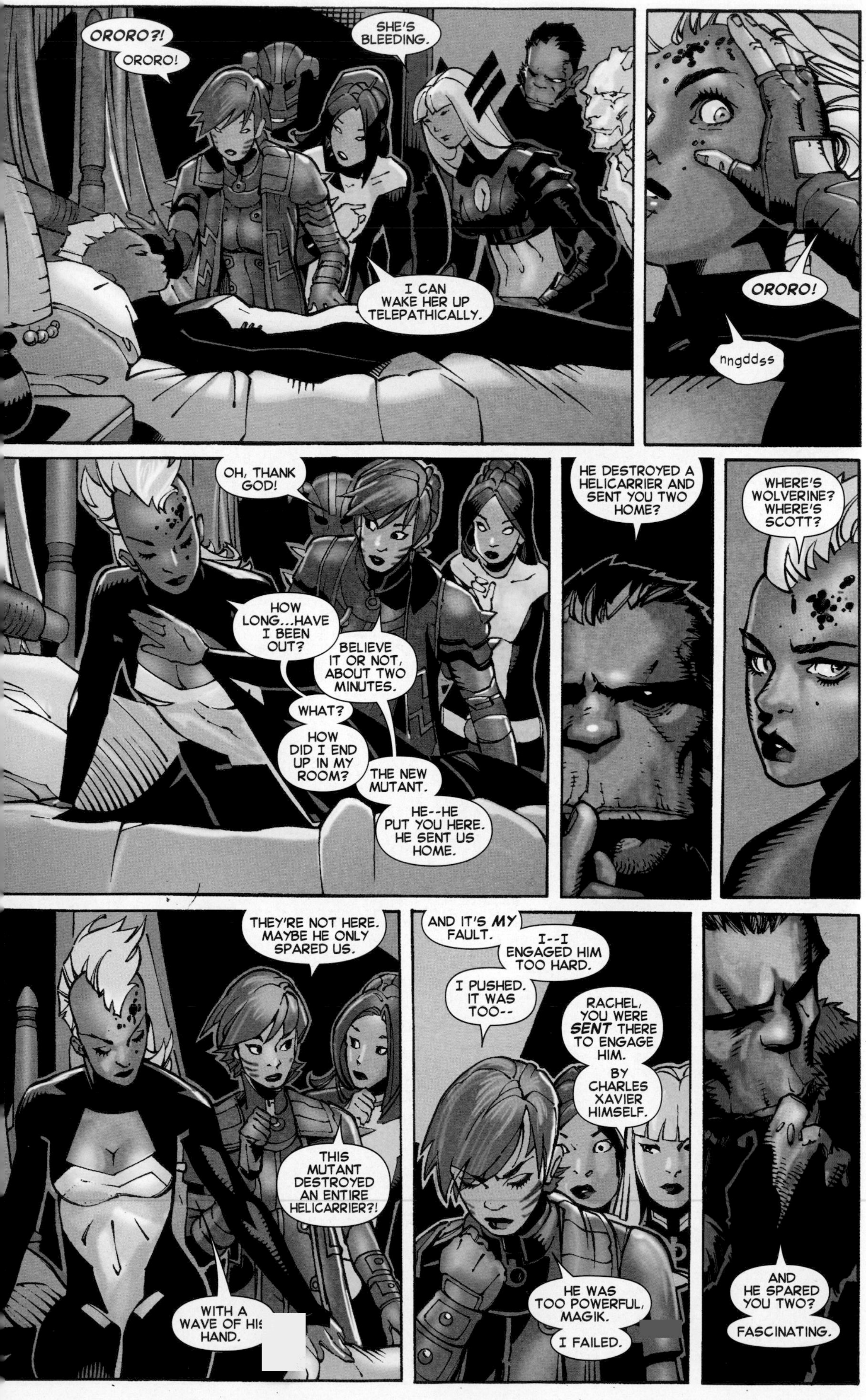
ORORO?!
ORORO!
SHE'S BLEEDING.
I CAN WAKE HER UP TELEPATHICALLY.
ORORO!
nngddss
OH, THANK GOD!
HOW LONG...HAVE I BEEN OUT?
BELIEVE IT OR NOT, ABOUT TWO MINUTES.
WHAT?
HOW DID I END UP IN MY ROOM?
THE NEW MUTANT.
HE--HE PUT YOU HERE. HE SENT US HOME.
HE DESTROYED A HELICARRIER AND SENT YOU TWO HOME?
WHERE'S WOLVERINE? WHERE'S SCOTT?
THEY'RE NOT HERE. MAYBE HE ONLY SPARED US.
THIS MUTANT DESTROYED AN ENTIRE HELICARRIER?!
WITH A WAVE OF HIS HAND.
AND IT'S MY FAULT.
I--I ENGAGED HIM TOO HARD.
I PUSHED. IT WAS TOO--
RACHEL, YOU WERE SENT THERE TO ENGAGE HIM.
BY CHARLES XAVIER HIMSELF.
HE WAS TOO POWERFUL, MAGIK.
I FAILED.
AND HE SPARED YOU TWO?
FASCINATING.

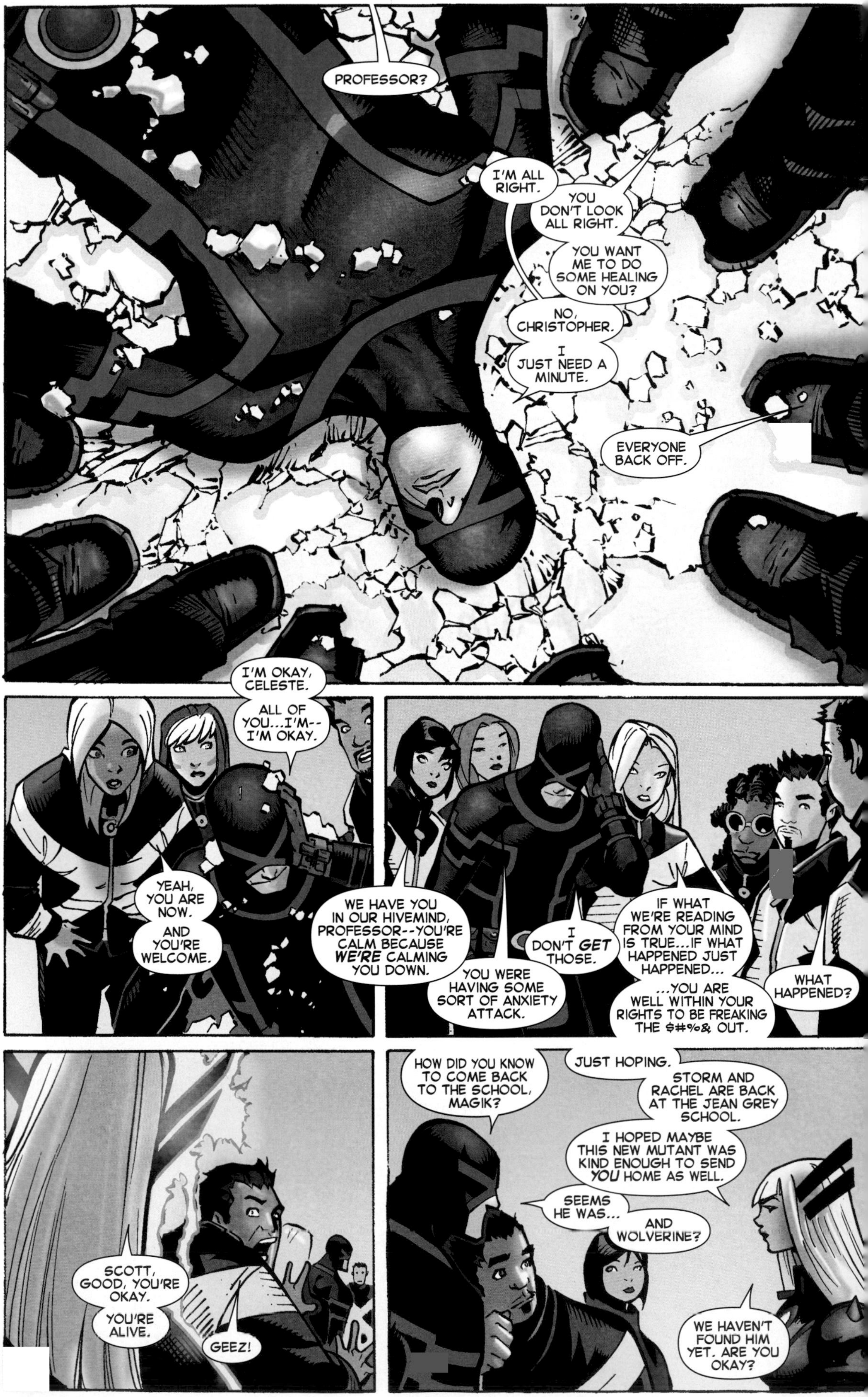
PROFESSOR?
I'M ALL RIGHT.
YOU DON'T LOOK ALL RIGHT.
YOU WANT ME TO DO SOME HEALING ON YOU?
NO, CHRISTOPHER.
I JUST NEED A MINUTE.
EVERYONE BACK OFF.
I'M OKAY, CELESTE.
ALL OF YOU...I'M-- I'M OKAY.
YEAH, YOU ARE NOW.
AND YOU'RE WELCOME.
WE HAVE YOU IN OUR HIVEMIND, PROFESSOR--YOU'RE CALM BECAUSE *WE'RE* CALMING YOU DOWN.
YOU WERE HAVING SOME SORT OF ANXIETY ATTACK.
I DON'T *GET* THOSE.
IF WHAT WE'RE READING FROM YOUR MIND IS TRUE...IF WHAT HAPPENED JUST HAPPENED...
...YOU ARE WELL WITHIN YOUR RIGHTS TO BE FREAKING THE $#%& OUT.
WHAT HAPPENED?
SCOTT, GOOD, YOU'RE OKAY.
YOU'RE ALIVE.
GEEZ!
HOW DID YOU KNOW TO COME BACK TO THE SCHOOL, MAGIK?
JUST HOPING.
STORM AND RACHEL ARE BACK AT THE JEAN GREY SCHOOL.
I HOPED MAYBE THIS NEW MUTANT WAS KIND ENOUGH TO SEND *YOU* HOME AS WELL.
SEEMS HE WAS...
AND WOLVERINE?
WE HAVEN'T FOUND HIM YET. ARE YOU OKAY?

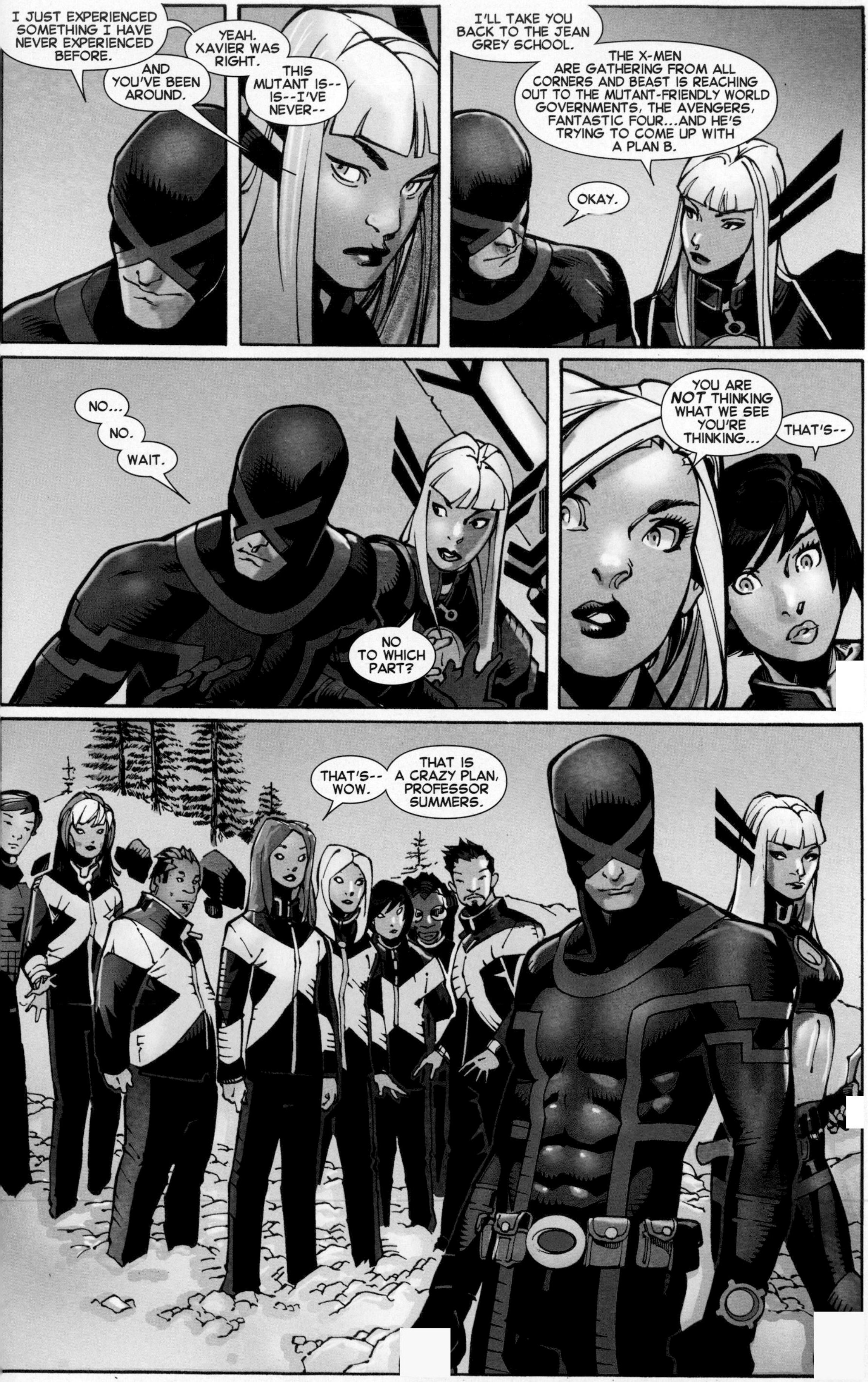
I JUST EXPERIENCED SOMETHING I HAVE NEVER EXPERIENCED BEFORE.
YEAH. XAVIER WAS RIGHT.
AND YOU'VE BEEN AROUND.
THIS MUTANT IS-- IS--I'VE NEVER--
I'LL TAKE YOU BACK TO THE JEAN GREY SCHOOL.
THE X-MEN ARE GATHERING FROM ALL CORNERS AND BEAST IS REACHING OUT TO THE MUTANT-FRIENDLY WORLD GOVERNMENTS, THE AVENGERS, FANTASTIC FOUR...AND HE'S TRYING TO COME UP WITH A PLAN B.
OKAY.
NO...
NO.
WAIT.
NO TO WHICH PART?
YOU ARE **NOT** THINKING WHAT WE SEE YOU'RE THINKING...
THAT'S--
THAT'S-- WOW.
THAT IS A CRAZY PLAN, PROFESSOR SUMMERS.

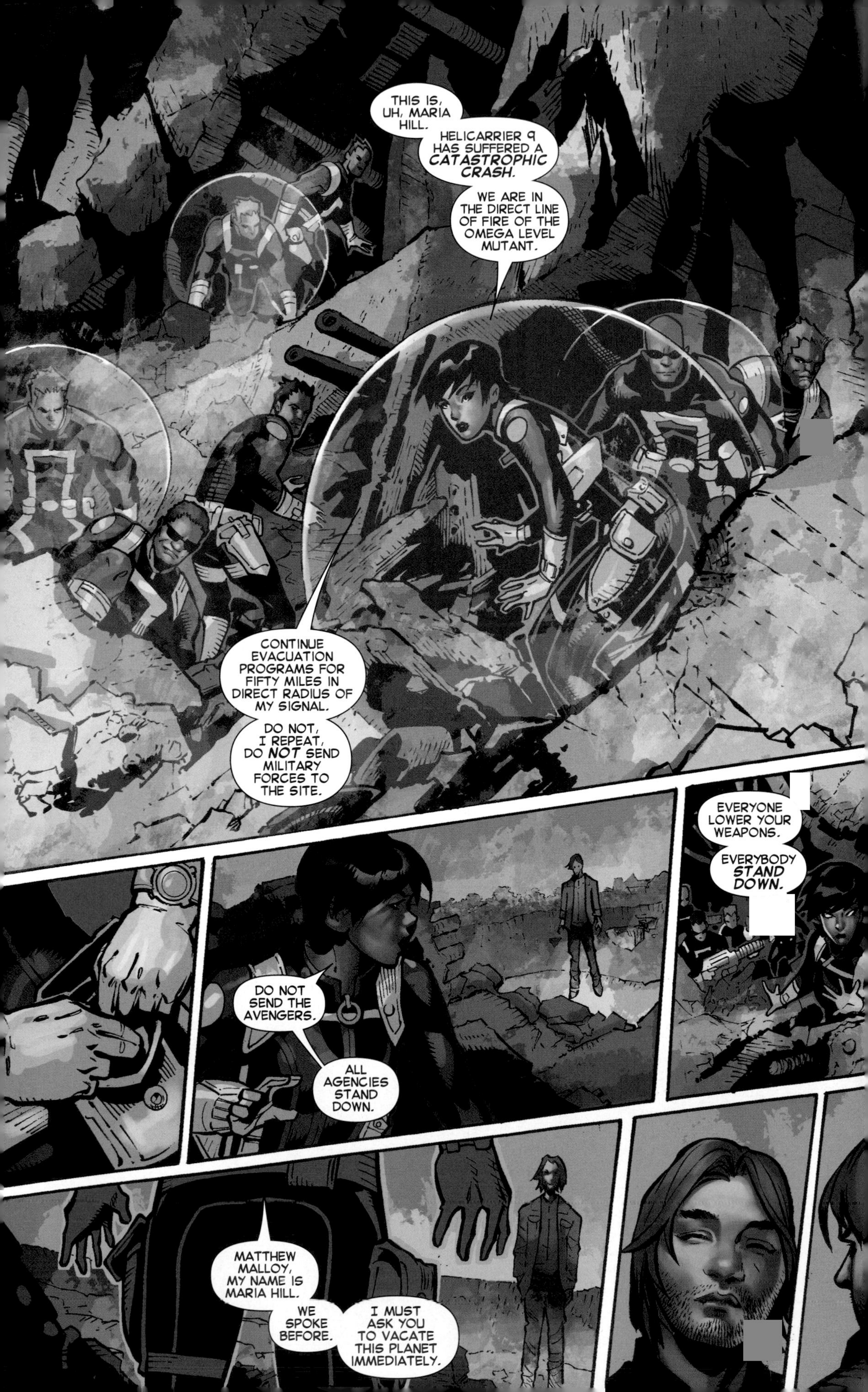
THIS IS, UH, MARIA HILL.
HELICARRIER 9 HAS SUFFERED A CATASTROPHIC CRASH.
WE ARE IN THE DIRECT LINE OF FIRE OF THE OMEGA LEVEL MUTANT.
CONTINUE EVACUATION PROGRAMS FOR FIFTY MILES IN DIRECT RADIUS OF MY SIGNAL.
DO NOT, I REPEAT, DO NOT SEND MILITARY FORCES TO THE SITE.
DO NOT SEND THE AVENGERS.
ALL AGENCIES STAND DOWN.
EVERYONE LOWER YOUR WEAPONS.
EVERYBODY STAND DOWN.
MATTHEW MALLOY, MY NAME IS MARIA HILL.
WE SPOKE BEFORE.
I MUST ASK YOU TO VACATE THIS PLANET IMMEDIATELY.

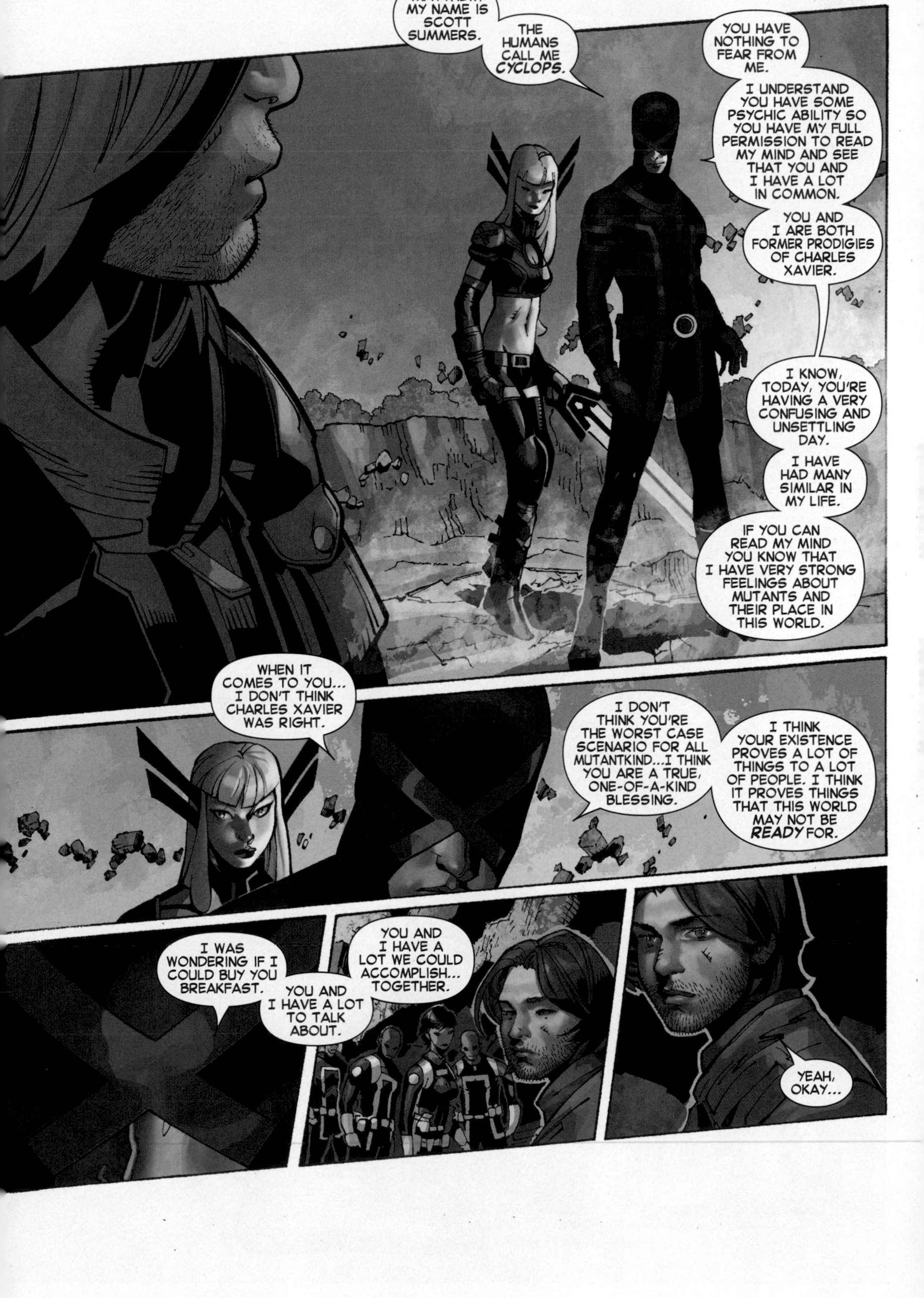
MATTHEW, MY NAME IS SCOTT SUMMERS.
THE HUMANS CALL ME CYCLOPS.
YOU HAVE NOTHING TO FEAR FROM ME.
I UNDERSTAND YOU HAVE SOME PSYCHIC ABILITY SO YOU HAVE MY FULL PERMISSION TO READ MY MIND AND SEE THAT YOU AND I HAVE A LOT IN COMMON.
YOU AND I ARE BOTH FORMER PRODIGIES OF CHARLES XAVIER.
I KNOW, TODAY, YOU'RE HAVING A VERY CONFUSING AND UNSETTLING DAY.
I HAVE HAD MANY SIMILAR IN MY LIFE.
IF YOU CAN READ MY MIND YOU KNOW THAT I HAVE VERY STRONG FEELINGS ABOUT MUTANTS AND THEIR PLACE IN THIS WORLD.
WHEN IT COMES TO YOU... I DON'T THINK CHARLES XAVIER WAS RIGHT.
I DON'T THINK YOU'RE THE WORST CASE SCENARIO FOR ALL MUTANTKIND...I THINK YOU ARE A TRUE, ONE-OF-A-KIND BLESSING.
I THINK YOUR EXISTENCE PROVES A LOT OF THINGS TO A LOT OF PEOPLE. I THINK IT PROVES THINGS THAT THIS WORLD MAY NOT BE READY FOR.
I WAS WONDERING IF I COULD BUY YOU BREAKFAST.
YOU AND I HAVE A LOT TO TALK ABOUT.
YOU AND I HAVE A LOT WE COULD ACCOMPLISH... TOGETHER.
YEAH, OKAY...

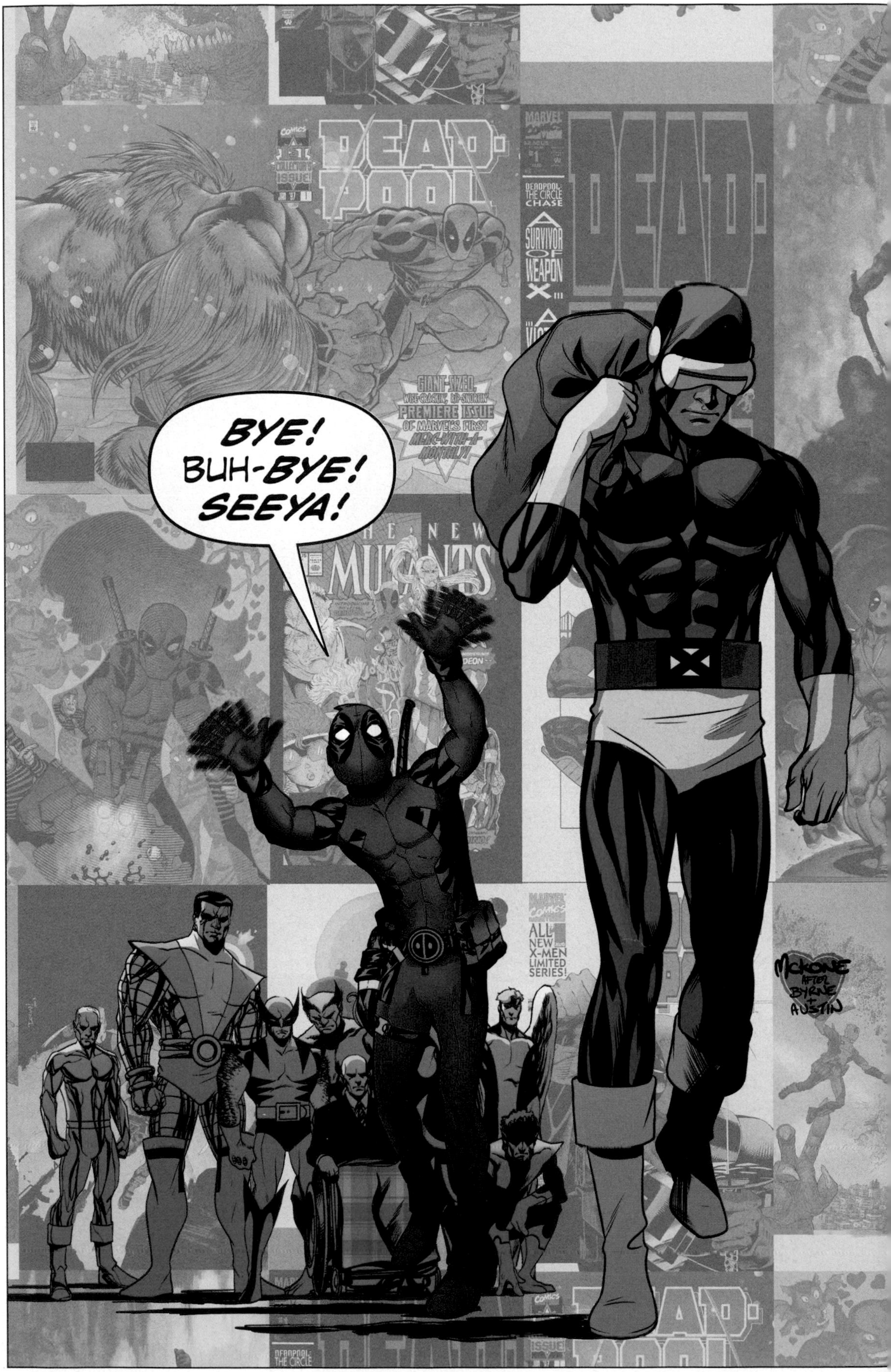
BYE! BUH-BYE! SEEYA!
MCKONE AFTER BYRNE + AUSTIN

**UNCANNY X-MEN #27** DEADPOOL 75TH ANNIVERSARY VARIANT
BY MIKE MCKONE & JASON KEITH

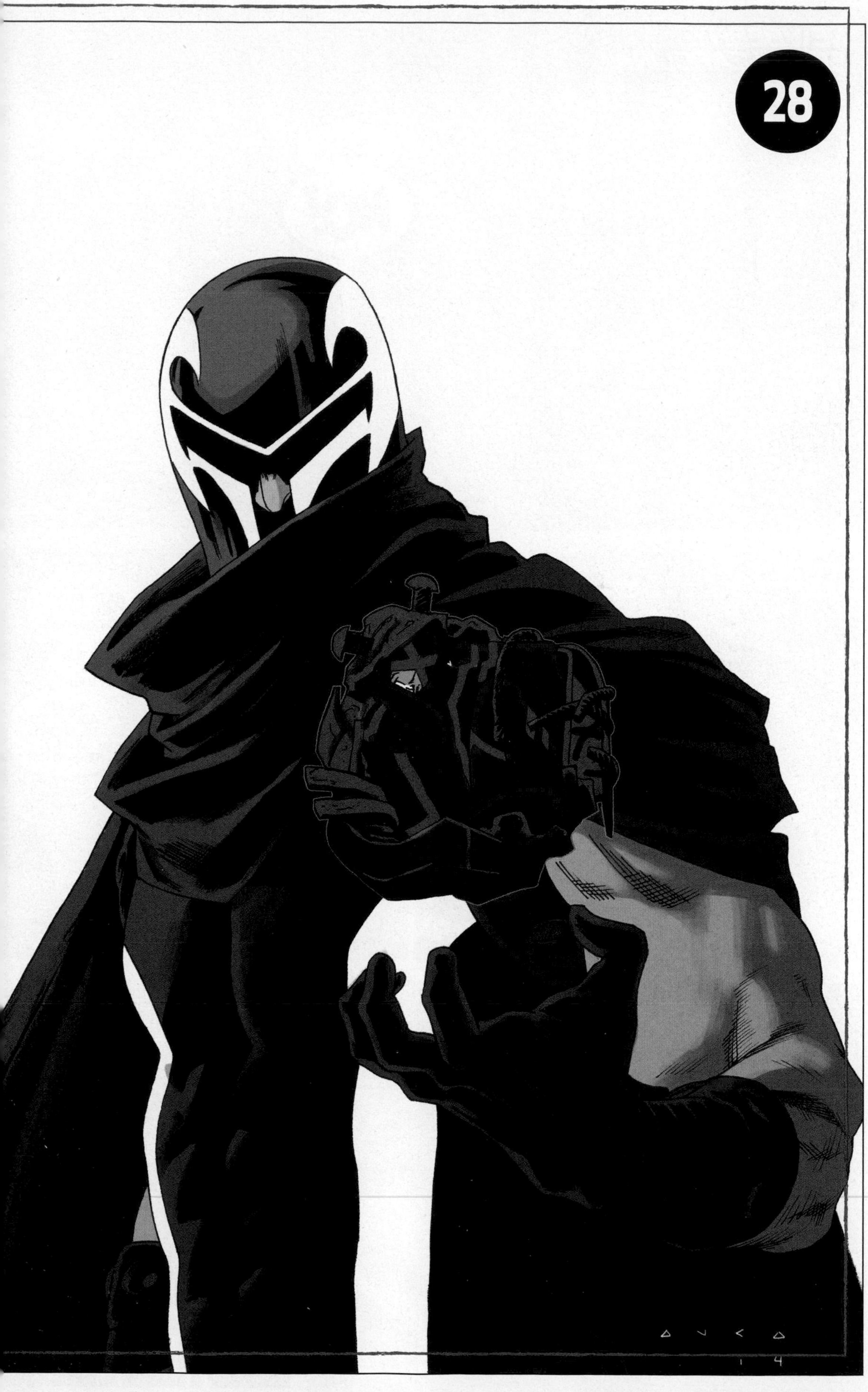
28

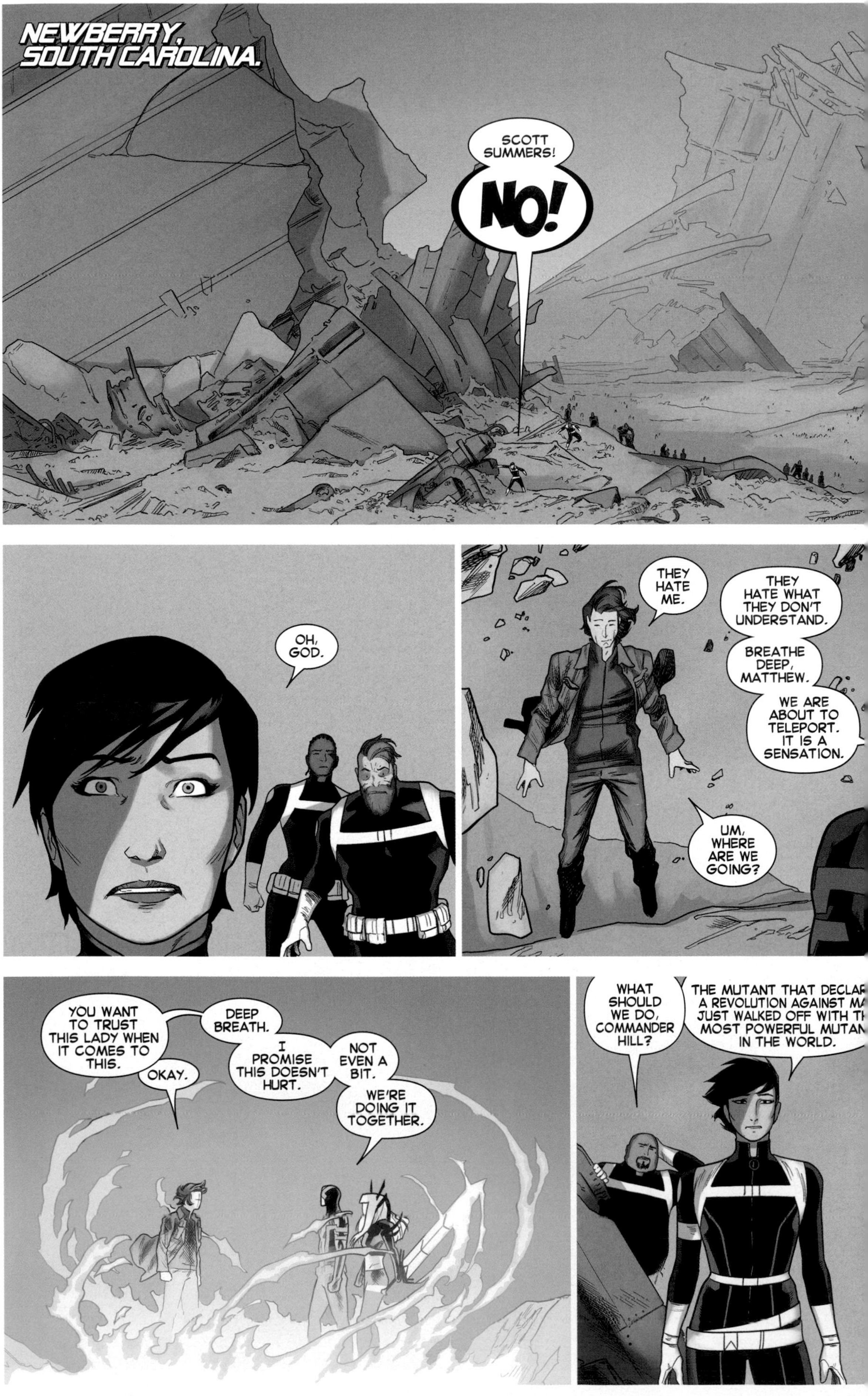
NEWBERRY, SOUTH CAROLINA.
SCOTT SUMMERS!
NO!
OH, GOD.
THEY HATE ME.
THEY HATE WHAT THEY DON'T UNDERSTAND.
BREATHE DEEP, MATTHEW.
WE ARE ABOUT TO TELEPORT. IT IS A SENSATION.
UM, WHERE ARE WE GOING?
YOU WANT TO TRUST THIS LADY WHEN IT COMES TO THIS.
DEEP BREATH.
OKAY.
I PROMISE THIS DOESN'T HURT.
NOT EVEN A BIT.
WE'RE DOING IT TOGETHER.
WHAT SHOULD WE DO, COMMANDER HILL?
THE MUTANT THAT DECLAR
A REVOLUTION AGAINST MA
JUST WALKED OFF WITH TH
MOST POWERFUL MUTAN
IN THE WORLD.

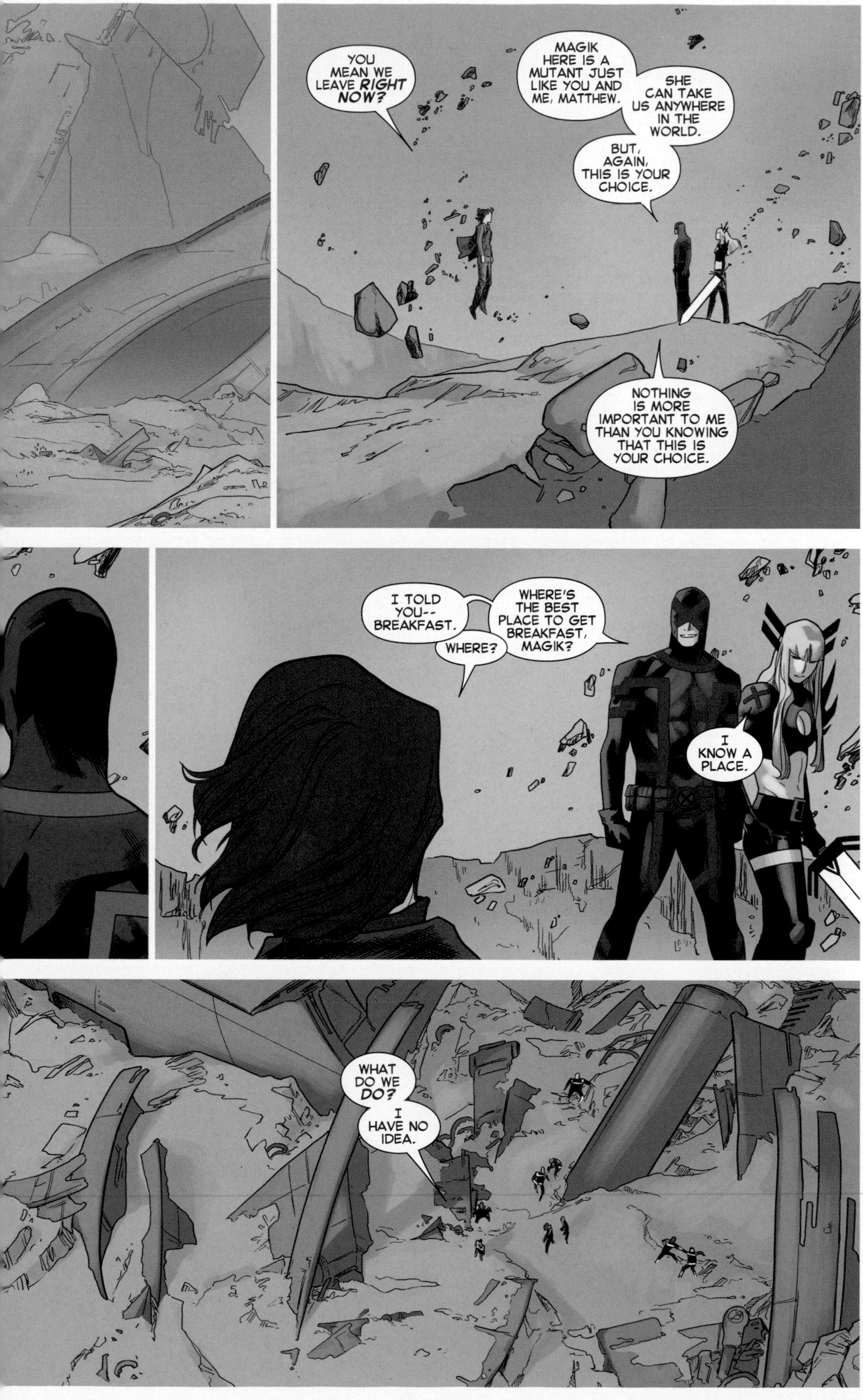
YOU MEAN WE LEAVE RIGHT NOW?
MAGIK HERE IS A MUTANT JUST LIKE YOU AND ME, MATTHEW.
SHE CAN TAKE US ANYWHERE IN THE WORLD.
BUT, AGAIN, THIS IS YOUR CHOICE.
NOTHING IS MORE IMPORTANT TO ME THAN YOU KNOWING THAT THIS IS YOUR CHOICE.
I TOLD YOU-- BREAKFAST.
WHERE?
WHERE'S THE BEST PLACE TO GET BREAKFAST, MAGIK?
I KNOW A PLACE.
WHAT DO WE DO?
I HAVE NO IDEA.

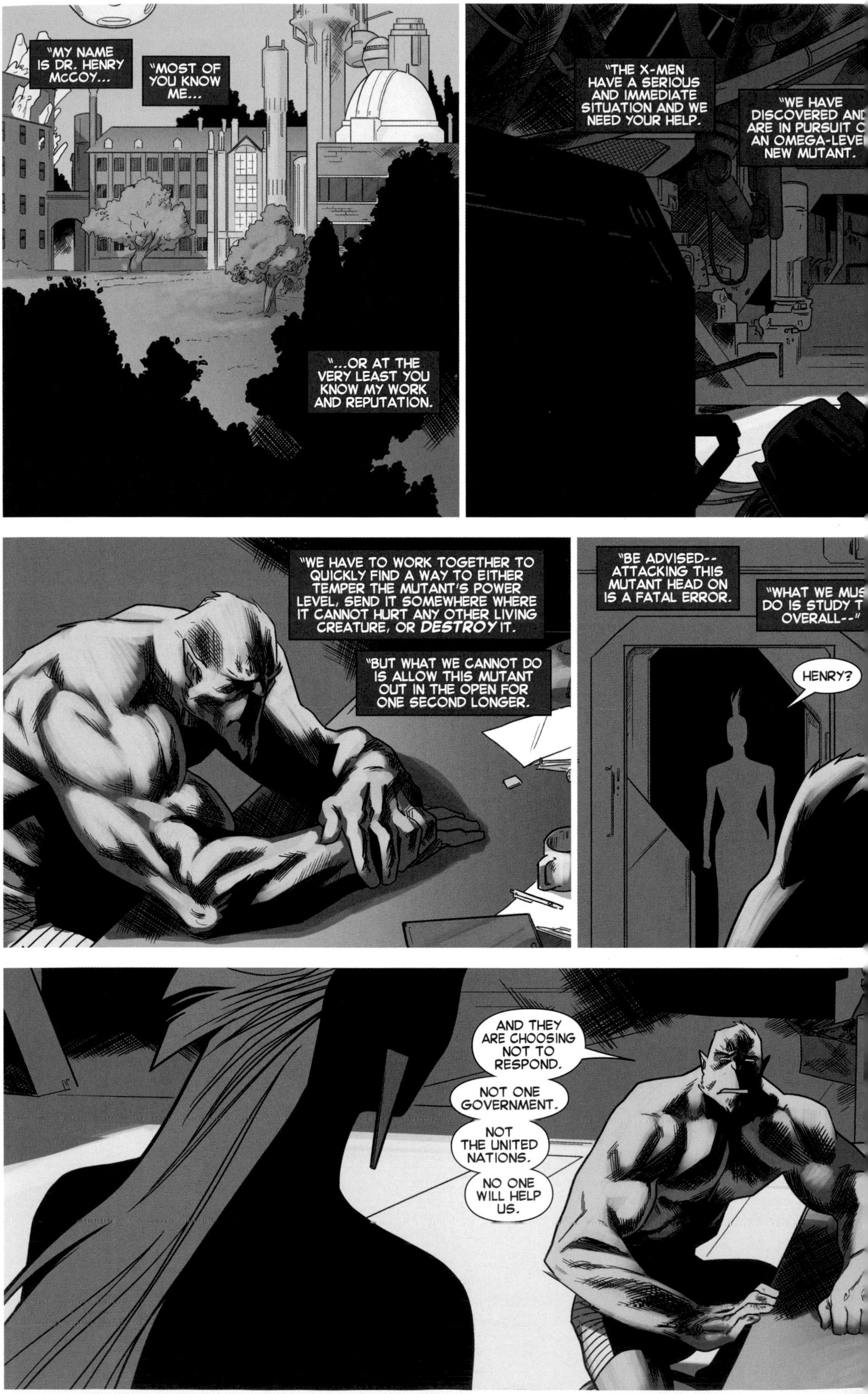
"MY NAME IS DR. HENRY McCOY...
"MOST OF YOU KNOW ME...
"...OR AT THE VERY LEAST YOU KNOW MY WORK AND REPUTATION.
"THE X-MEN HAVE A SERIOUS AND IMMEDIATE SITUATION AND WE NEED YOUR HELP.
"WE HAVE DISCOVERED AND ARE IN PURSUIT O AN OMEGA-LEVE NEW MUTANT.
"WE HAVE TO WORK TOGETHER TO QUICKLY FIND A WAY TO EITHER TEMPER THE MUTANT'S POWER LEVEL, SEND IT SOMEWHERE WHERE IT CANNOT HURT ANY OTHER LIVING CREATURE, OR DESTROY IT.
"BUT WHAT WE CANNOT DO IS ALLOW THIS MUTANT OUT IN THE OPEN FOR ONE SECOND LONGER.
"BE ADVISED--ATTACKING THIS MUTANT HEAD ON IS A FATAL ERROR.
"WHAT WE MUS DO IS STUDY T OVERALL--"
HENRY?
AND THEY ARE CHOOSING NOT TO RESPOND.
NOT ONE GOVERNMENT.
NOT THE UNITED NATIONS.
NO ONE WILL HELP US.

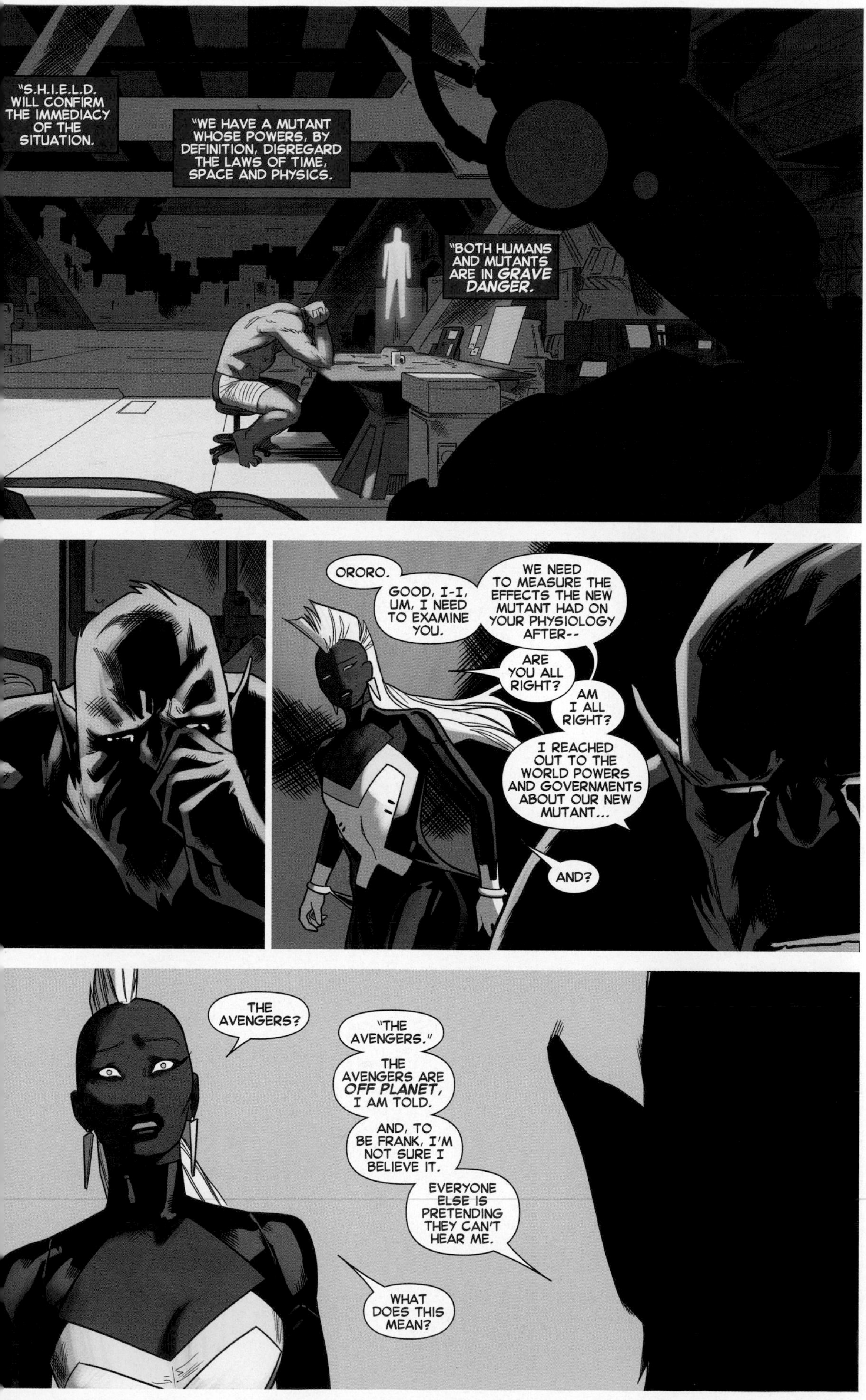
"S.H.I.E.L.D. WILL CONFIRM THE IMMEDIACY OF THE SITUATION.
"WE HAVE A MUTANT WHOSE POWERS, BY DEFINITION, DISREGARD THE LAWS OF TIME, SPACE AND PHYSICS.
"BOTH HUMANS AND MUTANTS ARE IN GRAVE DANGER.
ORORO.
GOOD, I-I, UM, I NEED TO EXAMINE YOU.
WE NEED TO MEASURE THE EFFECTS THE NEW MUTANT HAD ON YOUR PHYSIOLOGY AFTER--
ARE YOU ALL RIGHT?
AM I ALL RIGHT?
I REACHED OUT TO THE WORLD POWERS AND GOVERNMENTS ABOUT OUR NEW MUTANT...
AND?
THE AVENGERS?
"THE AVENGERS."
THE AVENGERS ARE OFF PLANET, I AM TOLD.
AND, TO BE FRANK, I'M NOT SURE I BELIEVE IT.
EVERYONE ELSE IS PRETENDING THEY CAN'T HEAR ME.
WHAT DOES THIS MEAN?

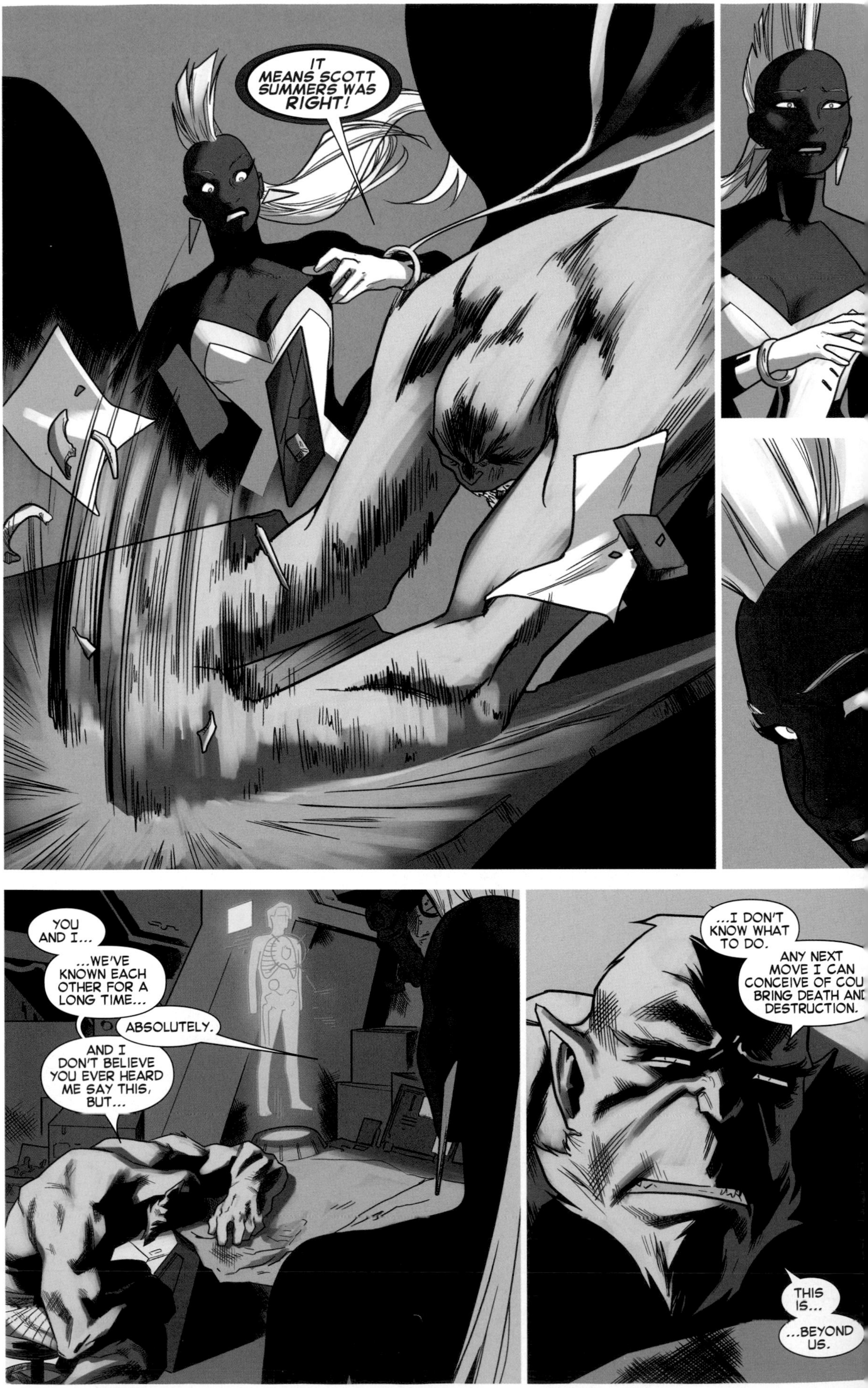
IT MEANS SCOTT SUMMERS WAS RIGHT!
YOU AND I...
...WE'VE KNOWN EACH OTHER FOR A LONG TIME...
ABSOLUTELY.
AND I DON'T BELIEVE YOU EVER HEARD ME SAY THIS, BUT...
...I DON'T KNOW WHAT TO DO.
ANY NEXT MOVE I CAN CONCEIVE OF
BRING DEATH AND DESTRUCTION.
THIS IS...
...BEYOND US.

THESE SHORTSIGHTED HUMANS CARE MORE ABOUT DISTANCING THEMSELVES FROM US THAN WORKING TOGETHER TO SOLVE THIS PROBLEM THAT AFFECTS US ALL!

YOU CAN EXAMINE ME LATER, HENRY.

WE NEED TO FIND SCOTT SUMMERS...AND WE NEED TO FIND HIM RIGHT NOW.

CAN YOU SEE SCOTT SUMMERS WITH CEREBRO?

WHY?

WHAT HAPPENED?

WHAT DID HE DO NOW?

HE TOOK THE NEW MUTANT.

HE TOOK HIM?

WE RECEIVED THIS INFORMATION DIRECTLY FROM S.H.I.E.L.D.

THE MUTANT CRASHED A HELICARRIER, FOR SOME REASON SPARED ALL OF THE X-MEN...

...AND THEN SCOTT SUMMERS SCOOPED HIM UP WHILE EVERYONE ELSE WAS RUNNING AROUND IN A PANIC.

PRETTY MUCH.

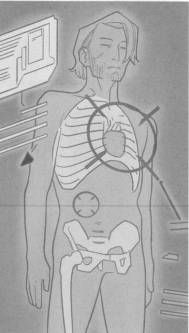

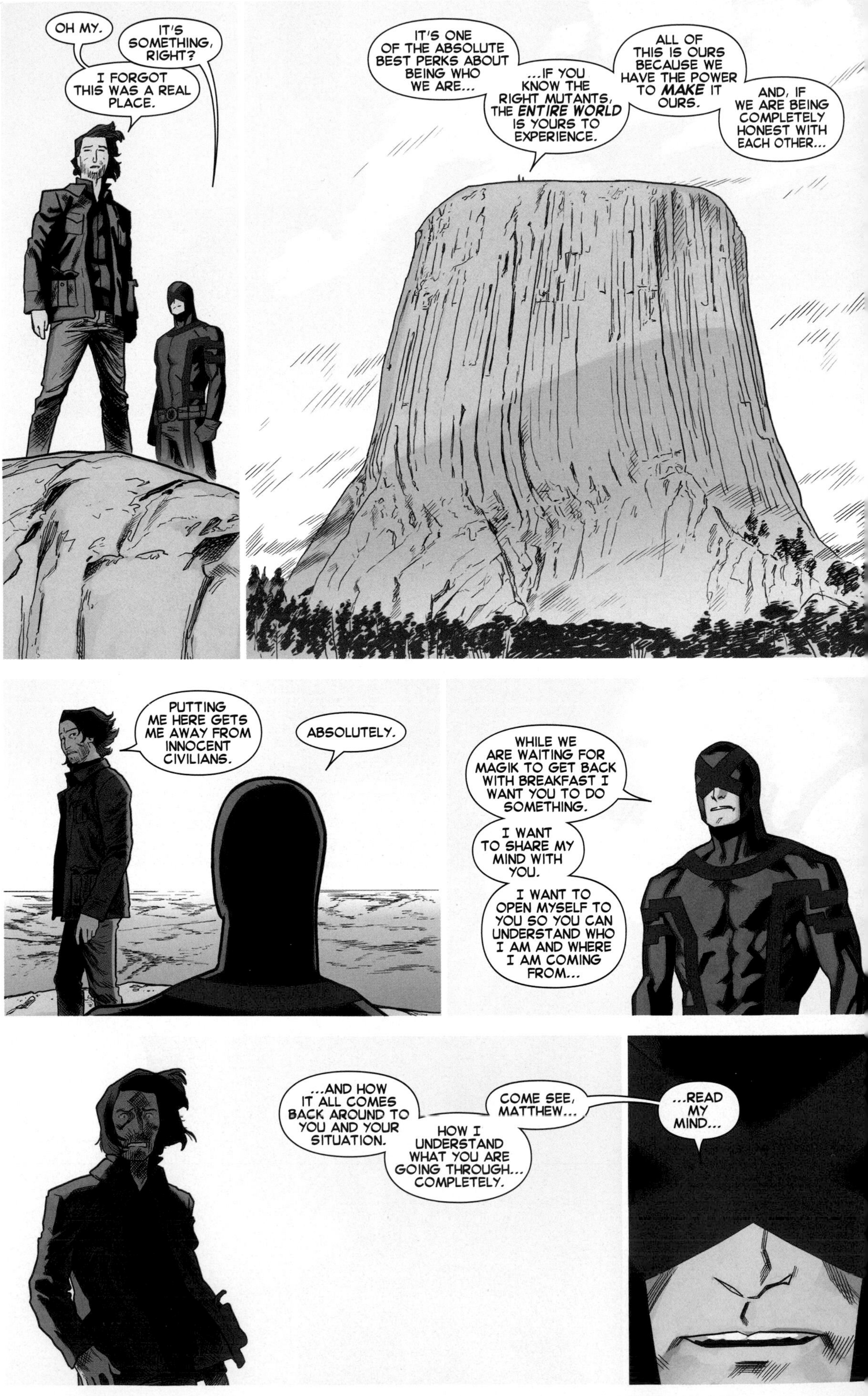
OH MY.
IT'S SOMETHING, RIGHT?
I FORGOT THIS WAS A REAL PLACE.
IT'S ONE OF THE ABSOLUTE BEST PERKS ABOUT BEING WHO WE ARE...
...IF YOU KNOW THE RIGHT MUTANTS, THE ENTIRE WORLD IS YOURS TO EXPERIENCE.
ALL OF THIS IS OURS BECAUSE WE HAVE THE POWER TO MAKE IT OURS.
AND, IF WE ARE BEING COMPLETELY HONEST WITH EACH OTHER...
PUTTING ME HERE GETS ME AWAY FROM INNOCENT CIVILIANS.
ABSOLUTELY.
WHILE WE ARE WAITING FOR MAGIK TO GET BACK WITH BREAKFAST I WANT YOU TO DO SOMETHING.
I WANT TO SHARE MY MIND WITH YOU.
I WANT TO OPEN MYSELF TO YOU SO YOU CAN UNDERSTAND WHO I AM AND WHERE I AM COMING FROM...
...AND HOW IT ALL COMES BACK AROUND TO YOU AND YOUR SITUATION.
HOW I UNDERSTAND WHAT YOU ARE GOING THROUGH... COMPLETELY.
COME SEE, MATTHEW...
...READ MY MIND...

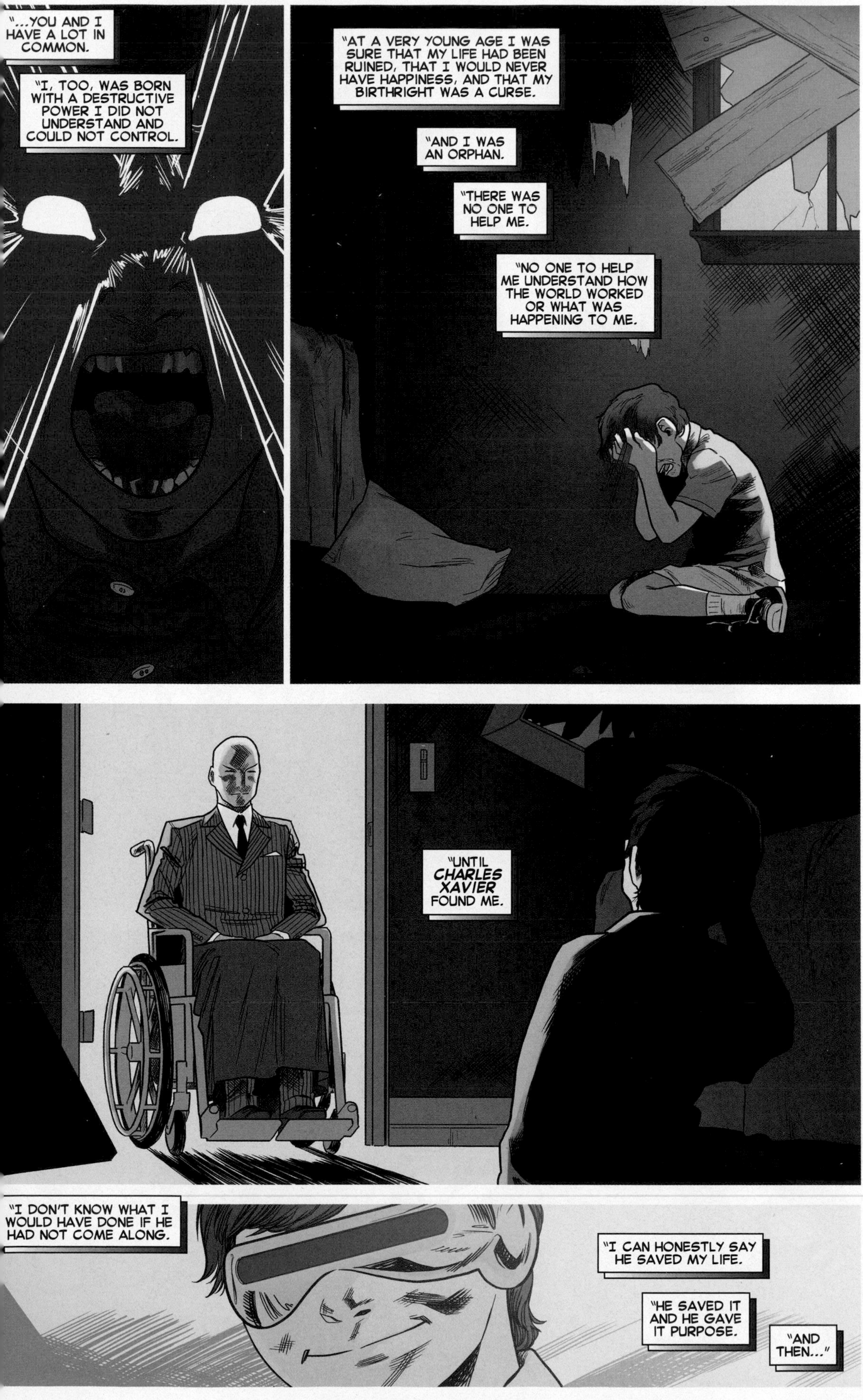
"...YOU AND I HAVE A LOT IN COMMON.
"I, TOO, WAS BORN WITH A DESTRUCTIVE POWER I DID NOT UNDERSTAND AND COULD NOT CONTROL.
"AT A VERY YOUNG AGE I WAS SURE THAT MY LIFE HAD BEEN RUINED, THAT I WOULD NEVER HAVE HAPPINESS, AND THAT MY BIRTHRIGHT WAS A CURSE.
"AND I WAS AN ORPHAN.
"THERE WAS NO ONE TO HELP ME.
"NO ONE TO HELP ME UNDERSTAND HOW THE WORLD WORKED OR WHAT WAS HAPPENING TO ME.
"UNTIL CHARLES XAVIER FOUND ME.
"I DON'T KNOW WHAT I WOULD HAVE DONE IF HE HAD NOT COME ALONG.
"I CAN HONESTLY SAY HE SAVED MY LIFE.
"HE SAVED IT AND HE GAVE IT PURPOSE.
"AND THEN..."

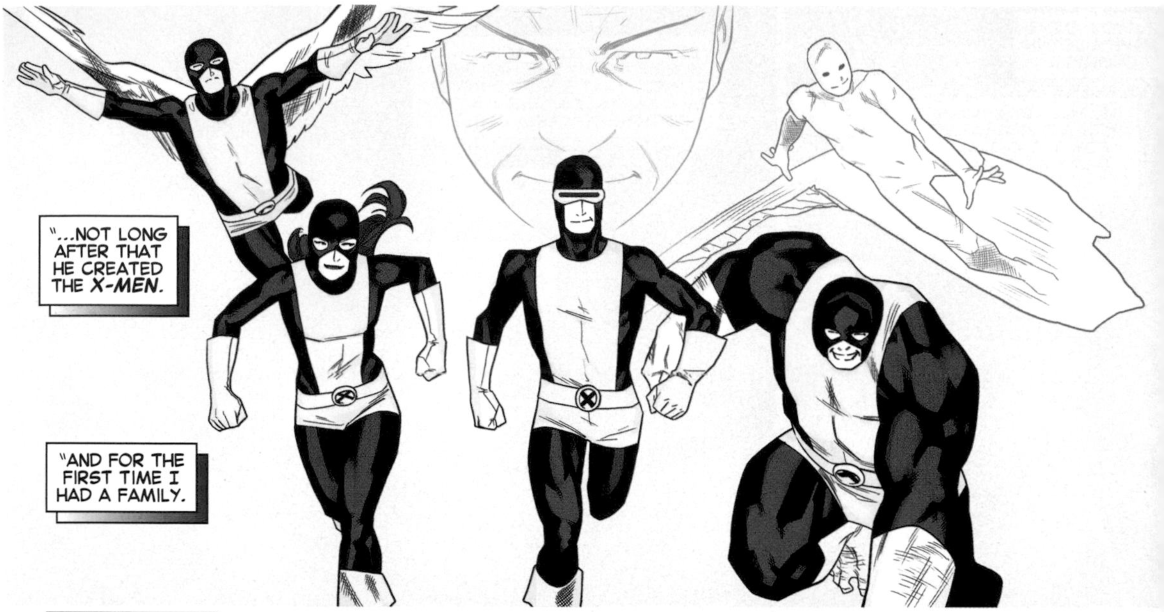
"...NOT LONG AFTER THAT HE CREATED THE *X-MEN*.
"AND FOR THE FIRST TIME I HAD A FAMILY.

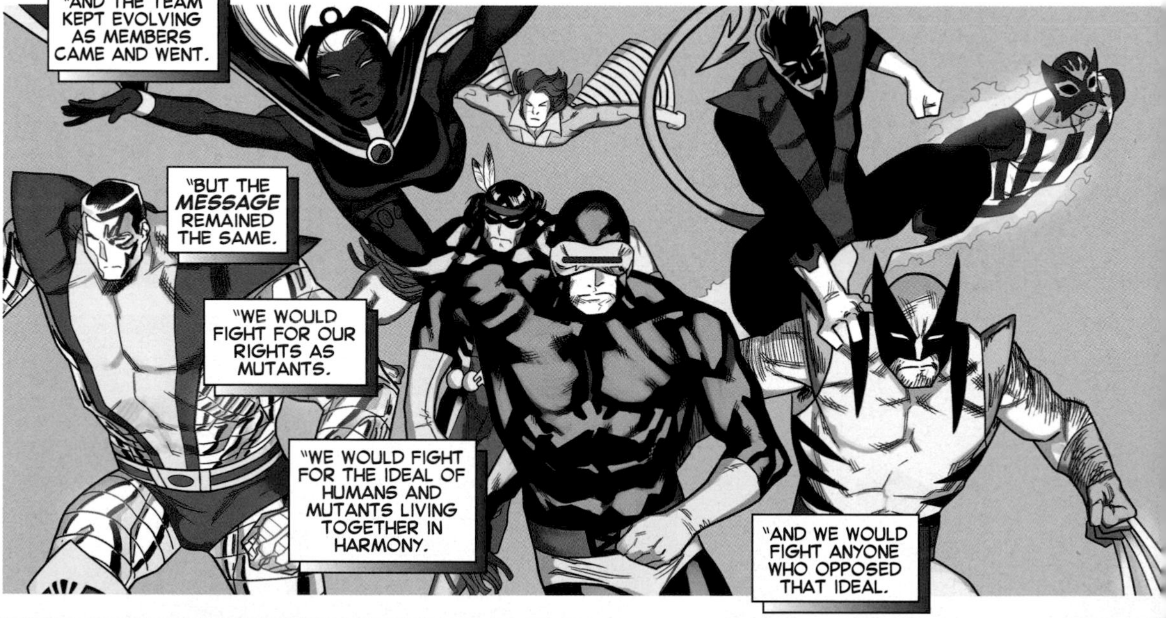
"AND THE TEAM KEPT EVOLVING AS MEMBERS CAME AND WENT.
"BUT THE *MESSAGE* REMAINED THE SAME.
"WE WOULD FIGHT FOR OUR RIGHTS AS MUTANTS.
"WE WOULD FIGHT FOR THE IDEAL OF HUMANS AND MUTANTS LIVING TOGETHER IN HARMONY.
"AND WE WOULD FIGHT ANYONE WHO OPPOSED THAT IDEAL.

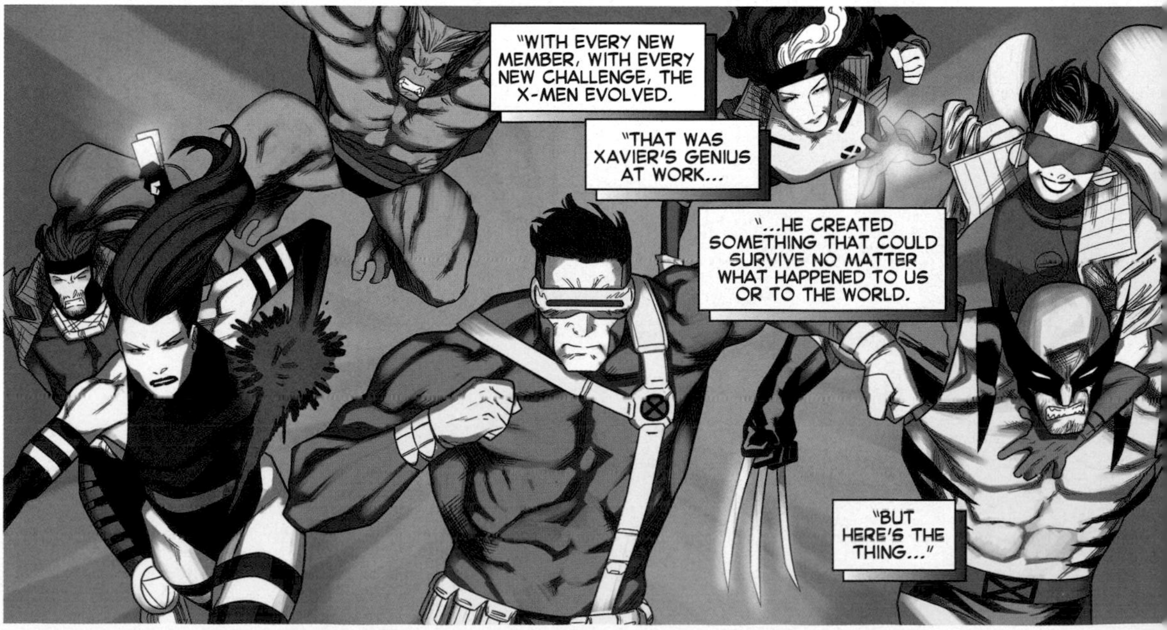
"WITH EVERY NEW MEMBER, WITH EVERY NEW CHALLENGE, THE X-MEN EVOLVED.
"THAT WAS XAVIER'S GENIUS AT WORK...
"...HE CREATED SOMETHING THAT COULD SURVIVE NO MATTER WHAT HAPPENED TO US OR TO THE WORLD.
"BUT HERE'S THE THING..."

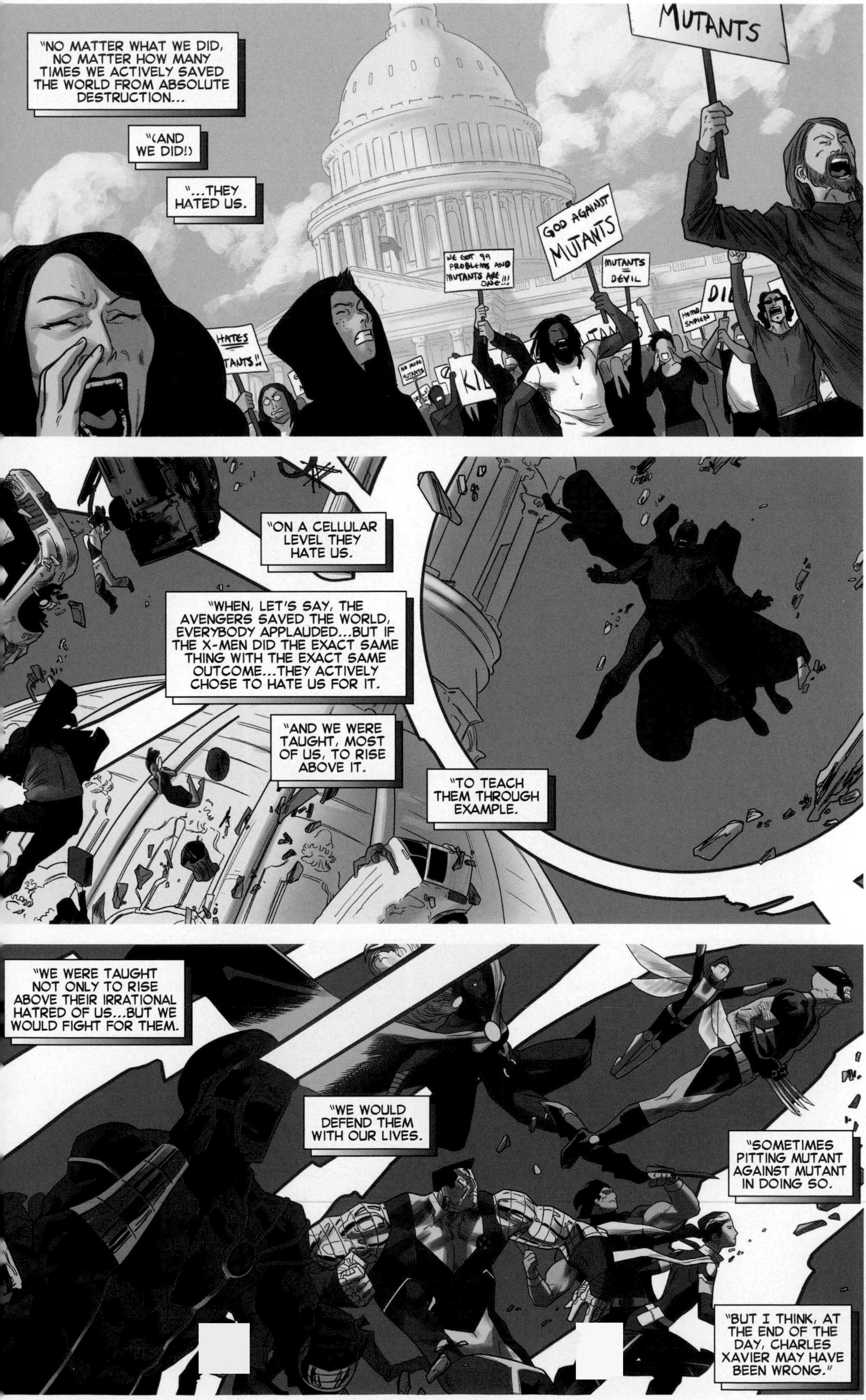
MUTANTS
"NO MATTER WHAT WE DID, NO MATTER HOW MANY TIMES WE ACTIVELY SAVED THE WORLD FROM ABSOLUTE DESTRUCTION...
"(AND WE DID!)
"...THEY HATED US.
GOD AGAINST MUTANTS
WE GOT 99 PROBLEMS AND MUTANTS ARE ONE!!!
MUTANTS = DEVIL
"ON A CELLULAR LEVEL THEY HATE US.
"WHEN, LET'S SAY, THE AVENGERS SAVED THE WORLD, EVERYBODY APPLAUDED...BUT IF THE X-MEN DID THE EXACT SAME THING WITH THE EXACT SAME OUTCOME...THEY ACTIVELY CHOSE TO HATE US FOR IT.
"AND WE WERE TAUGHT, MOST OF US, TO RISE ABOVE IT.
"TO TEACH THEM THROUGH EXAMPLE.
"WE WERE TAUGHT NOT ONLY TO RISE ABOVE THEIR IRRATIONAL HATRED OF US...BUT WE WOULD FIGHT FOR THEM.
"WE WOULD DEFEND THEM WITH OUR LIVES.
"SOMETIMES PITTING MUTANT AGAINST MUTANT IN DOING SO.
"BUT I THINK, AT THE END OF THE DAY, CHARLES XAVIER MAY HAVE BEEN WRONG."

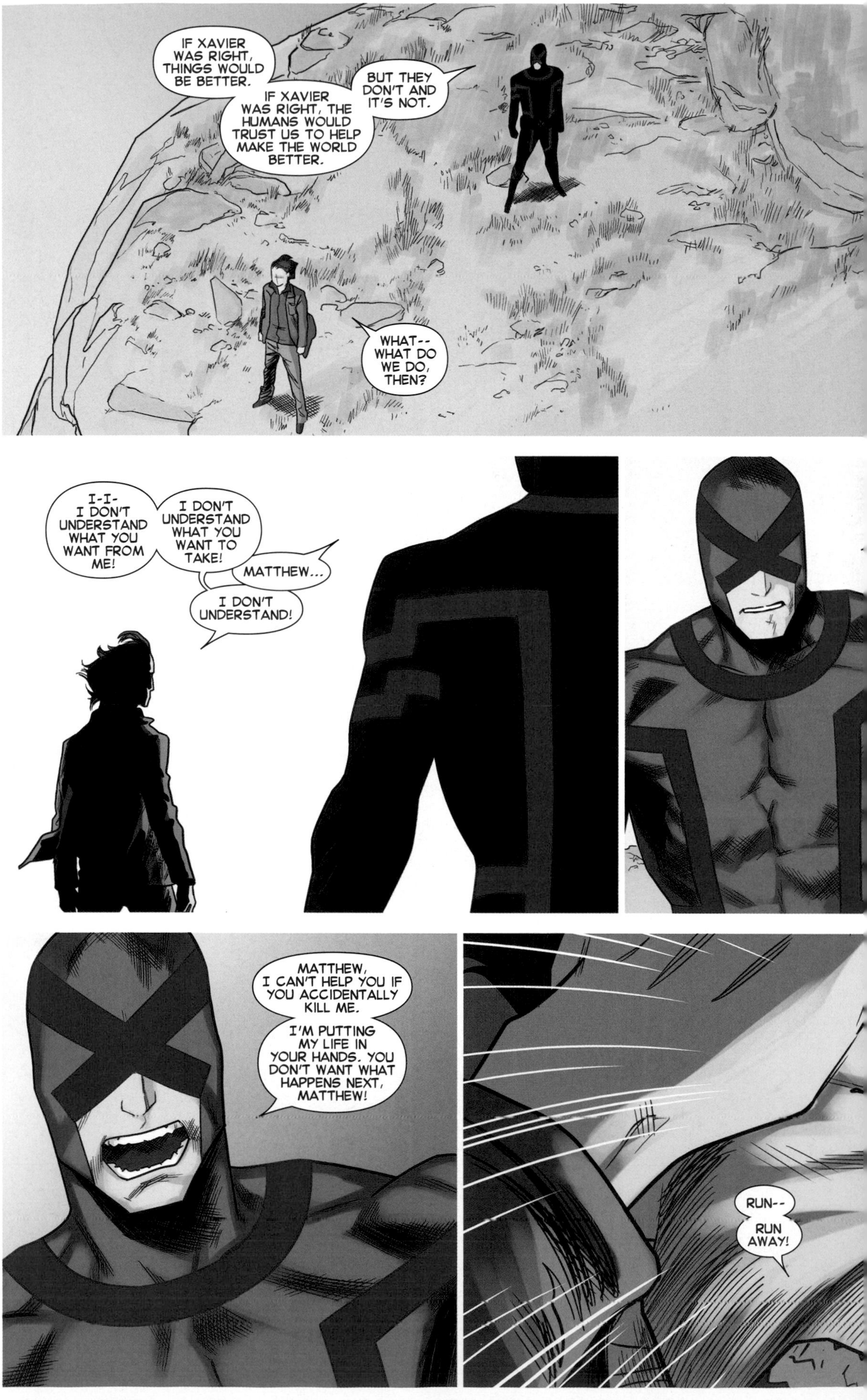
IF XAVIER WAS RIGHT, THINGS WOULD BE BETTER.
IF XAVIER WAS RIGHT, THE HUMANS WOULD TRUST US TO HELP MAKE THE WORLD BETTER.
BUT THEY DON'T AND IT'S NOT.
WHAT-- WHAT DO WE DO, THEN?
I-I- I DON'T UNDERSTAND WHAT YOU WANT FROM ME!
I DON'T UNDERSTAND WHAT YOU WANT TO TAKE!
MATTHEW...
I DON'T UNDERSTAND!
MATTHEW, I CAN'T HELP YOU IF YOU ACCIDENTALLY KILL ME.
I'M PUTTING MY LIFE IN YOUR HANDS. YOU DON'T WANT WHAT HAPPENS NEXT, MATTHEW!
RUN--
RUN AWAY!

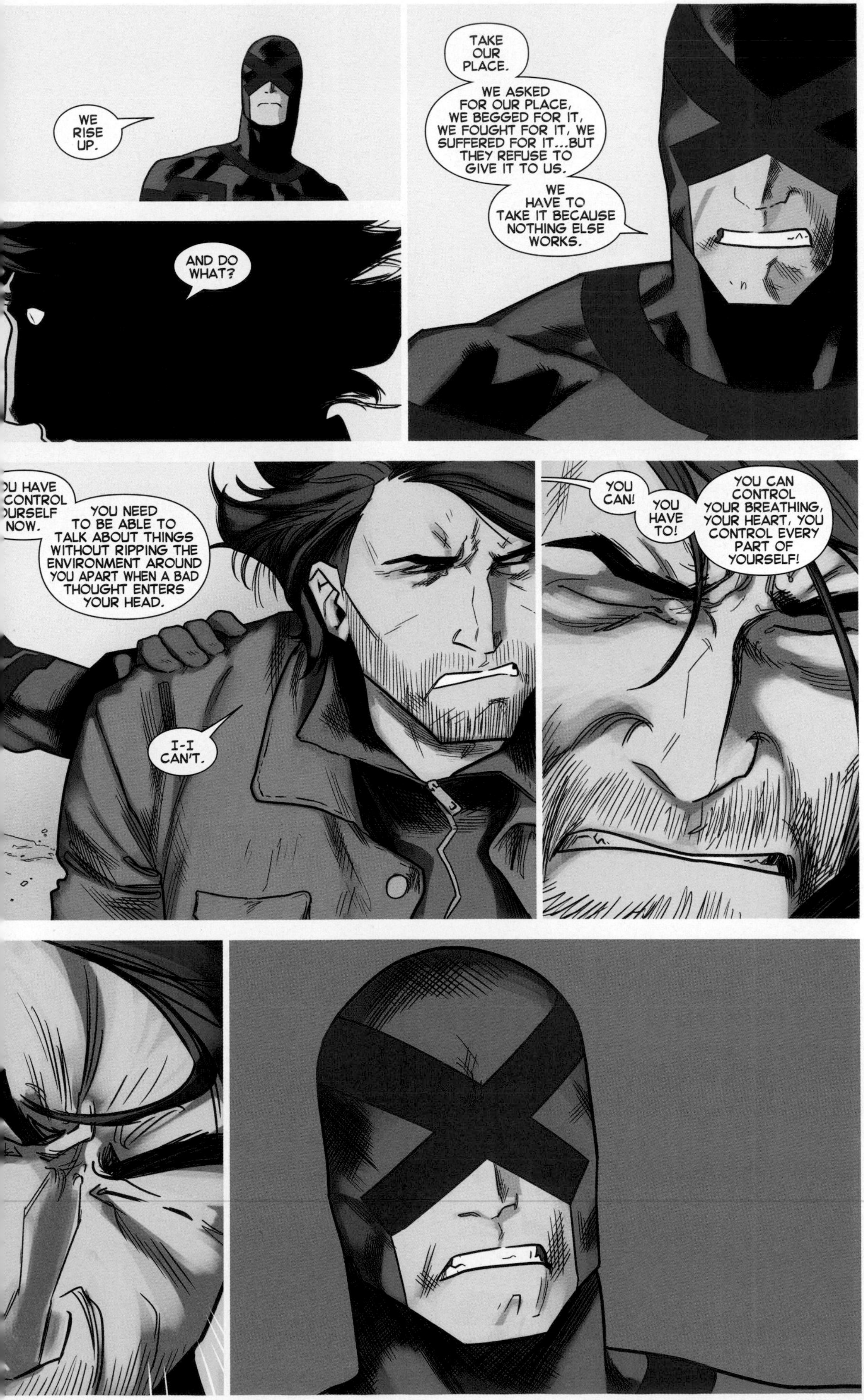
WE RISE UP.
TAKE OUR PLACE.
WE ASKED FOR OUR PLACE, WE BEGGED FOR IT, WE FOUGHT FOR IT, WE SUFFERED FOR IT...BUT THEY REFUSE TO GIVE IT TO US.
AND DO WHAT?
WE HAVE TO TAKE IT BECAUSE NOTHING ELSE WORKS.
OU HAVE CONTROL OURSELF NOW.
YOU NEED TO BE ABLE TO TALK ABOUT THINGS WITHOUT RIPPING THE ENVIRONMENT AROUND YOU APART WHEN A BAD THOUGHT ENTERS YOUR HEAD.
I-I CAN'T.
YOU CAN!
YOU HAVE TO!
YOU CAN CONTROL YOUR BREATHING, YOUR HEART, YOU CONTROL EVERY PART OF YOURSELF!

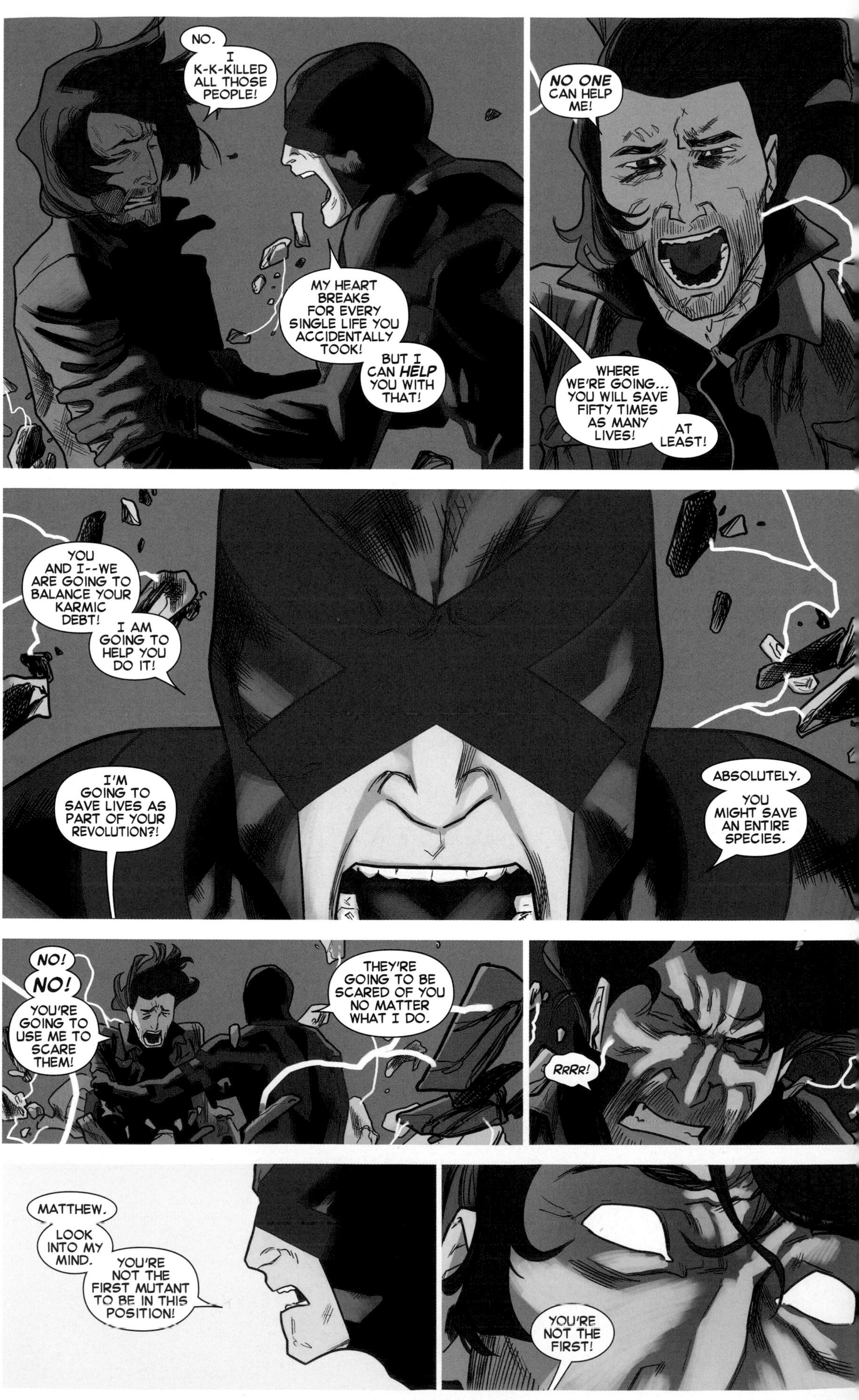
NO.
I K-K-KILLED ALL THOSE PEOPLE!
MY HEART BREAKS FOR EVERY SINGLE LIFE YOU ACCIDENTALLY TOOK!
BUT I CAN *HELP* YOU WITH THAT!
*NO ONE* CAN HELP ME!
WHERE WE'RE GOING... YOU WILL SAVE FIFTY TIMES AS MANY LIVES!
AT LEAST!
YOU AND I--WE ARE GOING TO BALANCE YOUR KARMIC DEBT!
I AM GOING TO HELP YOU DO IT!
I'M GOING TO SAVE LIVES AS PART OF YOUR REVOLUTION?!
ABSOLUTELY.
YOU MIGHT SAVE AN ENTIRE SPECIES.
*NO!*
*NO!*
YOU'RE GOING TO USE ME TO SCARE THEM!
THEY'RE GOING TO BE SCARED OF YOU NO MATTER WHAT I DO.
*RRRR!*
MATTHEW.
LOOK INTO MY MIND.
YOU'RE NOT THE FIRST MUTANT TO BE IN THIS POSITION!
YOU'RE NOT THE FIRST!

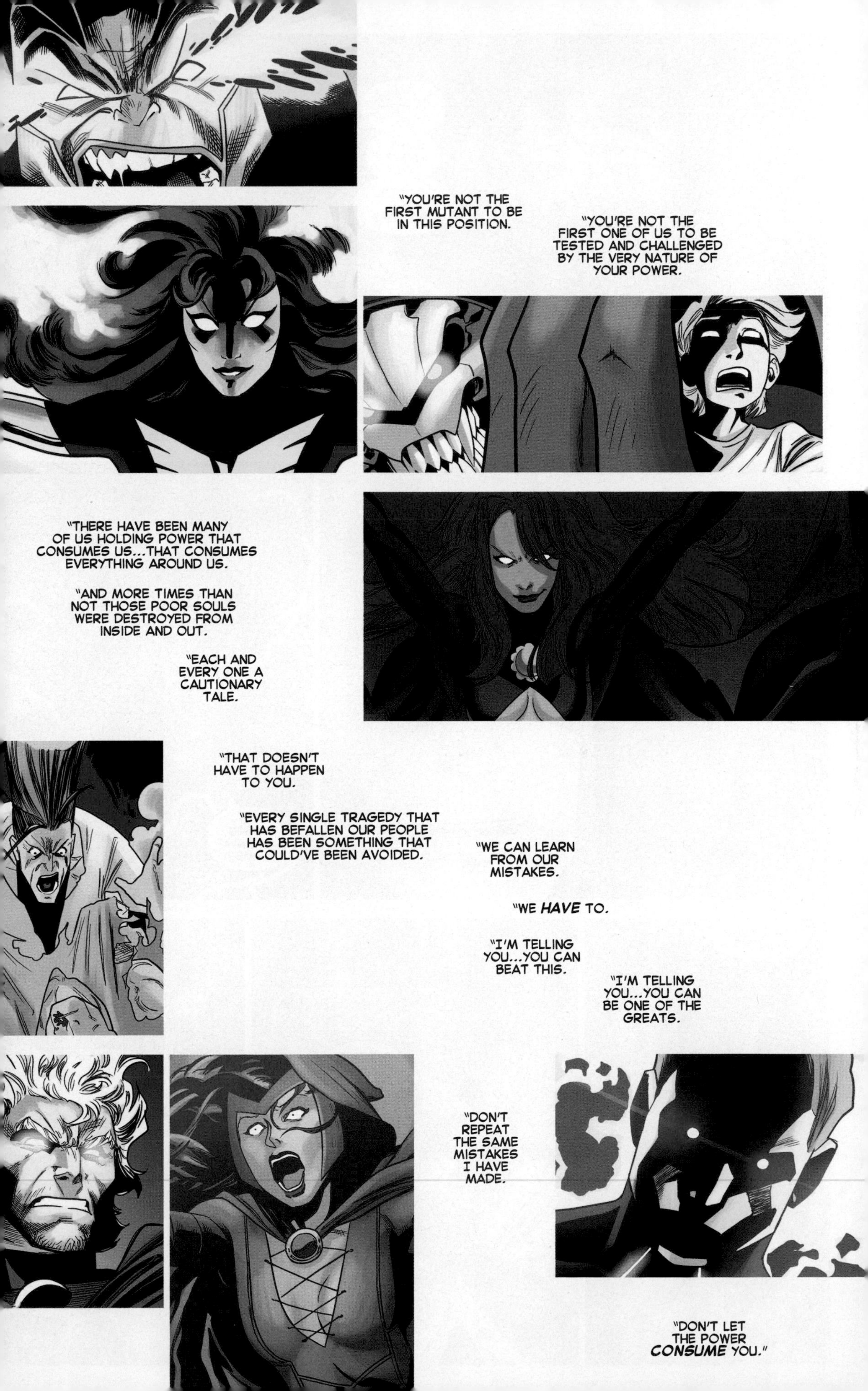
"YOU'RE NOT THE FIRST MUTANT TO BE IN THIS POSITION.
"YOU'RE NOT THE FIRST ONE OF US TO BE TESTED AND CHALLENGED BY THE VERY NATURE OF YOUR POWER.
"THERE HAVE BEEN MANY OF US HOLDING POWER THAT CONSUMES US...THAT CONSUMES EVERYTHING AROUND US.
"AND MORE TIMES THAN NOT THOSE POOR SOULS WERE DESTROYED FROM INSIDE AND OUT.
"EACH AND EVERY ONE A CAUTIONARY TALE.
"THAT DOESN'T HAVE TO HAPPEN TO YOU.
"EVERY SINGLE TRAGEDY THAT HAS BEFALLEN OUR PEOPLE HAS BEEN SOMETHING THAT COULD'VE BEEN AVOIDED.
"WE CAN LEARN FROM OUR MISTAKES.
"WE *HAVE* TO.
"I'M TELLING YOU...YOU CAN BEAT THIS.
"I'M TELLING YOU...YOU CAN BE ONE OF THE GREATS.
"DON'T REPEAT THE SAME MISTAKES I HAVE MADE.
"DON'T LET THE POWER *CONSUME* YOU."

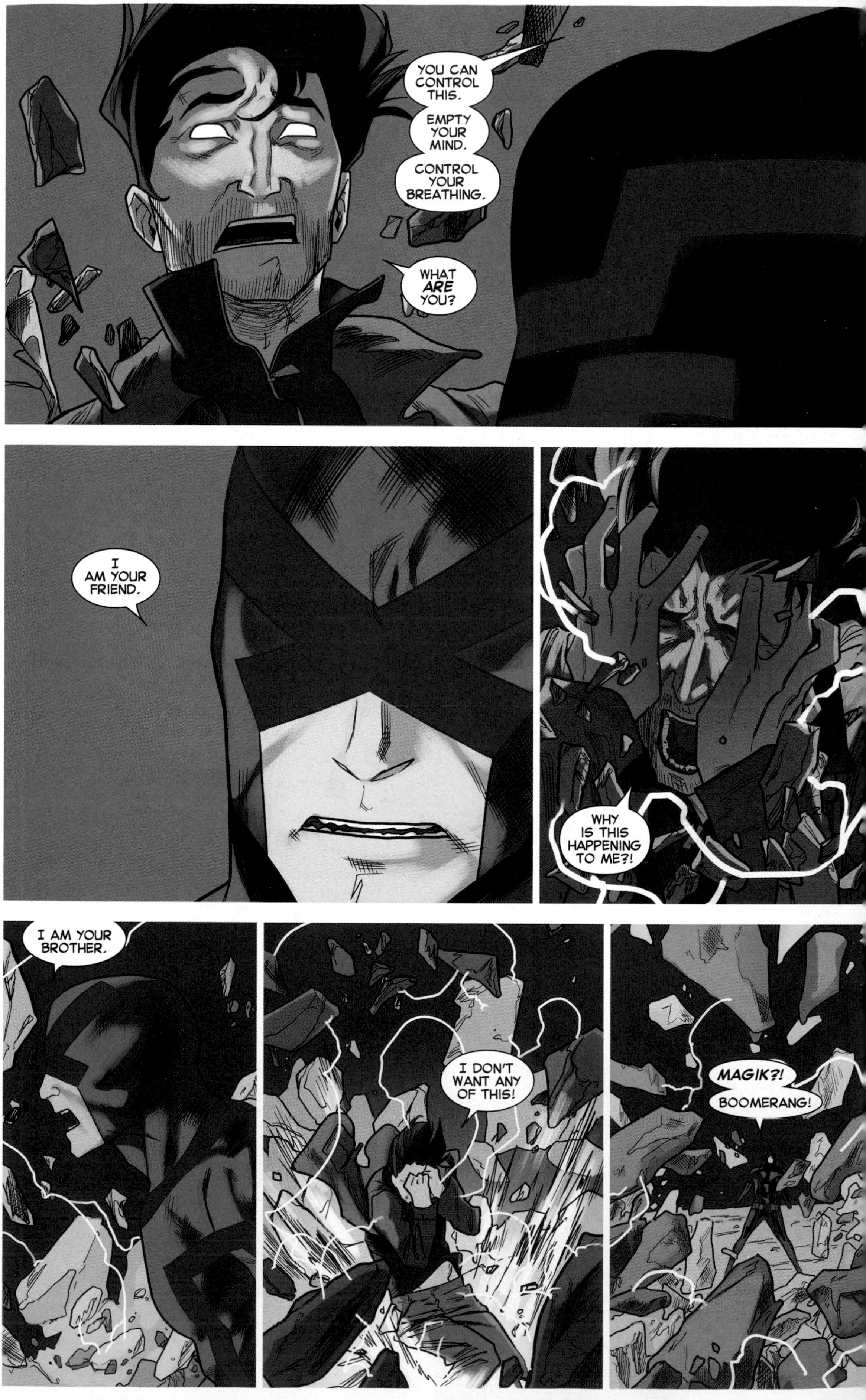
YOU CAN CONTROL THIS.
EMPTY YOUR MIND.
CONTROL YOUR BREATHING.
WHAT ARE YOU?
I AM YOUR FRIEND.
WHY IS THIS HAPPENING TO ME?!
I AM YOUR BROTHER.
I DON'T WANT ANY OF THIS!
MAGIK?!
BOOMERANG!

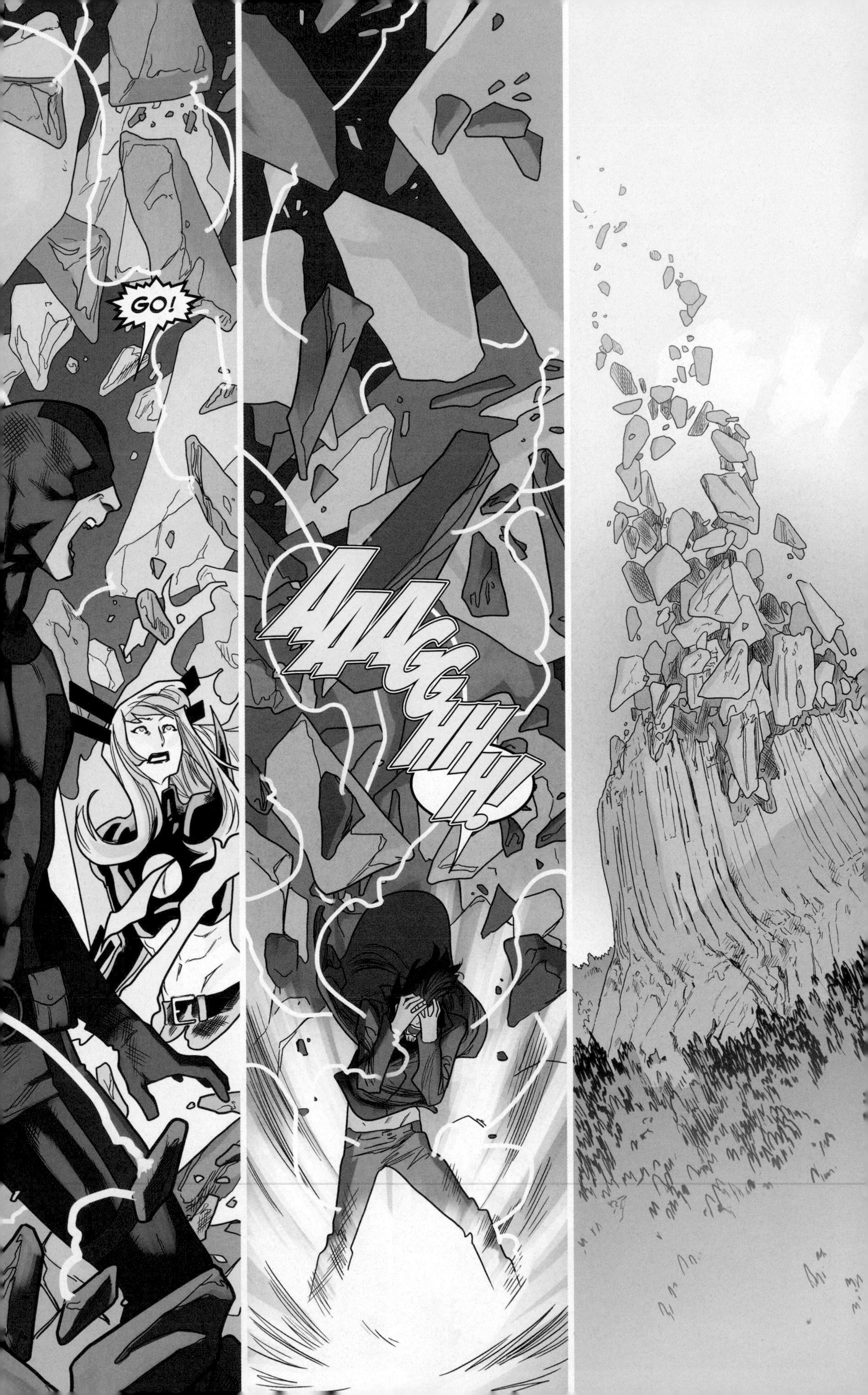
GO!
AAAGGHHH!

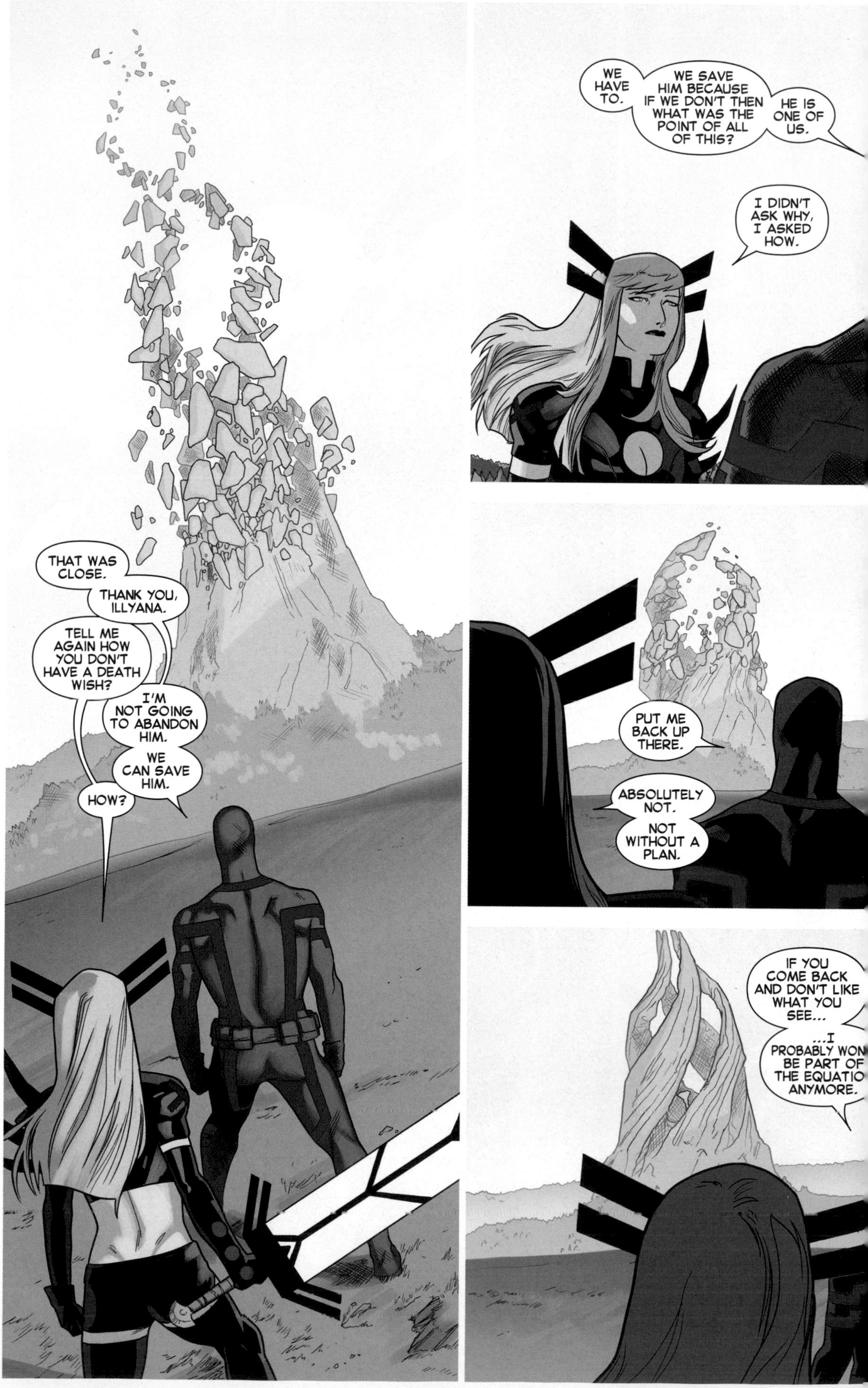
THAT WAS CLOSE.
THANK YOU, ILLYANA.
TELL ME AGAIN HOW YOU DON'T HAVE A DEATH WISH?
I'M NOT GOING TO ABANDON HIM.
WE CAN SAVE HIM.
HOW?
WE HAVE TO.
WE SAVE HIM BECAUSE IF WE DON'T THEN WHAT WAS THE POINT OF ALL OF THIS?
HE IS ONE OF US.
I DIDN'T ASK WHY, I ASKED HOW.
PUT ME BACK UP THERE.
ABSOLUTELY NOT.
NOT WITHOUT A PLAN.
IF YOU COME BACK AND DON'T LIKE WHAT YOU SEE...
...I PROBABLY WON BE PART OF THE EQUATIO ANYMORE.

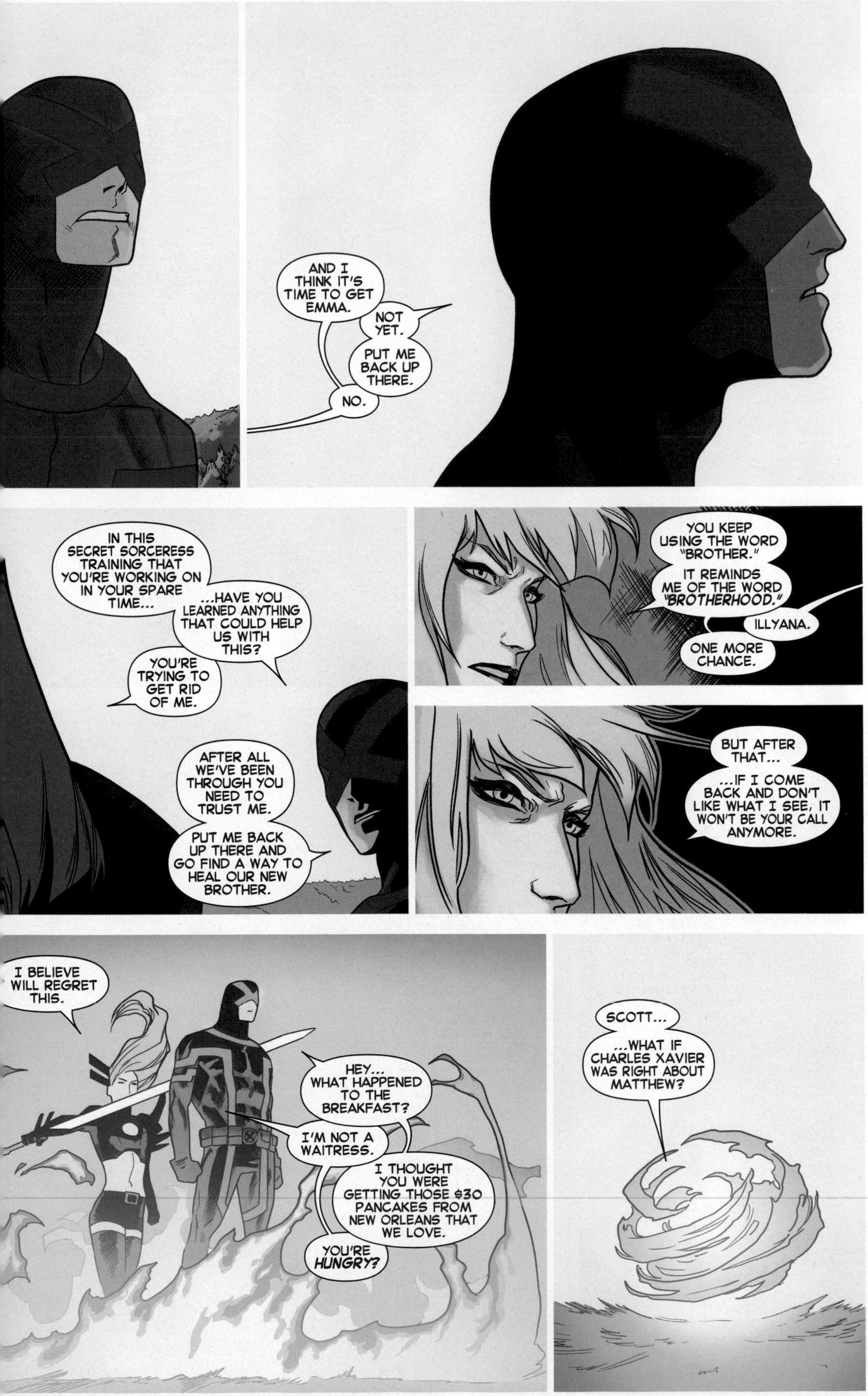
AND I THINK IT'S TIME TO GET EMMA.
NOT YET.
PUT ME BACK UP THERE.
NO.
IN THIS SECRET SORCERESS TRAINING THAT YOU'RE WORKING ON IN YOUR SPARE TIME...
...HAVE YOU LEARNED ANYTHING THAT COULD HELP US WITH THIS?
YOU'RE TRYING TO GET RID OF ME.
AFTER ALL WE'VE BEEN THROUGH YOU NEED TO TRUST ME.
PUT ME BACK UP THERE AND GO FIND A WAY TO HEAL OUR NEW BROTHER.
YOU KEEP USING THE WORD "BROTHER."
IT REMINDS ME OF THE WORD "BROTHERHOOD."
ILLYANA.
ONE MORE CHANCE.
BUT AFTER THAT...
...IF I COME BACK AND DON'T LIKE WHAT I SEE, IT WON'T BE YOUR CALL ANYMORE.
I BELIEVE WILL REGRET THIS.
HEY... WHAT HAPPENED TO THE BREAKFAST?
I'M NOT A WAITRESS.
I THOUGHT YOU WERE GETTING THOSE $30 PANCAKES FROM NEW ORLEANS THAT WE LOVE.
YOU'RE HUNGRY?
SCOTT...
...WHAT IF CHARLES XAVIER WAS RIGHT ABOUT MATTHEW?

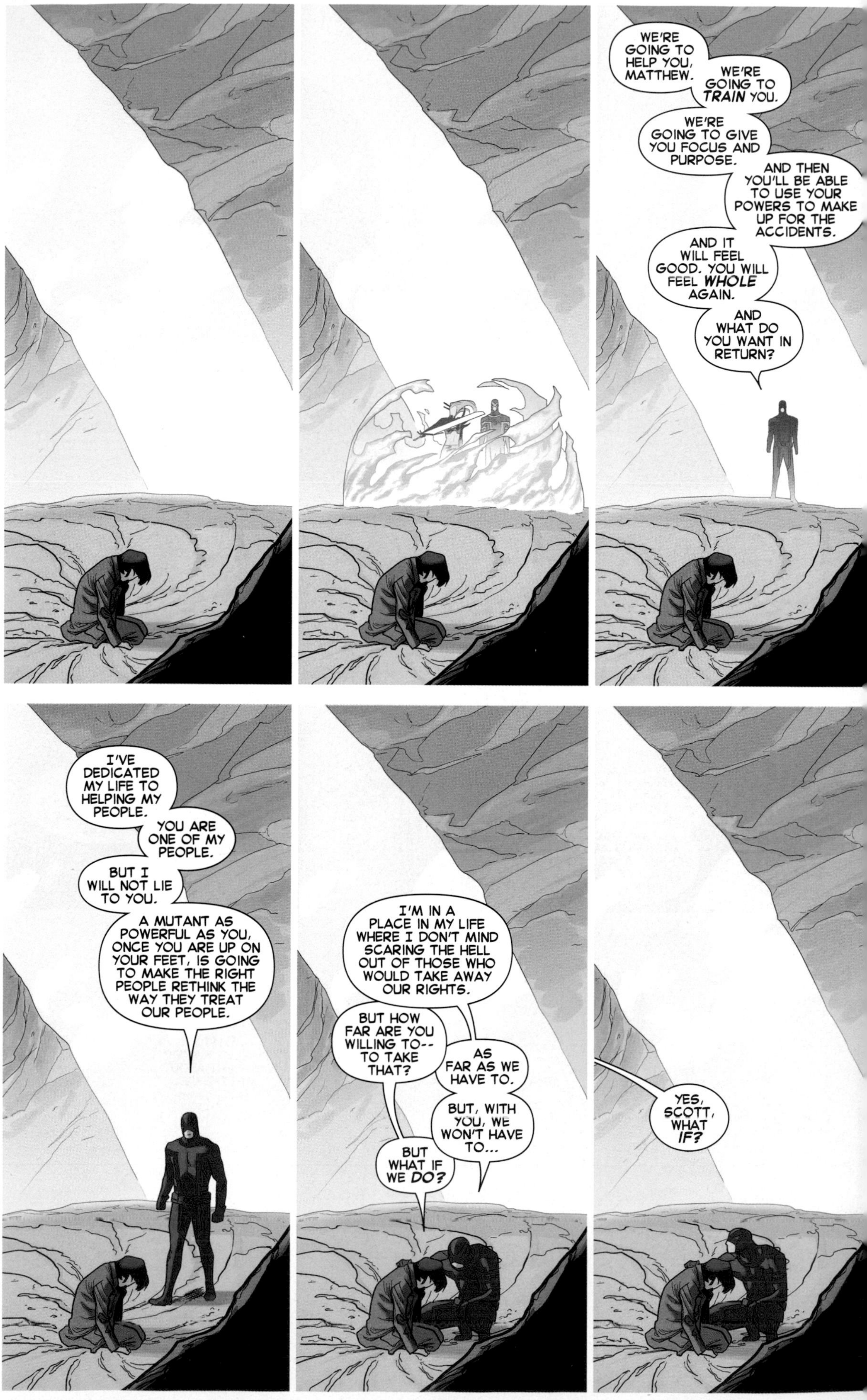
WE'RE GOING TO HELP YOU, MATTHEW.
WE'RE GOING TO TRAIN YOU.
WE'RE GOING TO GIVE YOU FOCUS AND PURPOSE.
AND THEN YOU'LL BE ABLE TO USE YOUR POWERS TO MAKE UP FOR THE ACCIDENTS.
AND IT WILL FEEL GOOD. YOU WILL FEEL WHOLE AGAIN.
AND WHAT DO YOU WANT IN RETURN?
I'VE DEDICATED MY LIFE TO HELPING MY PEOPLE.
YOU ARE ONE OF MY PEOPLE.
BUT I WILL NOT LIE TO YOU.
A MUTANT AS POWERFUL AS YOU, ONCE YOU ARE UP ON YOUR FEET, IS GOING TO MAKE THE RIGHT PEOPLE RETHINK THE WAY THEY TREAT OUR PEOPLE.
I'M IN A PLACE IN MY LIFE WHERE I DON'T MIND SCARING THE HELL OUT OF THOSE WHO WOULD TAKE AWAY OUR RIGHTS.
BUT HOW FAR ARE YOU WILLING TO-- TO TAKE THAT?
AS FAR AS WE HAVE TO.
BUT, WITH YOU, WE WON'T HAVE TO...
BUT WHAT IF WE DO?
YES, SCOTT, WHAT IF?

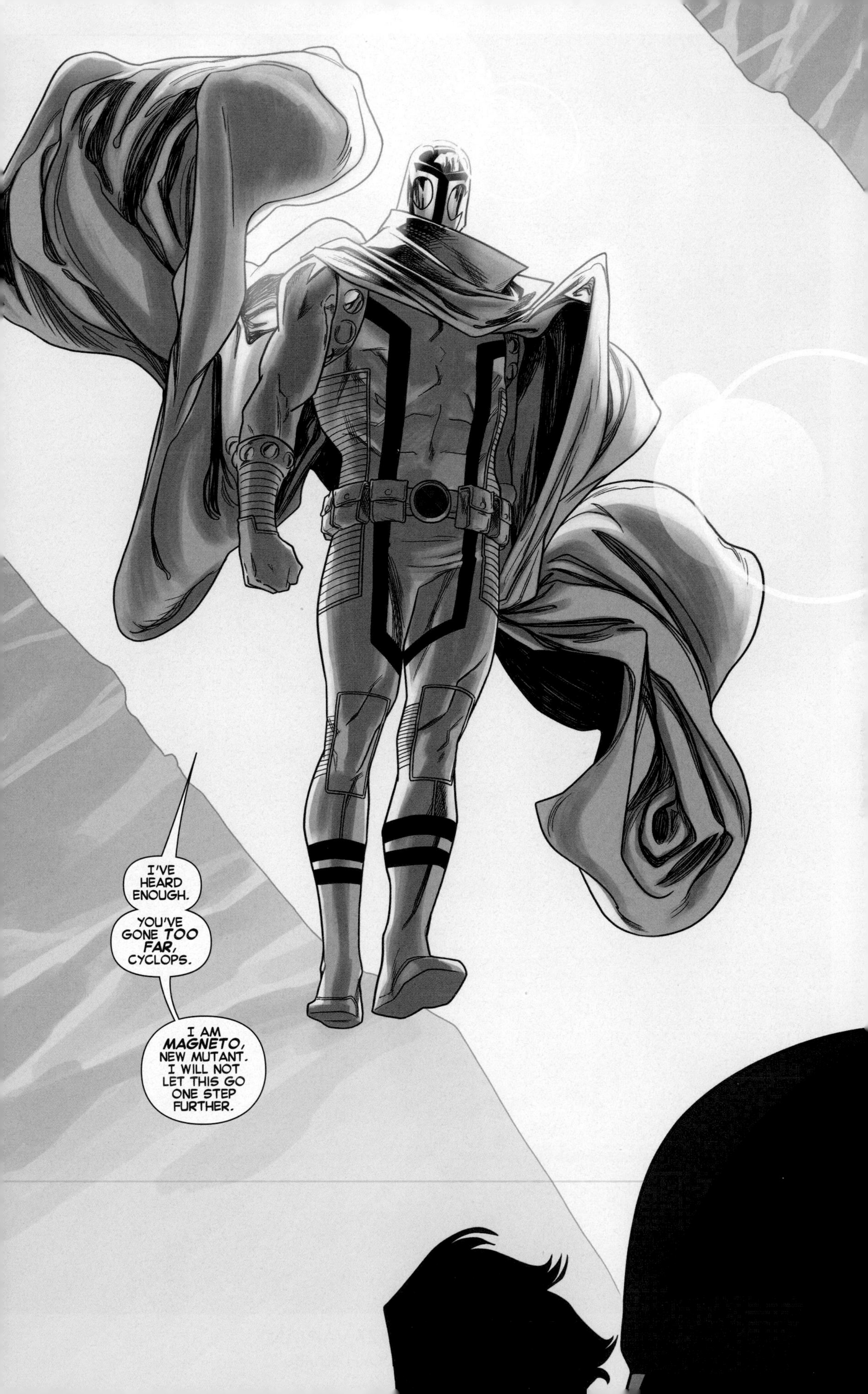

I'VE HEARD ENOUGH.
YOU'VE GONE *TOO FAR*, CYCLOPS.
I AM *MAGNETO*, NEW MUTANT. I WILL NOT LET THIS GO ONE STEP FURTHER.

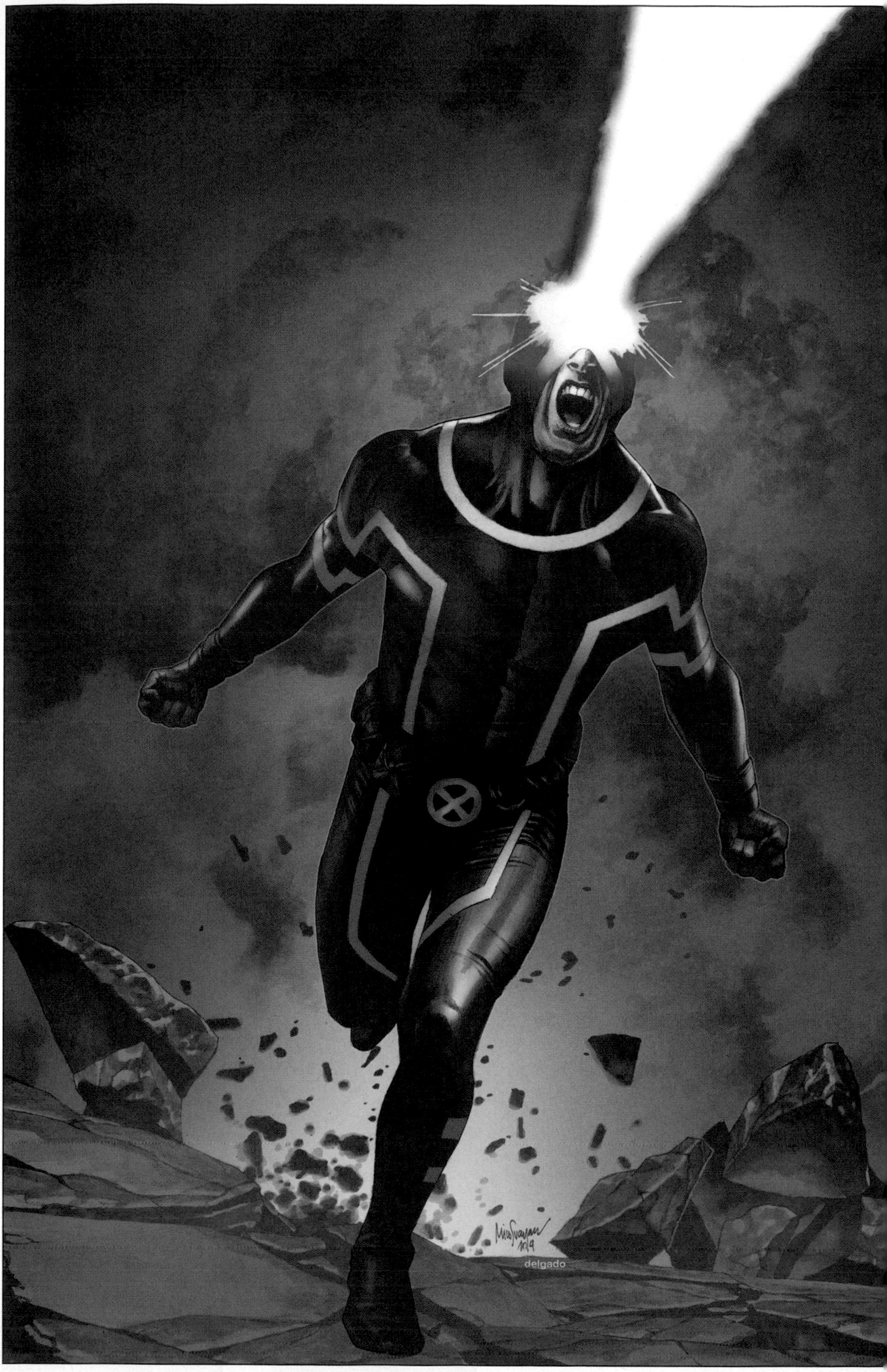
delgado

**UNCANNY X-MEN #27** VARIANT
BY MICO SUAYAN & EDGAR DELGADO

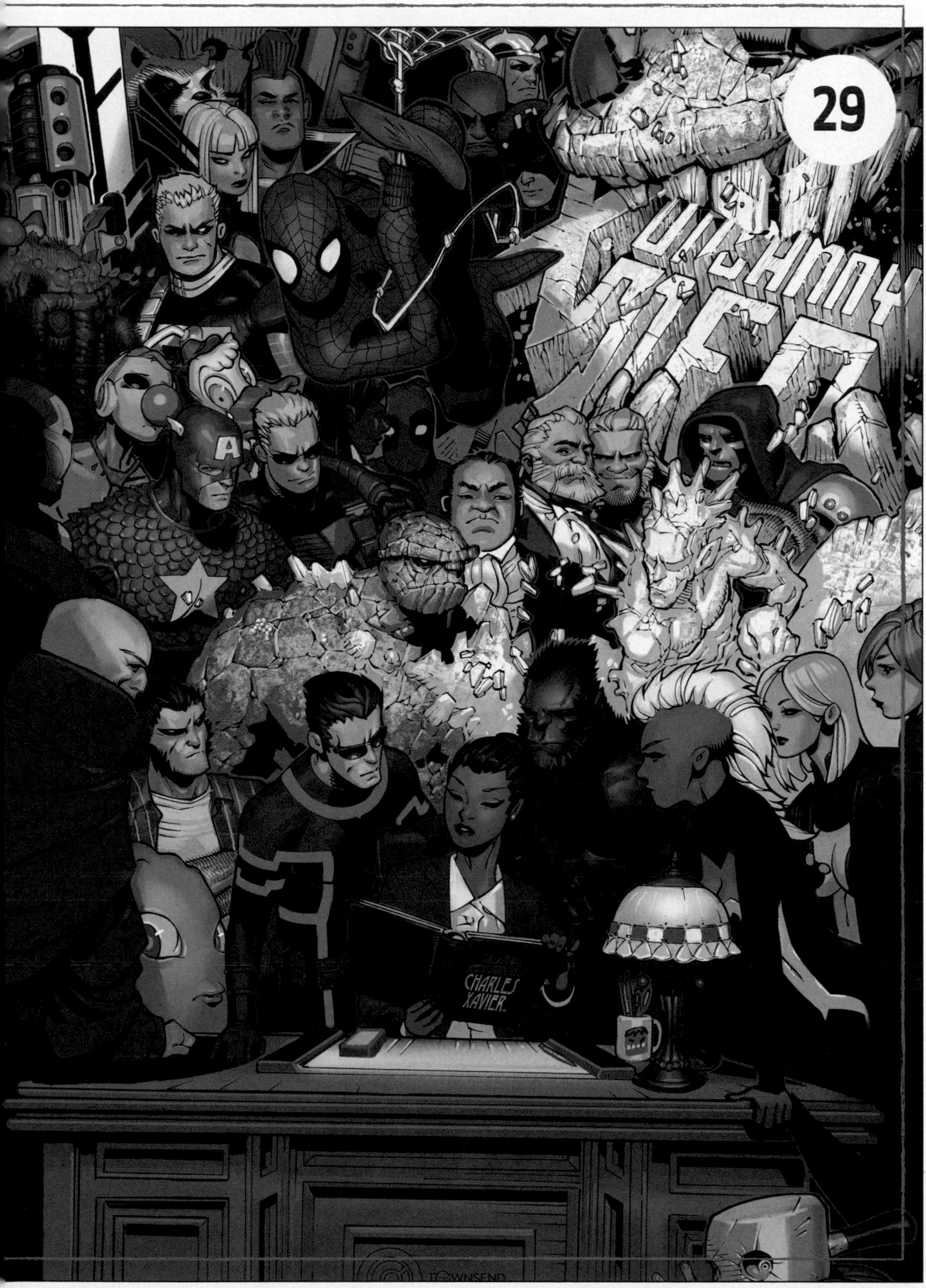
29
CHARLES XAVIER

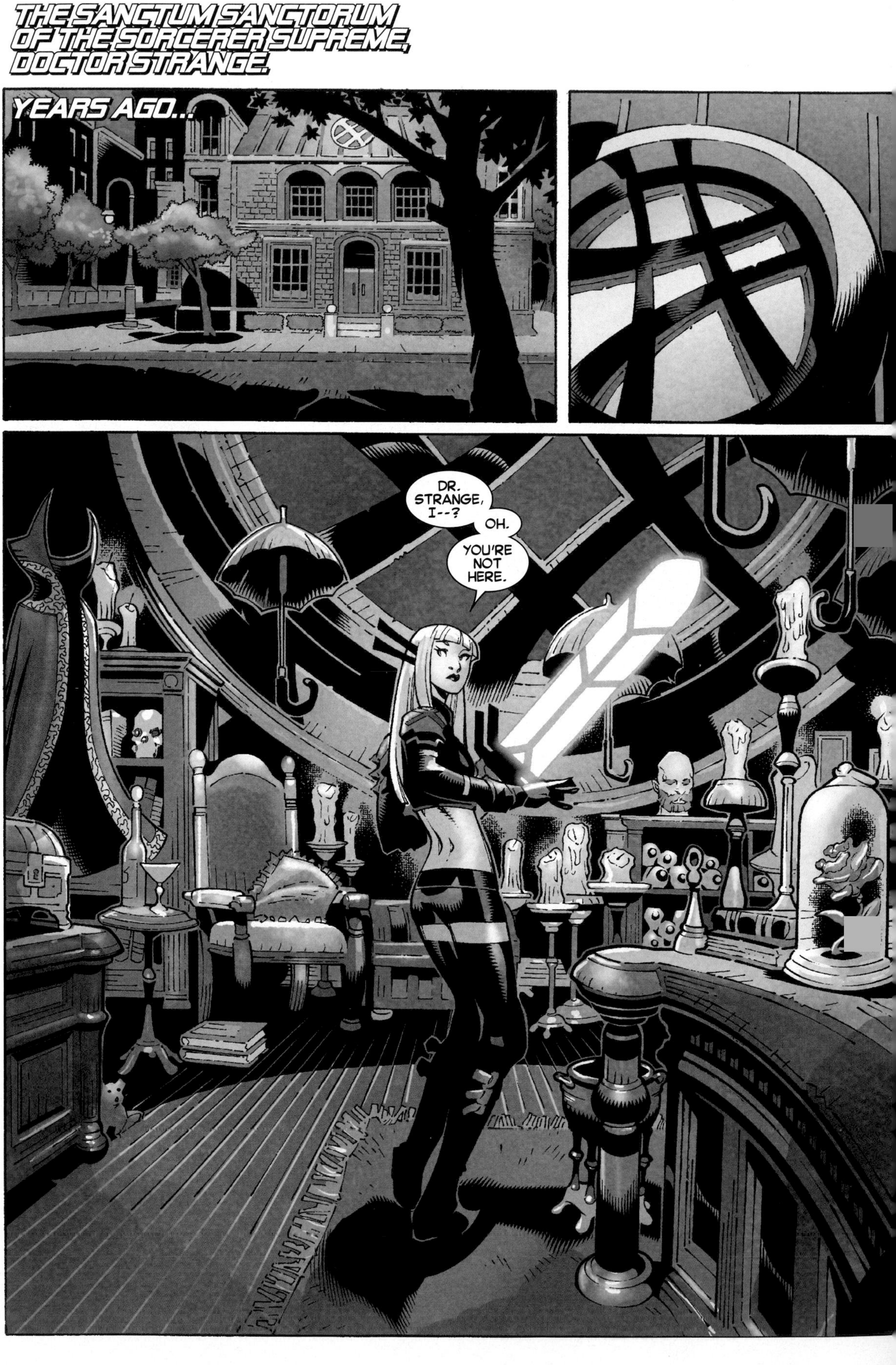
THE SANCTUM SANCTORUM OF THE SORCERER SUPREME, DOCTOR STRANGE.
YEARS AGO...
DR. STRANGE, I--?
OH.
YOU'RE NOT HERE.

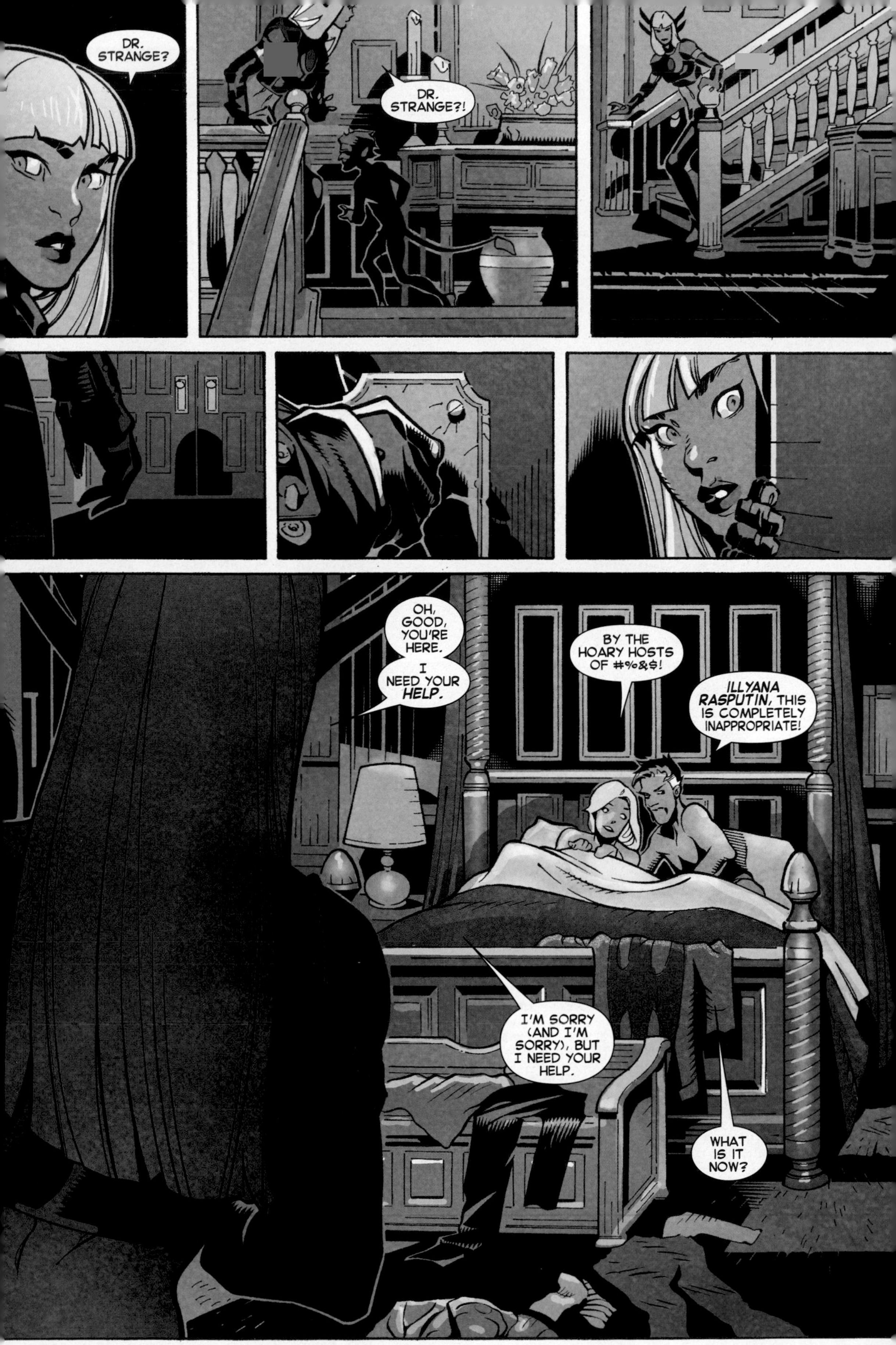
DR. STRANGE?
DR. STRANGE?!
OH, GOOD, YOU'RE HERE.
I NEED YOUR *HELP.*
BY THE HOARY HOSTS OF #%&$!
*ILLYANA RASPUTIN,* THIS IS COMPLETELY INAPPROPRIATE!
I'M SORRY (AND I'M SORRY), BUT I NEED YOUR HELP.
WHAT IS IT NOW?

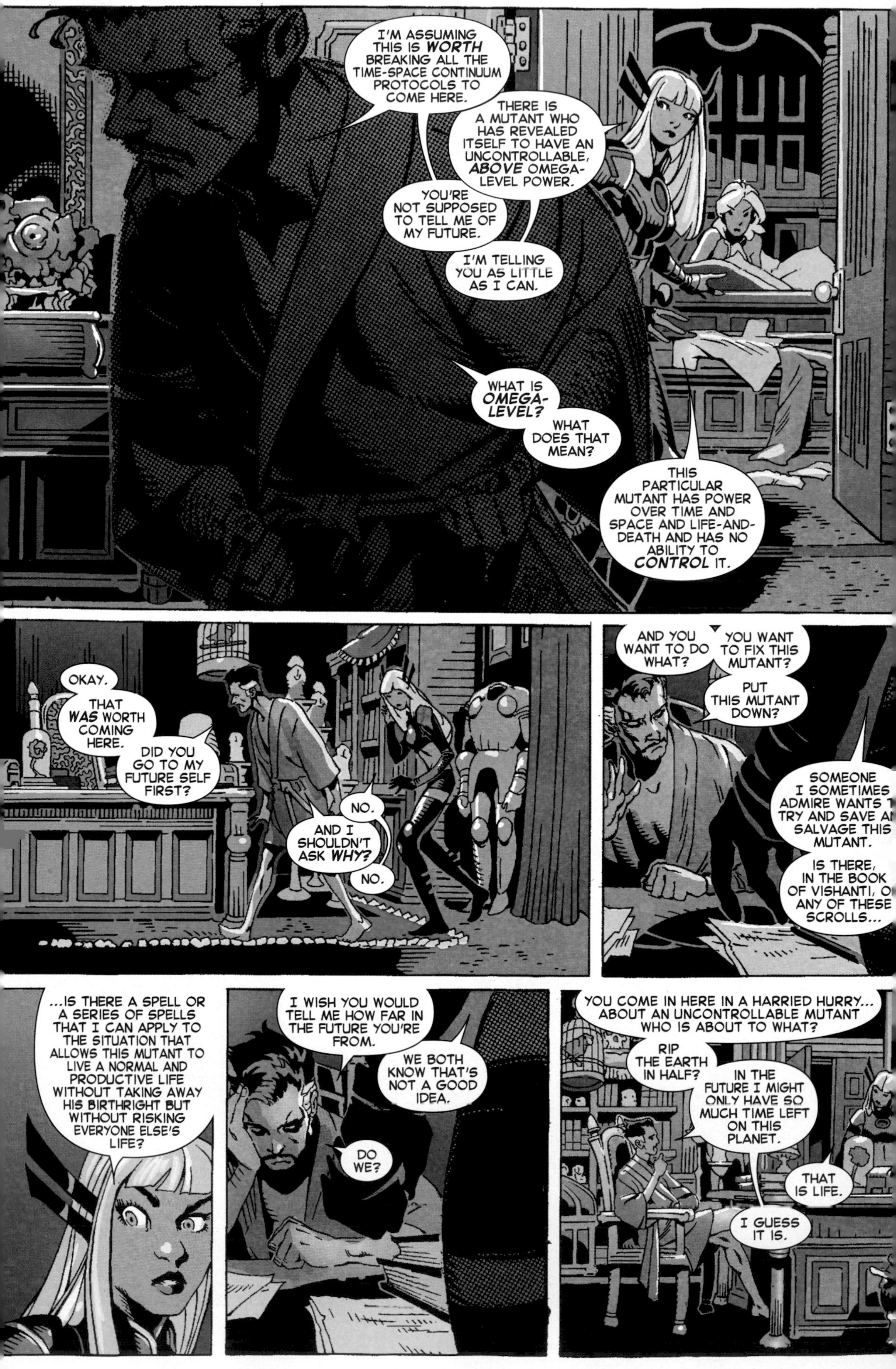

I'M ASSUMING THIS IS WORTH BREAKING ALL THE TIME-SPACE CONTINUUM PROTOCOLS TO COME HERE.
THERE IS A MUTANT WHO HAS REVEALED ITSELF TO HAVE AN UNCONTROLLABLE, ABOVE OMEGA-LEVEL POWER.
YOU'RE NOT SUPPOSED TO TELL ME OF MY FUTURE.
I'M TELLING YOU AS LITTLE AS I CAN.
WHAT IS OMEGA-LEVEL?
WHAT DOES THAT MEAN?
THIS PARTICULAR MUTANT HAS POWER OVER TIME AND SPACE AND LIFE-AND-DEATH AND HAS NO ABILITY TO CONTROL IT.
OKAY.
THAT WAS WORTH COMING HERE.
DID YOU GO TO MY FUTURE SELF FIRST?
NO.
AND I SHOULDN'T ASK WHY?
NO.
AND YOU WANT TO DO WHAT?
YOU WANT TO FIX THIS MUTANT?
PUT THIS MUTANT DOWN?
SOMEONE I SOMETIMES ADMIRE WANTS T TRY AND SAVE AI SALVAGE THIS MUTANT.
IS THERE, IN THE BOOK OF VISHANTI, O ANY OF THESE SCROLLS...
...IS THERE A SPELL OR A SERIES OF SPELLS THAT I CAN APPLY TO THE SITUATION THAT ALLOWS THIS MUTANT TO LIVE A NORMAL AND PRODUCTIVE LIFE WITHOUT TAKING AWAY HIS BIRTHRIGHT BUT WITHOUT RISKING EVERYONE ELSE'S LIFE?
I WISH YOU WOULD TELL ME HOW FAR IN THE FUTURE YOU'RE FROM.
WE BOTH KNOW THAT'S NOT A GOOD IDEA.
DO WE?
YOU COME IN HERE IN A HARRIED HURRY... ABOUT AN UNCONTROLLABLE MUTANT WHO IS ABOUT TO WHAT?
RIP THE EARTH IN HALF?
IN THE FUTURE I MIGHT ONLY HAVE SO MUCH TIME LEFT ON THIS PLANET.
THAT IS LIFE.
I GUESS IT IS.

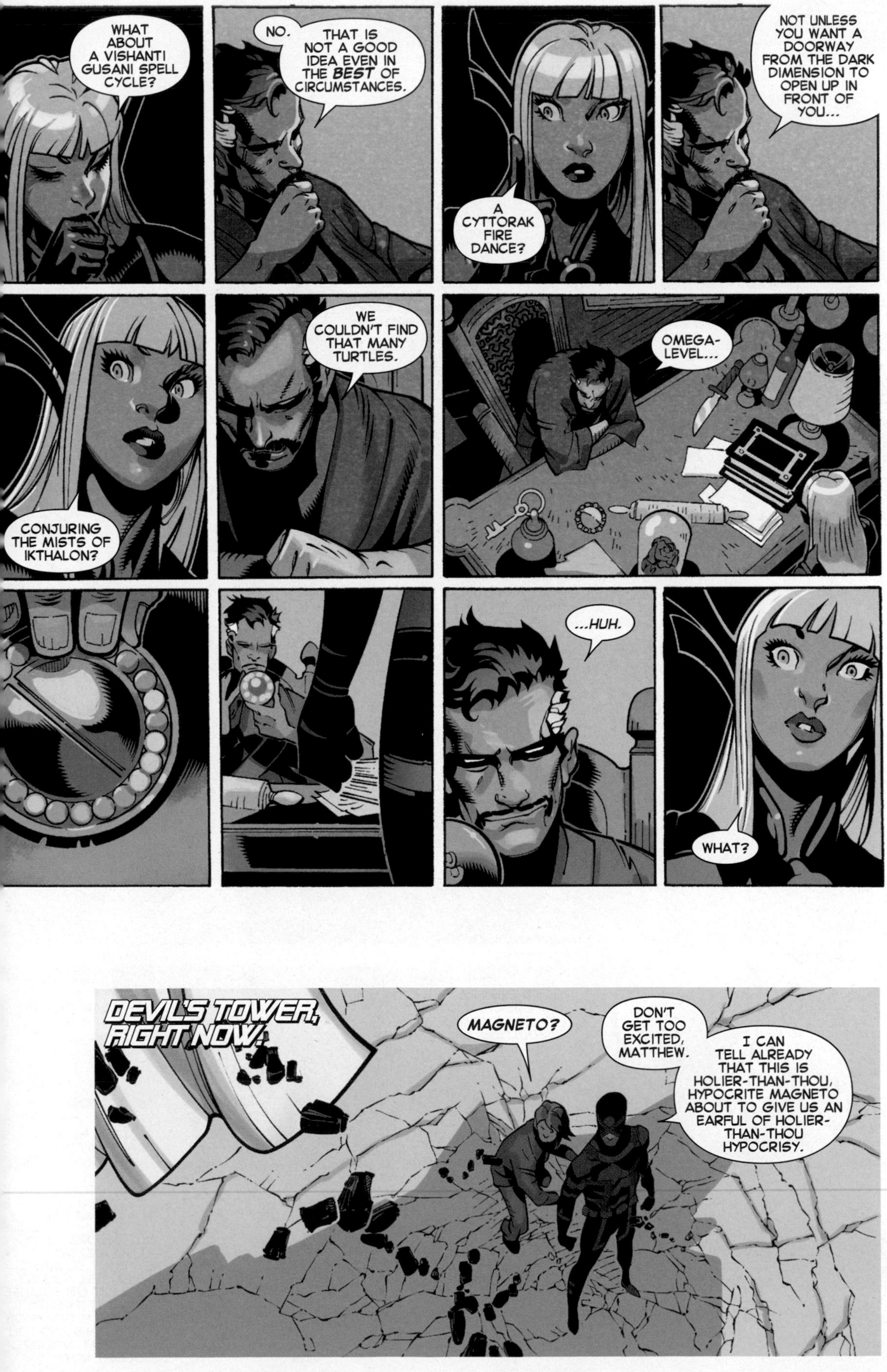
WHAT ABOUT A VISHANTI GUSANI SPELL CYCLE?
NO.
THAT IS NOT A GOOD IDEA EVEN IN THE BEST OF CIRCUMSTANCES.
A CYTTORAK FIRE DANCE?
NOT UNLESS YOU WANT A DOORWAY FROM THE DARK DIMENSION TO OPEN UP IN FRONT OF YOU...
CONJURING THE MISTS OF IKTHALON?
WE COULDN'T FIND THAT MANY TURTLES.
OMEGA-LEVEL...
...HUH.
WHAT?
DEVIL'S TOWER, RIGHT NOW.
MAGNETO?
DON'T GET TOO EXCITED, MATTHEW.
I CAN TELL ALREADY THAT THIS IS HOLIER-THAN-THOU, HYPOCRITE MAGNETO ABOUT TO GIVE US AN EARFUL OF HOLIER-THAN-THOU HYPOCRISY.

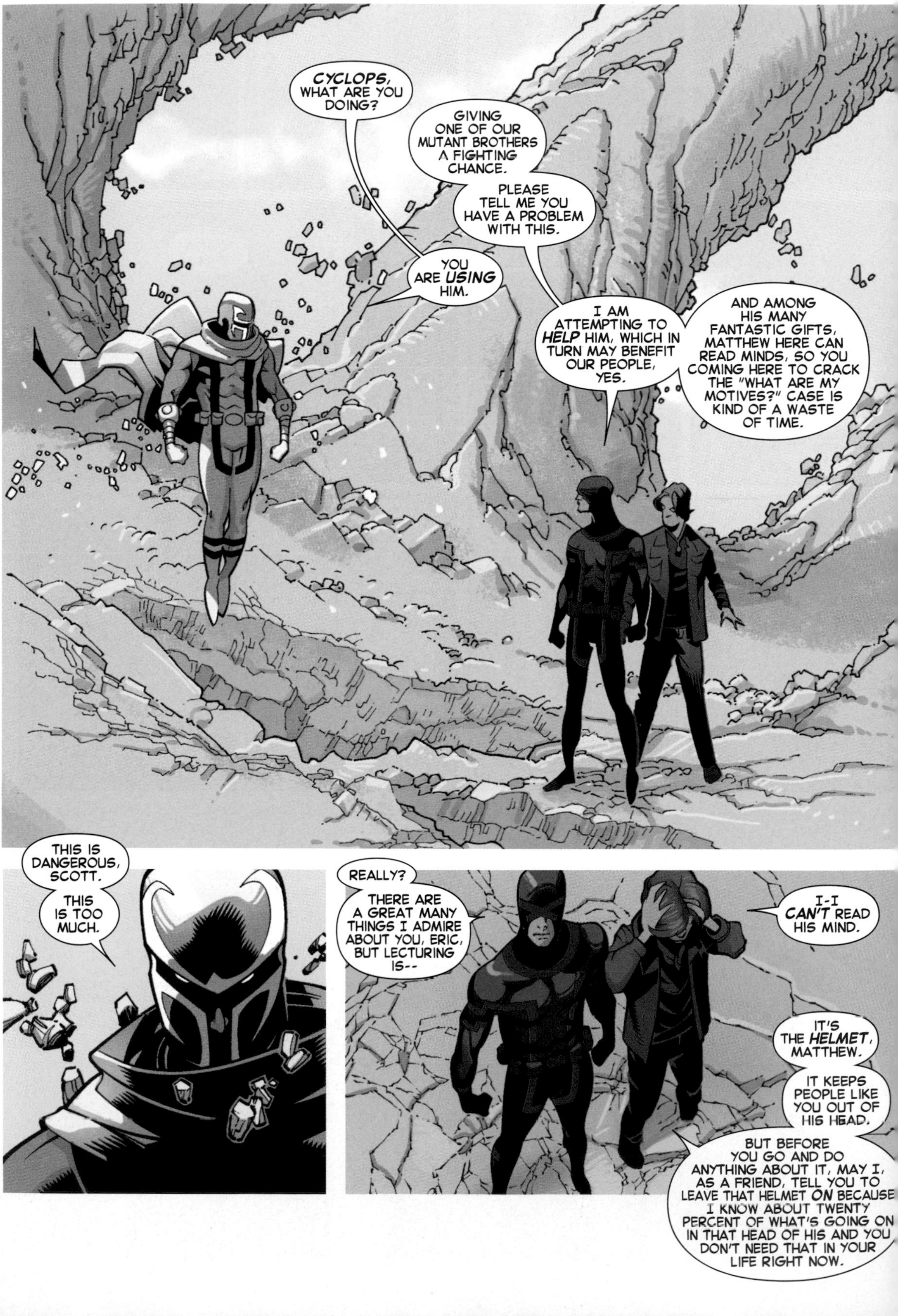
CYCLOPS, WHAT ARE YOU DOING?
GIVING ONE OF OUR MUTANT BROTHERS A FIGHTING CHANCE.
PLEASE TELL ME YOU HAVE A PROBLEM WITH THIS.
YOU ARE USING HIM.
I AM ATTEMPTING TO HELP HIM, WHICH IN TURN MAY BENEFIT OUR PEOPLE, YES.
AND AMONG HIS MANY FANTASTIC GIFTS, MATTHEW HERE CAN READ MINDS, SO YOU COMING HERE TO CRACK THE "WHAT ARE MY MOTIVES?" CASE IS KIND OF A WASTE OF TIME.
THIS IS DANGEROUS, SCOTT.
THIS IS TOO MUCH.
REALLY?
THERE ARE A GREAT MANY THINGS I ADMIRE ABOUT YOU, ERIC, BUT LECTURING IS--
I-I CAN'T READ HIS MIND.
IT'S THE HELMET, MATTHEW.
IT KEEPS PEOPLE LIKE YOU OUT OF HIS HEAD.
BUT BEFORE YOU GO AND DO ANYTHING ABOUT IT, MAY I, AS A FRIEND, TELL YOU TO LEAVE THAT HELMET ON BECAUSE I KNOW ABOUT TWENTY PERCENT OF WHAT'S GOING ON IN THAT HEAD OF HIS AND YOU DON'T NEED THAT IN YOUR LIFE RIGHT NOW.

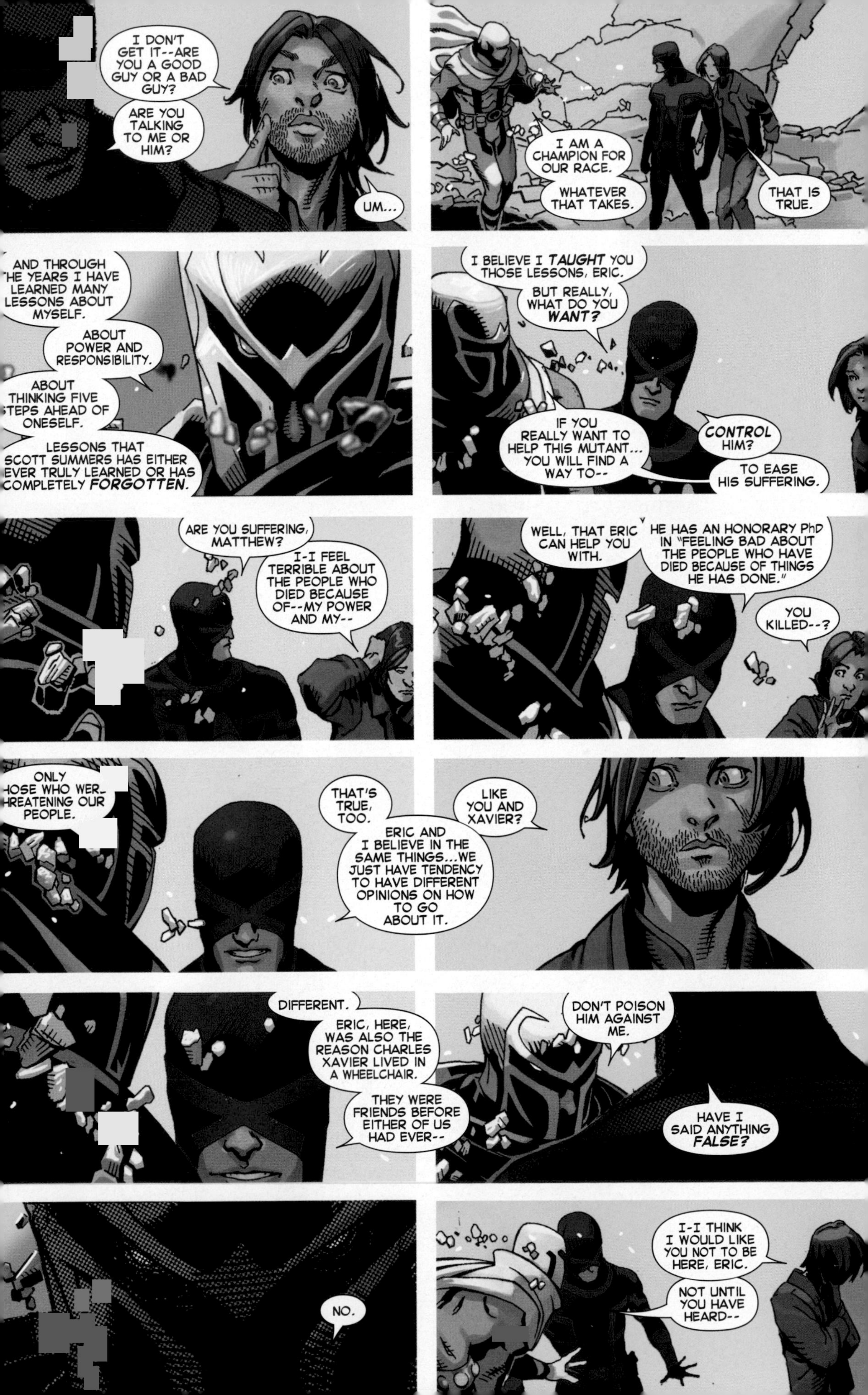
I DON'T GET IT--ARE YOU A GOOD GUY OR A BAD GUY?
ARE YOU TALKING TO ME OR HIM?
UM...
I AM A CHAMPION FOR OUR RACE.
WHATEVER THAT TAKES.
THAT IS TRUE.
AND THROUGH THE YEARS I HAVE LEARNED MANY LESSONS ABOUT MYSELF.
ABOUT POWER AND RESPONSIBILITY.
ABOUT THINKING FIVE STEPS AHEAD OF ONESELF.
LESSONS THAT SCOTT SUMMERS HAS EITHER NEVER TRULY LEARNED OR HAS COMPLETELY FORGOTTEN.
I BELIEVE I TAUGHT YOU THOSE LESSONS, ERIC.
BUT REALLY, WHAT DO YOU WANT?
IF YOU REALLY WANT TO HELP THIS MUTANT... YOU WILL FIND A WAY TO--
CONTROL HIM?
TO EASE HIS SUFFERING.
ARE YOU SUFFERING, MATTHEW?
I-I FEEL TERRIBLE ABOUT THE PEOPLE WHO DIED BECAUSE OF--MY POWER AND MY--
WELL, THAT ERIC CAN HELP YOU WITH.
HE HAS AN HONORARY PhD IN "FEELING BAD ABOUT THE PEOPLE WHO HAVE DIED BECAUSE OF THINGS HE HAS DONE."
YOU KILLED--?
ONLY THOSE WHO WERE THREATENING OUR PEOPLE.
THAT'S TRUE, TOO.
ERIC AND I BELIEVE IN THE SAME THINGS...WE JUST HAVE TENDENCY TO HAVE DIFFERENT OPINIONS ON HOW TO GO ABOUT IT.
LIKE YOU AND XAVIER?
DIFFERENT.
ERIC, HERE, WAS ALSO THE REASON CHARLES XAVIER LIVED IN A WHEELCHAIR.
THEY WERE FRIENDS BEFORE EITHER OF US HAD EVER--
DON'T POISON HIM AGAINST ME.
HAVE I SAID ANYTHING FALSE?
NO.
I-I THINK I WOULD LIKE YOU NOT TO BE HERE, ERIC.
NOT UNTIL YOU HAVE HEARD--

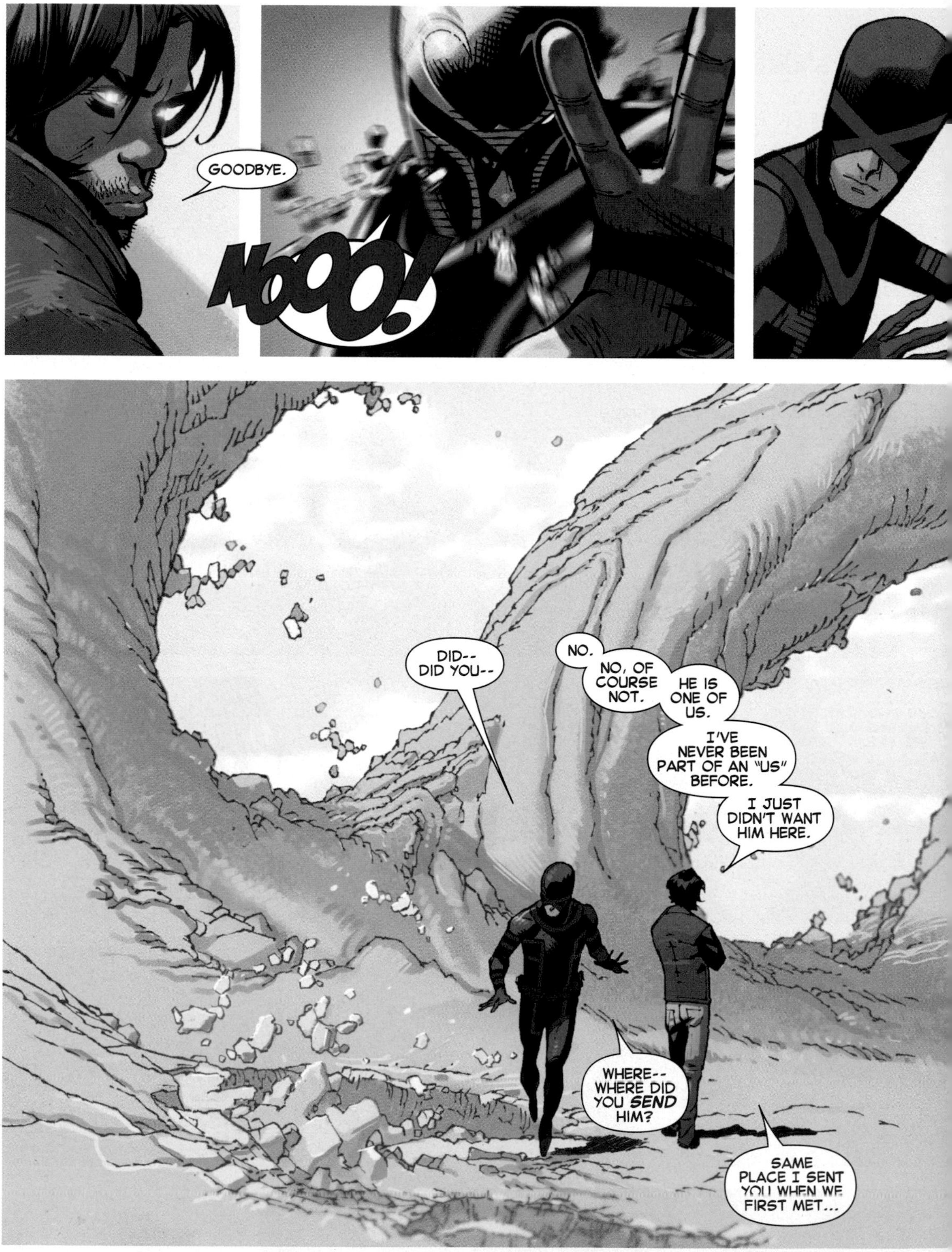
GOODBYE.
NOOOO!
DID-- DID YOU--
NO.
NO, OF COURSE NOT.
HE IS ONE OF US.
I'VE NEVER BEEN PART OF AN "US" BEFORE.
I JUST DIDN'T WANT HIM HERE.
WHERE-- WHERE DID YOU SEND HIM?
SAME PLACE I SENT YOU WHEN WE FIRST MET...

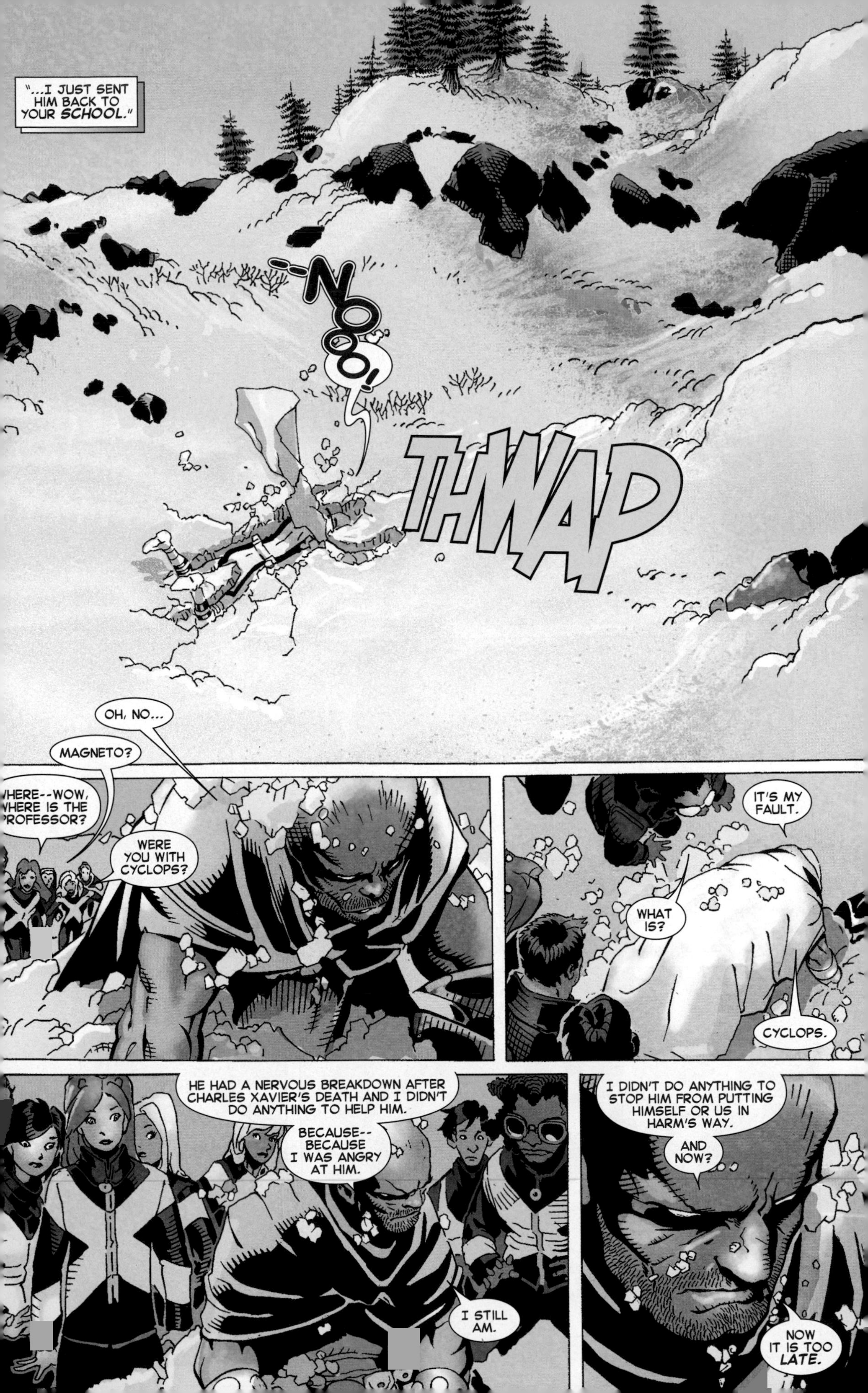
"...I JUST SENT HIM BACK TO YOUR SCHOOL."
--NOOOO!
THWAP
OH, NO...
MAGNETO?
WHERE--WOW, WHERE IS THE PROFESSOR?
WERE YOU WITH CYCLOPS?
IT'S MY FAULT.
WHAT IS?
CYCLOPS.
HE HAD A NERVOUS BREAKDOWN AFTER CHARLES XAVIER'S DEATH AND I DIDN'T DO ANYTHING TO HELP HIM.
BECAUSE-- BECAUSE I WAS ANGRY AT HIM.
I STILL AM.
I DIDN'T DO ANYTHING TO STOP HIM FROM PUTTING HIMSELF OR US IN HARM'S WAY.
AND NOW?
NOW IT IS TOO LATE.

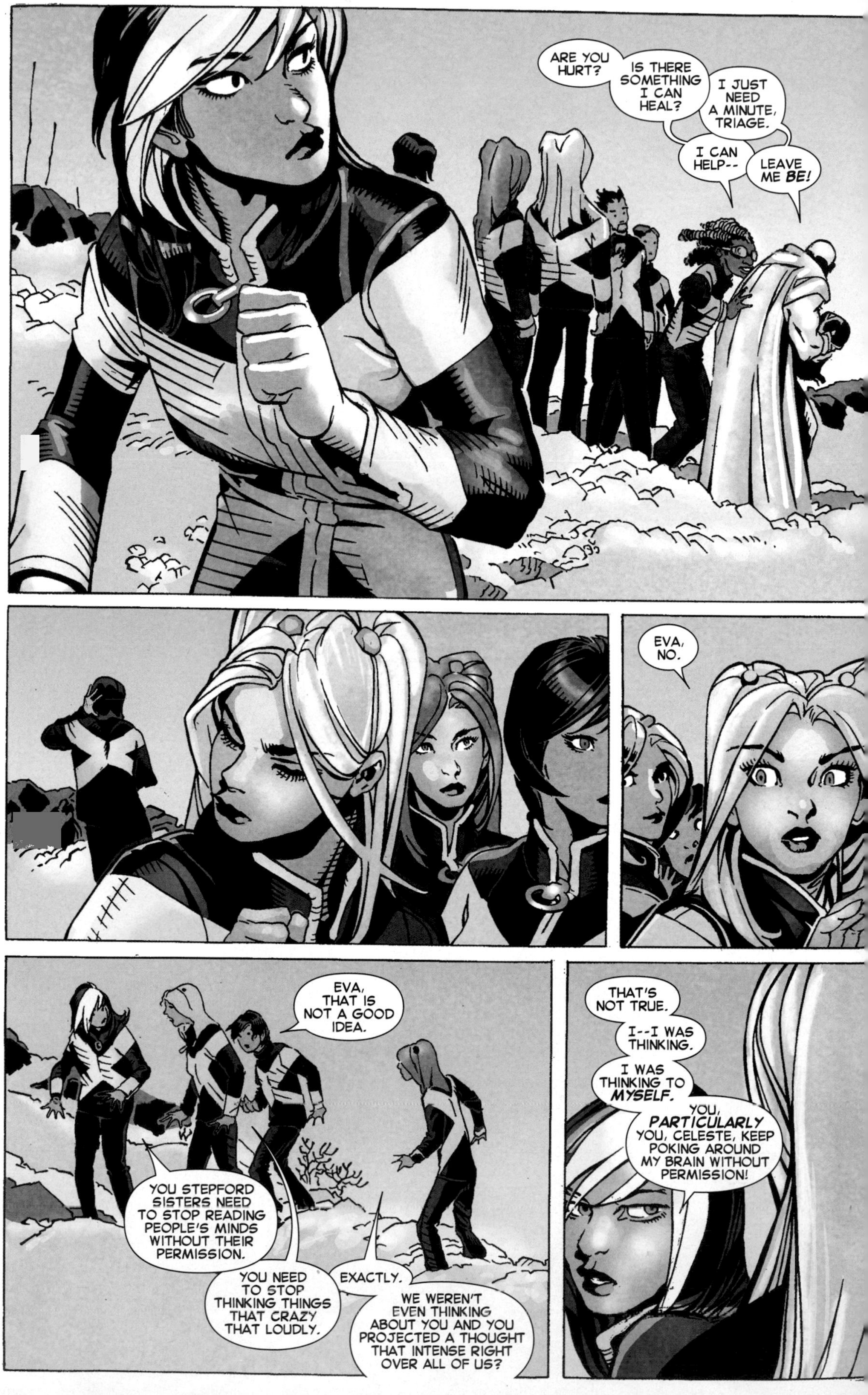
ARE YOU HURT?
IS THERE SOMETHING I CAN HEAL?
I JUST NEED A MINUTE, TRIAGE.
I CAN HELP--
LEAVE ME *BE!*
EVA, NO.
EVA, THAT IS NOT A GOOD IDEA.
YOU STEPFORD SISTERS NEED TO STOP READING PEOPLE'S MINDS WITHOUT THEIR PERMISSION.
YOU NEED TO STOP THINKING THINGS THAT CRAZY THAT LOUDLY.
EXACTLY.
WE WEREN'T EVEN THINKING ABOUT YOU AND YOU PROJECTED A THOUGHT THAT INTENSE RIGHT OVER ALL OF US?
THAT'S NOT TRUE.
I--I WAS THINKING.
I WAS THINKING TO *MYSELF.*
YOU, *PARTICULARLY* YOU, CELESTE, KEEP POKING AROUND MY BRAIN WITHOUT PERMISSION!

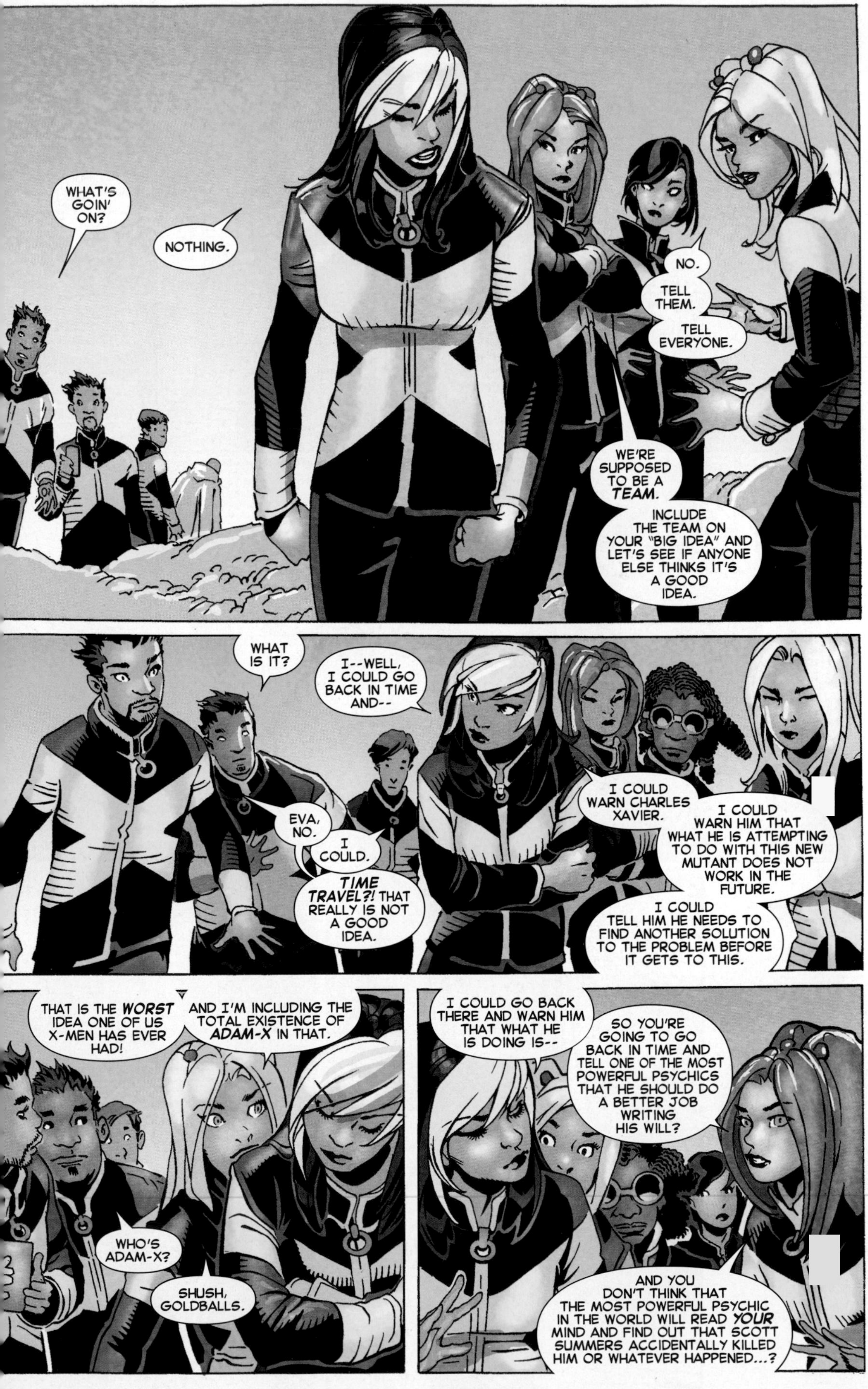
WHAT'S GOIN' ON?
NOTHING.
NO.
TELL THEM.
TELL EVERYONE.
WE'RE SUPPOSED TO BE A TEAM.
INCLUDE THE TEAM ON YOUR "BIG IDEA" AND LET'S SEE IF ANYONE ELSE THINKS IT'S A GOOD IDEA.
WHAT IS IT?
I--WELL, I COULD GO BACK IN TIME AND--
EVA, NO.
I COULD.
TIME TRAVEL?! THAT REALLY IS NOT A GOOD IDEA.
I COULD WARN CHARLES XAVIER.
I COULD WARN HIM THAT WHAT HE IS ATTEMPTING TO DO WITH THIS NEW MUTANT DOES NOT WORK IN THE FUTURE.
I COULD TELL HIM HE NEEDS TO FIND ANOTHER SOLUTION TO THE PROBLEM BEFORE IT GETS TO THIS.
THAT IS THE WORST IDEA ONE OF US X-MEN HAS EVER HAD!
AND I'M INCLUDING THE TOTAL EXISTENCE OF ADAM-X IN THAT.
WHO'S ADAM-X?
SHUSH, GOLDBALLS.
I COULD GO BACK THERE AND WARN HIM THAT WHAT HE IS DOING IS--
SO YOU'RE GOING TO GO BACK IN TIME AND TELL ONE OF THE MOST POWERFUL PSYCHICS THAT HE SHOULD DO A BETTER JOB WRITING HIS WILL?
AND YOU DON'T THINK THAT THE MOST POWERFUL PSYCHIC IN THE WORLD WILL READ YOUR MIND AND FIND OUT THAT SCOTT SUMMERS ACCIDENTALLY KILLED HIM OR WHATEVER HAPPENED...?

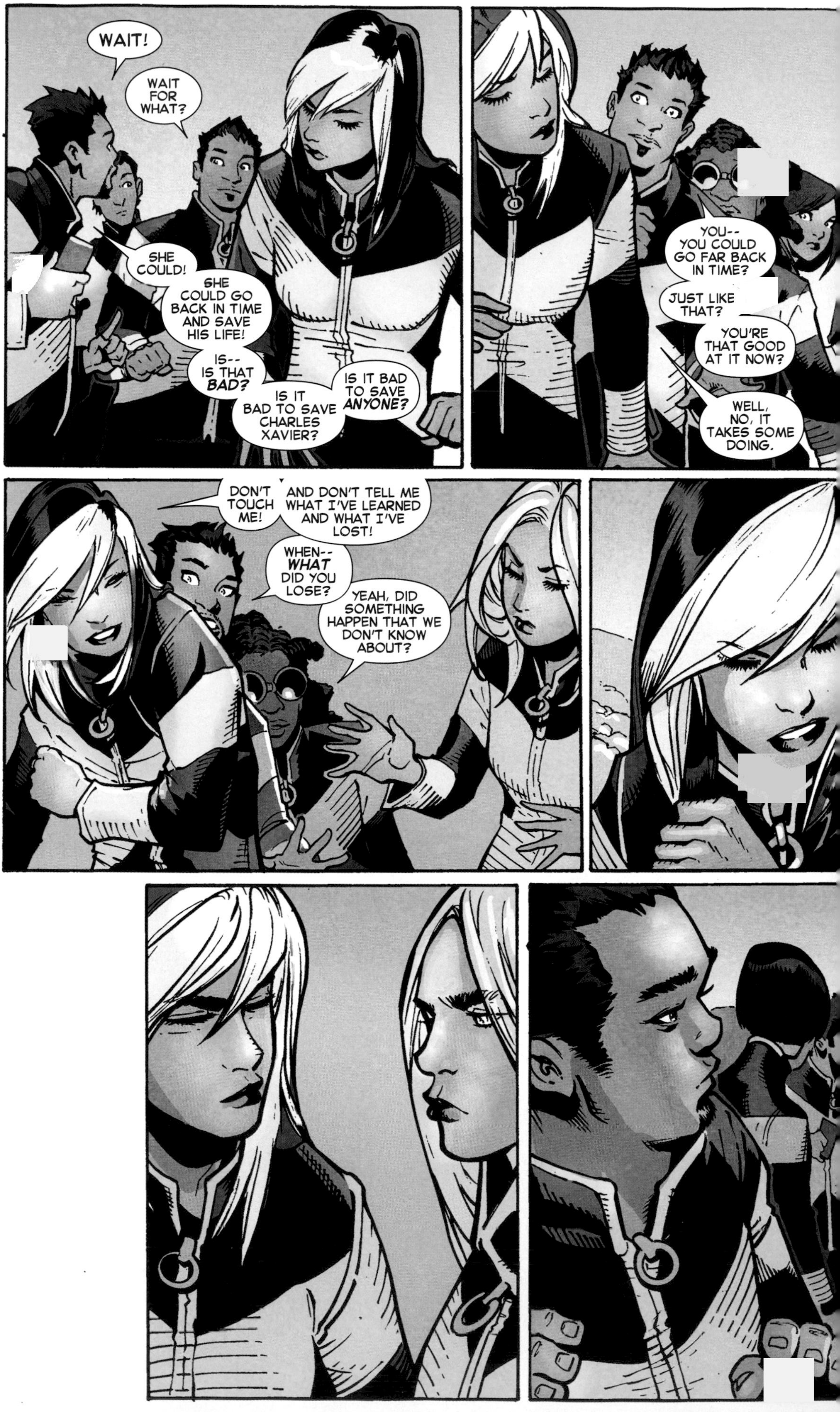
WAIT!
WAIT FOR WHAT?
SHE COULD!
SHE COULD GO BACK IN TIME AND SAVE HIS LIFE!
IS-- IS THAT BAD?
IS IT BAD TO SAVE CHARLES XAVIER?
IS IT BAD TO SAVE ANYONE?
YOU-- YOU COULD GO FAR BACK IN TIME?
JUST LIKE THAT?
YOU'RE THAT GOOD AT IT NOW?
WELL, NO, IT TAKES SOME DOING.
DON'T TOUCH ME!
AND DON'T TELL ME WHAT I'VE LEARNED AND WHAT I'VE LOST!
WHEN-- WHAT DID YOU LOSE?
YEAH, DID SOMETHING HAPPEN THAT WE DON'T KNOW ABOUT?

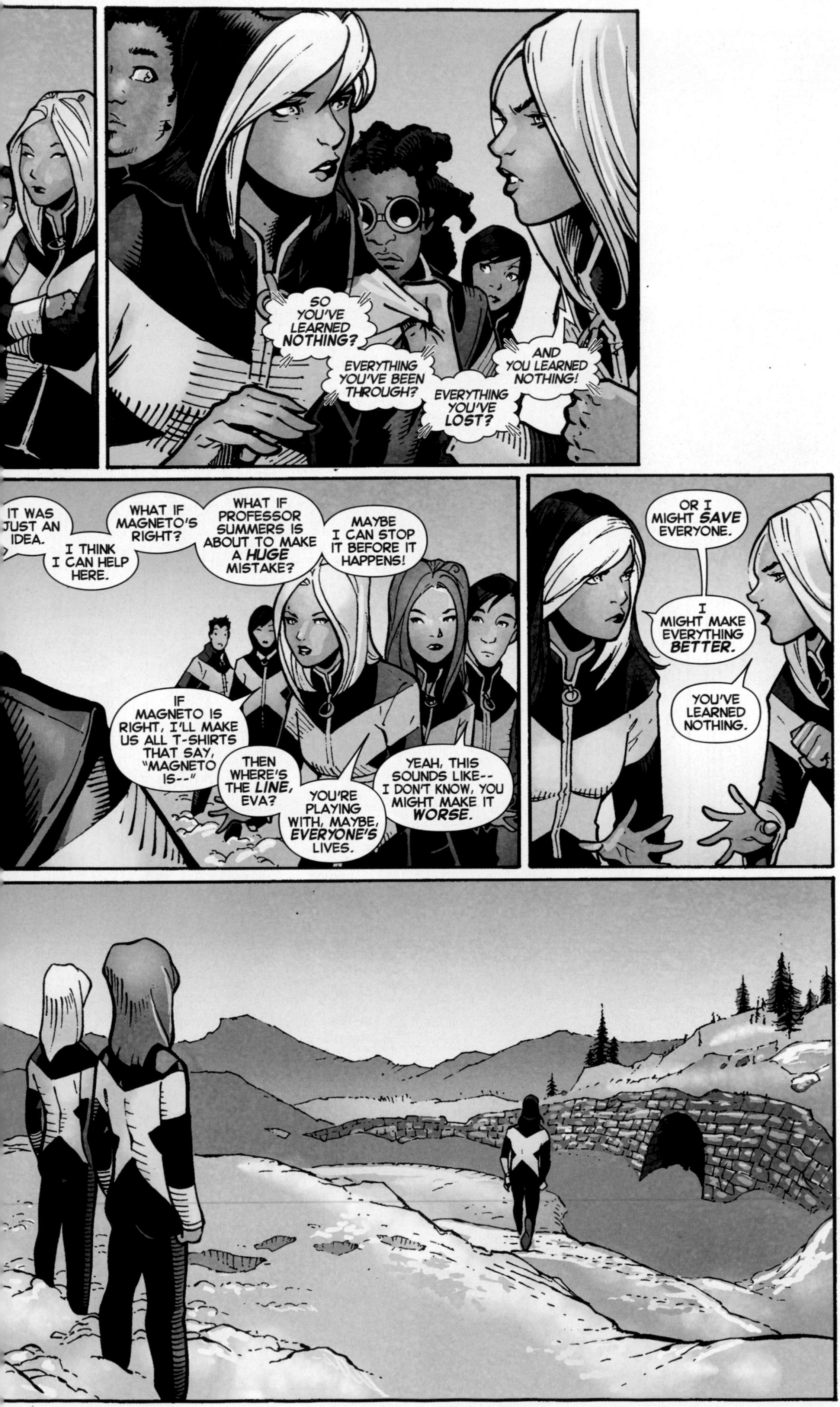
SO YOU'VE LEARNED NOTHING?
EVERYTHING YOU'VE BEEN THROUGH?
EVERYTHING YOU'VE LOST?
AND YOU LEARNED NOTHING!
IT WAS JUST AN IDEA.
I THINK I CAN HELP HERE.
WHAT IF MAGNETO'S RIGHT?
WHAT IF PROFESSOR SUMMERS IS ABOUT TO MAKE A HUGE MISTAKE?
MAYBE I CAN STOP IT BEFORE IT HAPPENS!
IF MAGNETO IS RIGHT, I'LL MAKE US ALL T-SHIRTS THAT SAY, "MAGNETO IS--"
THEN WHERE'S THE LINE, EVA?
YOU'RE PLAYING WITH, MAYBE, EVERYONE'S LIVES.
YEAH, THIS SOUNDS LIKE-- I DON'T KNOW, YOU MIGHT MAKE IT WORSE.
OR I MIGHT SAVE EVERYONE.
I MIGHT MAKE EVERYTHING BETTER.
YOU'VE LEARNED NOTHING.

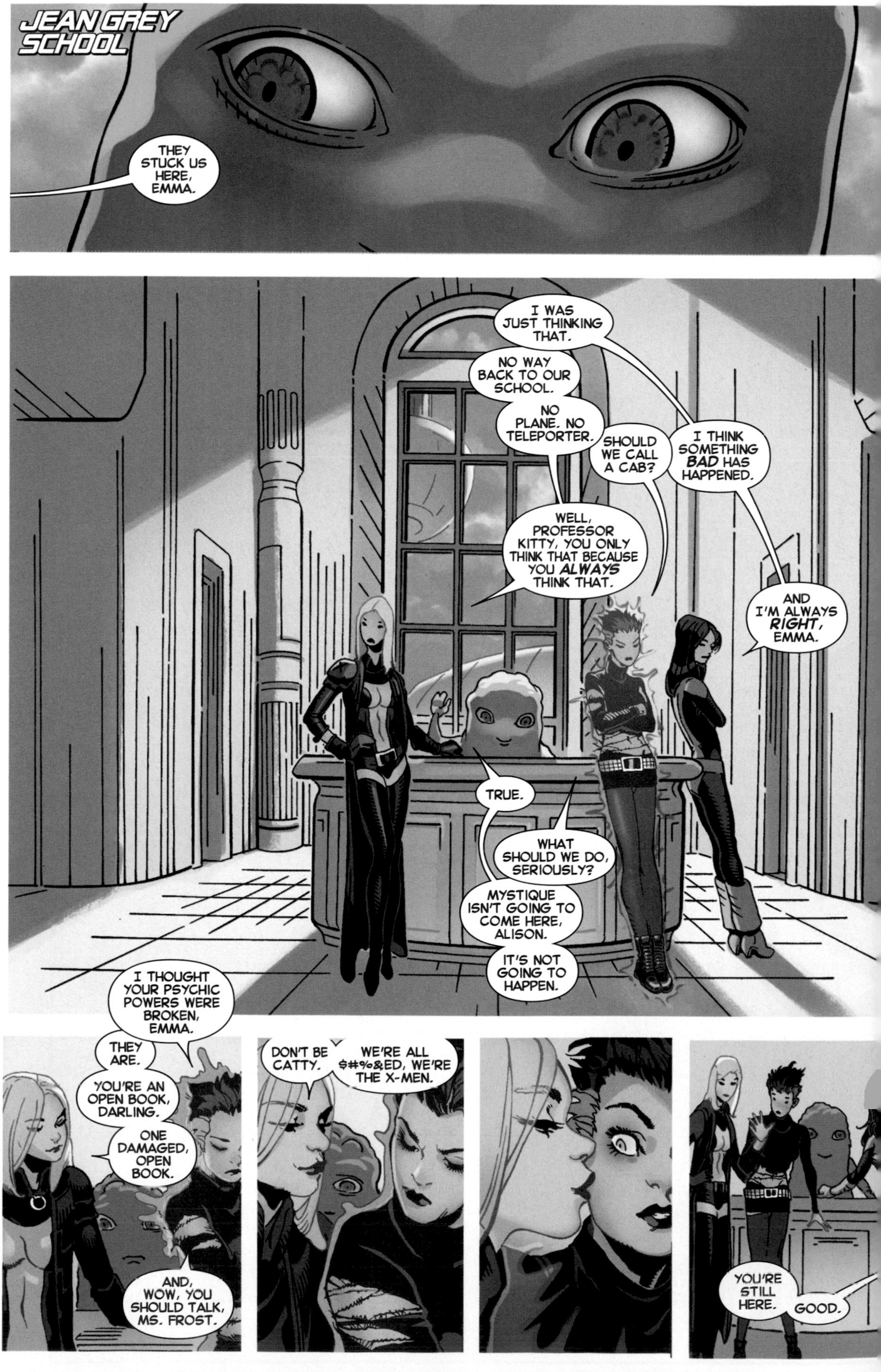
JEAN GREY SCHOOL
THEY STUCK US HERE, EMMA.
I WAS JUST THINKING THAT.
NO WAY BACK TO OUR SCHOOL.
NO PLANE. NO TELEPORTER.
SHOULD WE CALL A CAB?
I THINK SOMETHING BAD HAS HAPPENED.
WELL, PROFESSOR KITTY, YOU ONLY THINK THAT BECAUSE YOU ALWAYS THINK THAT.
AND I'M ALWAYS RIGHT, EMMA.
TRUE.
WHAT SHOULD WE DO, SERIOUSLY?
MYSTIQUE ISN'T GOING TO COME HERE, ALISON.
IT'S NOT GOING TO HAPPEN.
I THOUGHT YOUR PSYCHIC POWERS WERE BROKEN, EMMA.
THEY ARE.
YOU'RE AN OPEN BOOK, DARLING.
ONE DAMAGED, OPEN BOOK.
AND, WOW, YOU SHOULD TALK, MS. FROST.
DON'T BE CATTY.
WE'RE ALL $#%&ED, WE'RE THE X-MEN.
YOU'RE STILL HERE.
GOOD.

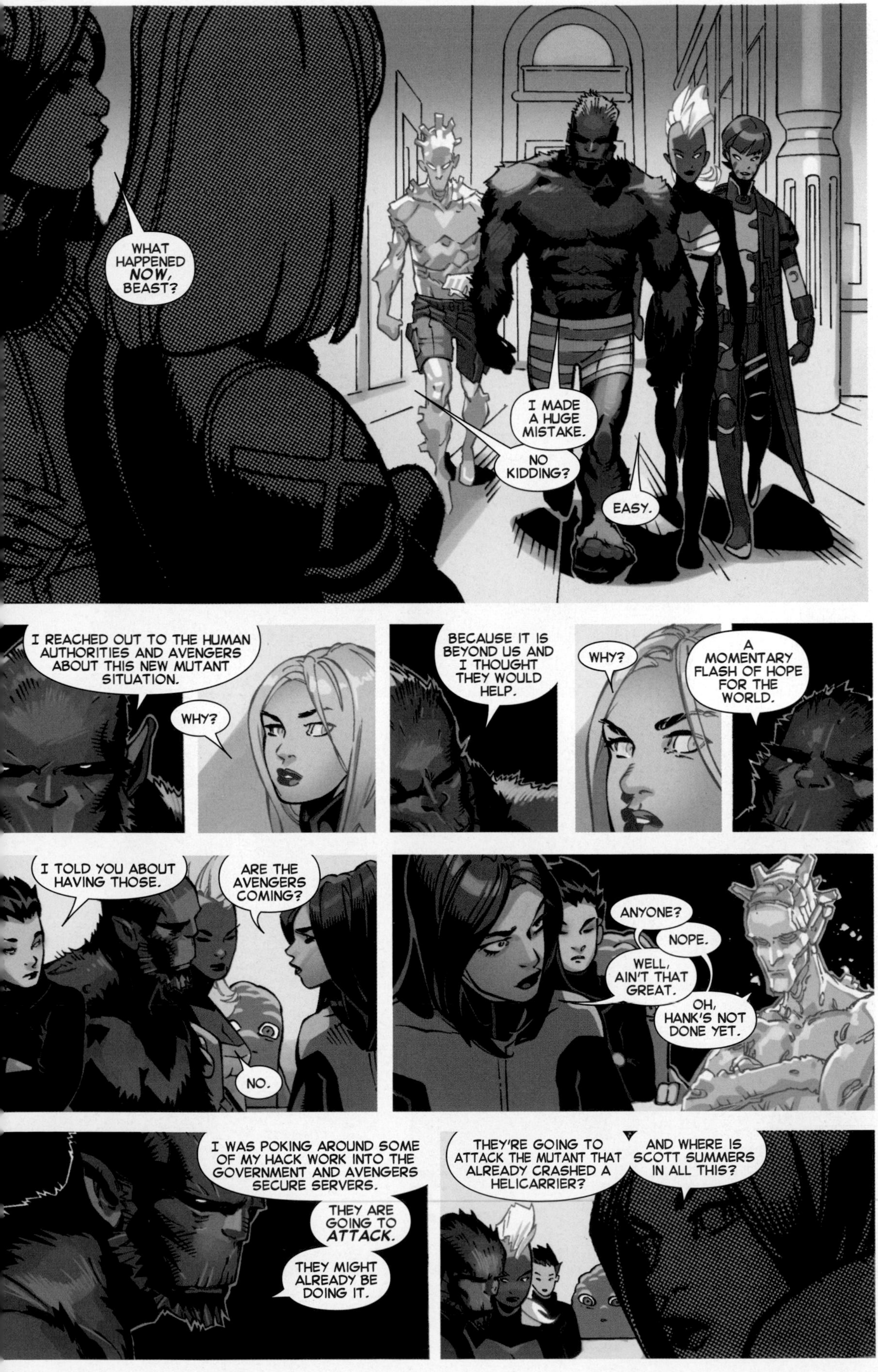
WHAT HAPPENED NOW, BEAST?
I MADE A HUGE MISTAKE.
NO KIDDING?
EASY.
I REACHED OUT TO THE HUMAN AUTHORITIES AND AVENGERS ABOUT THIS NEW MUTANT SITUATION.
WHY?
BECAUSE IT IS BEYOND US AND I THOUGHT THEY WOULD HELP.
WHY?
A MOMENTARY FLASH OF HOPE FOR THE WORLD.
I TOLD YOU ABOUT HAVING THOSE.
ARE THE AVENGERS COMING?
NO.
ANYONE?
NOPE.
WELL, AIN'T THAT GREAT.
OH, HANK'S NOT DONE YET.
I WAS POKING AROUND SOME OF MY HACK WORK INTO THE GOVERNMENT AND AVENGERS SECURE SERVERS.
THEY ARE GOING TO ATTACK.
THEY MIGHT ALREADY BE DOING IT.
THEY'RE GOING TO ATTACK THE MUTANT THAT ALREADY CRASHED A HELICARRIER?
AND WHERE IS SCOTT SUMMERS IN ALL THIS?

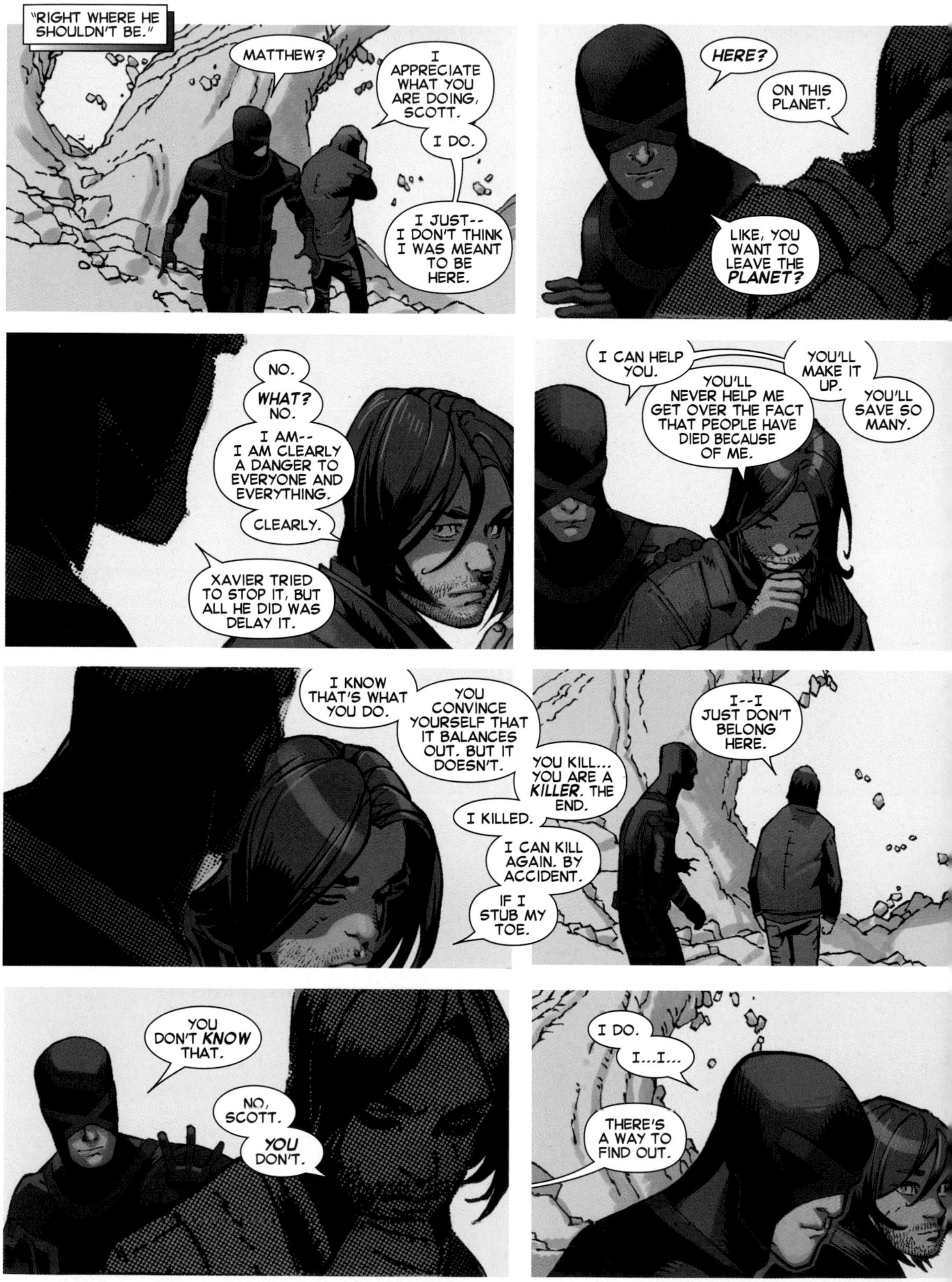
"RIGHT WHERE HE SHOULDN'T BE."
MATTHEW?
I APPRECIATE WHAT YOU ARE DOING, SCOTT.
I DO.
I JUST-- I DON'T THINK I WAS MEANT TO BE HERE.
HERE?
ON THIS PLANET.
LIKE, YOU WANT TO LEAVE THE PLANET?
NO.
WHAT? NO.
I AM-- I AM CLEARLY A DANGER TO EVERYONE AND EVERYTHING.
CLEARLY.
XAVIER TRIED TO STOP IT, BUT ALL HE DID WAS DELAY IT.
I CAN HELP YOU.
YOU'LL NEVER HELP ME GET OVER THE FACT THAT PEOPLE HAVE DIED BECAUSE OF ME.
YOU'LL MAKE IT UP.
YOU'LL SAVE SO MANY.
I KNOW THAT'S WHAT YOU DO.
YOU CONVINCE YOURSELF THAT IT BALANCES OUT. BUT IT DOESN'T.
YOU KILL... YOU ARE A KILLER. THE END.
I KILLED.
I CAN KILL AGAIN. BY ACCIDENT.
IF I STUB MY TOE.
I--I JUST DON'T BELONG HERE.
YOU DON'T KNOW THAT.
NO, SCOTT.
YOU DON'T.
I DO.
I...I...
THERE'S A WAY TO FIND OUT.

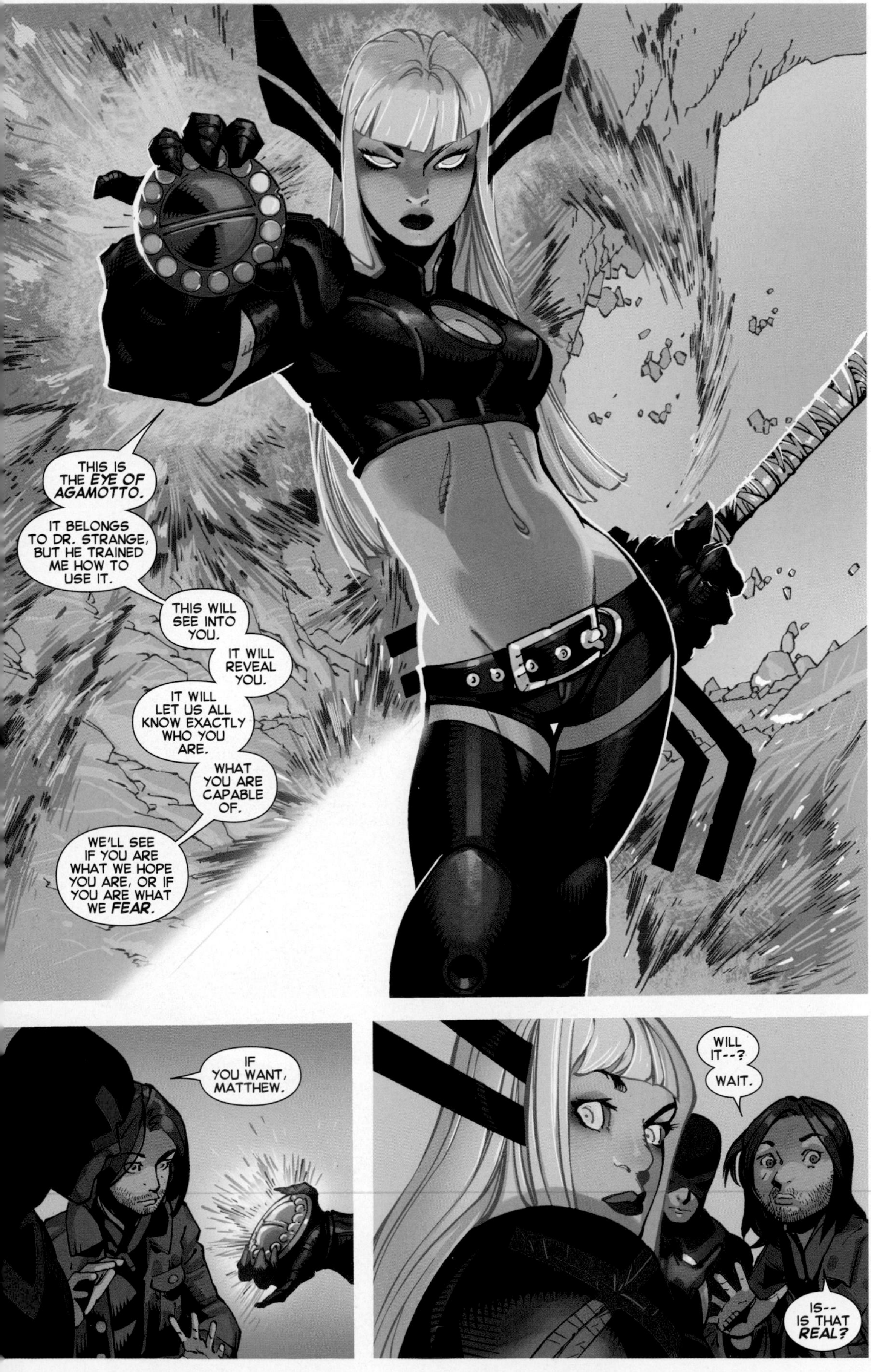
THIS IS THE *EYE OF AGAMOTTO.*
IT BELONGS TO DR. STRANGE, BUT HE TRAINED ME HOW TO USE IT.
THIS WILL SEE INTO YOU.
IT WILL REVEAL YOU.
IT WILL LET US ALL KNOW EXACTLY WHO YOU ARE.
WHAT YOU ARE CAPABLE OF.
WE'LL SEE IF YOU ARE WHAT WE HOPE YOU ARE, OR IF YOU ARE WHAT WE *FEAR.*
IF YOU WANT, MATTHEW.
WILL IT--?
WAIT.
IS-- IS THAT *REAL?*

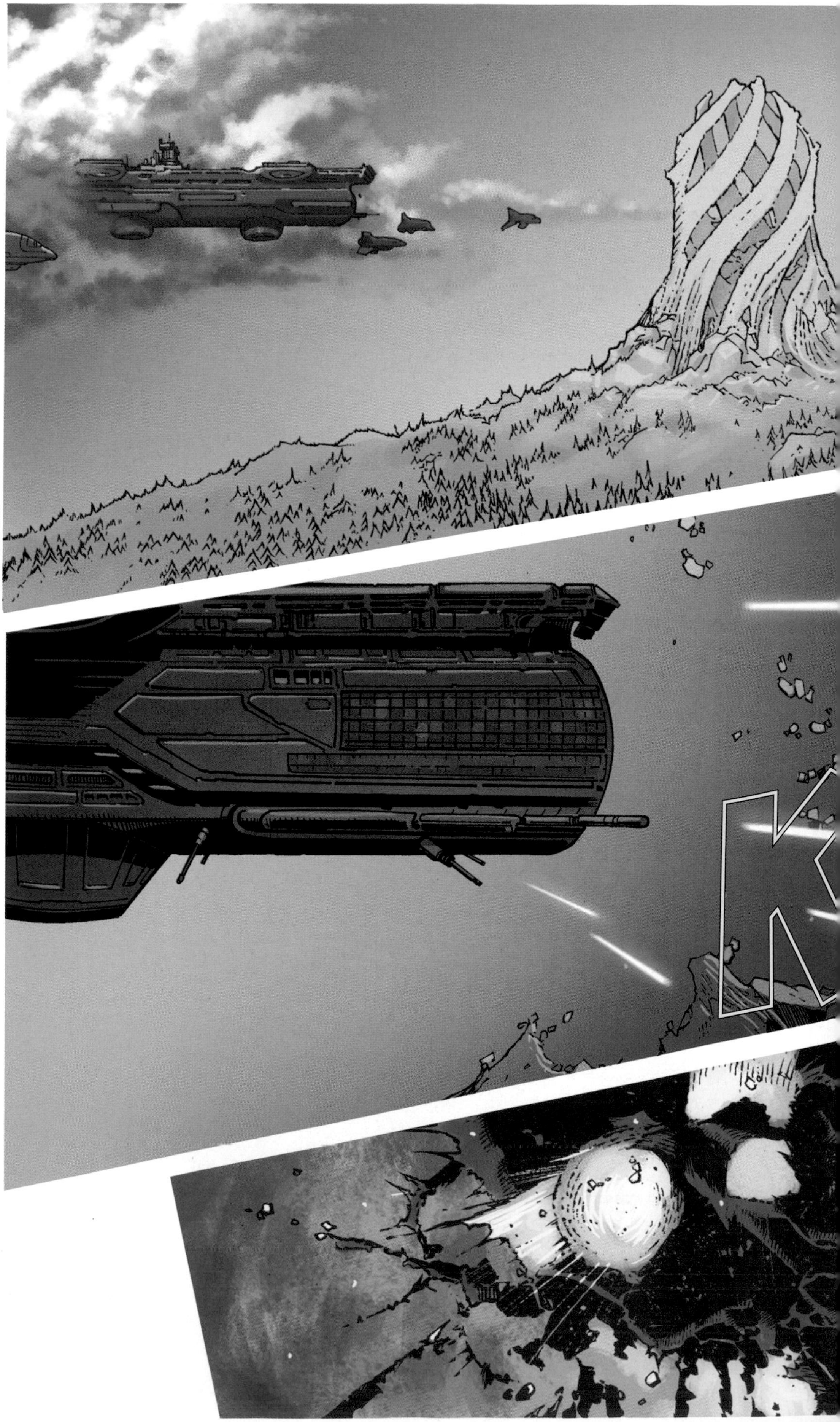

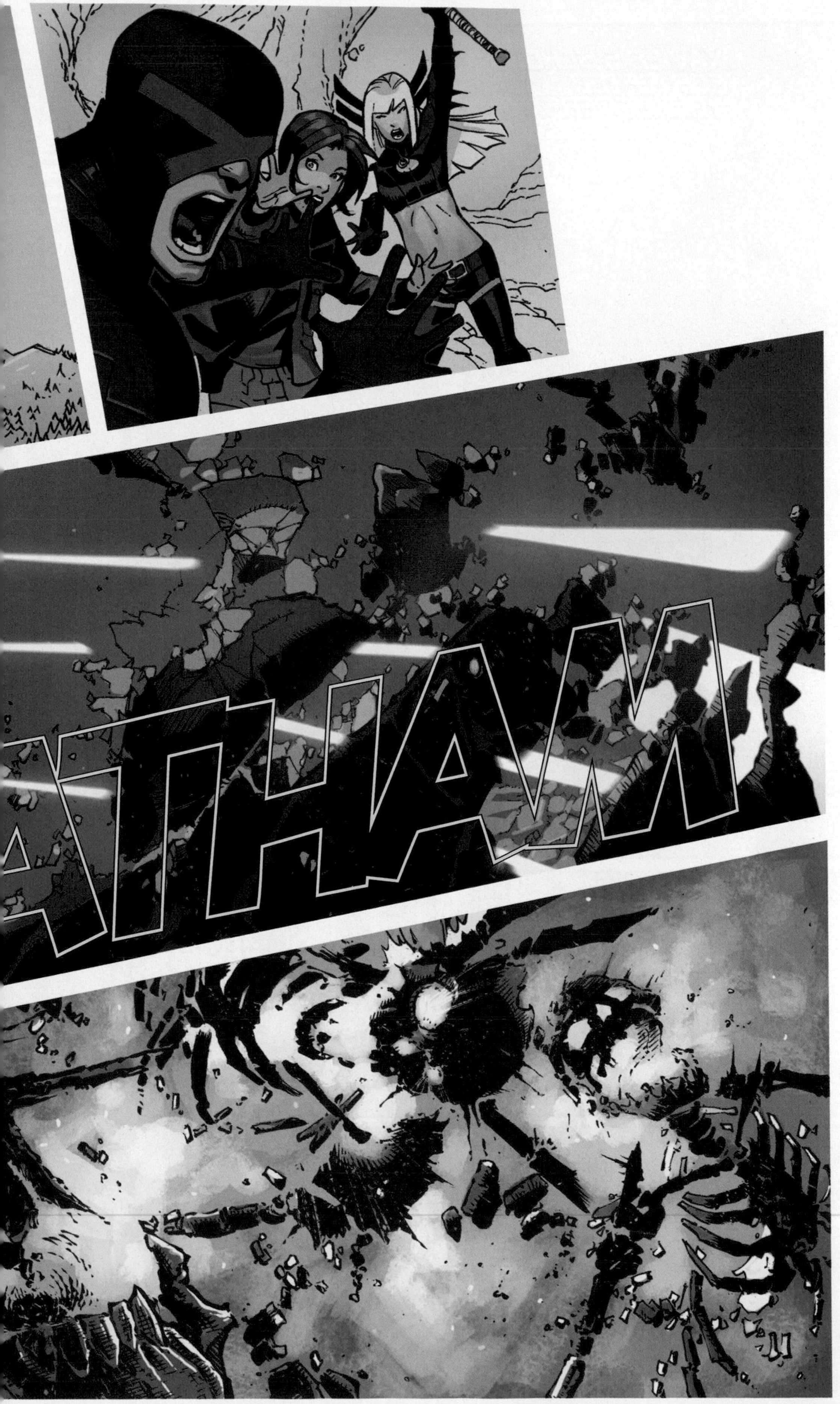
THAM

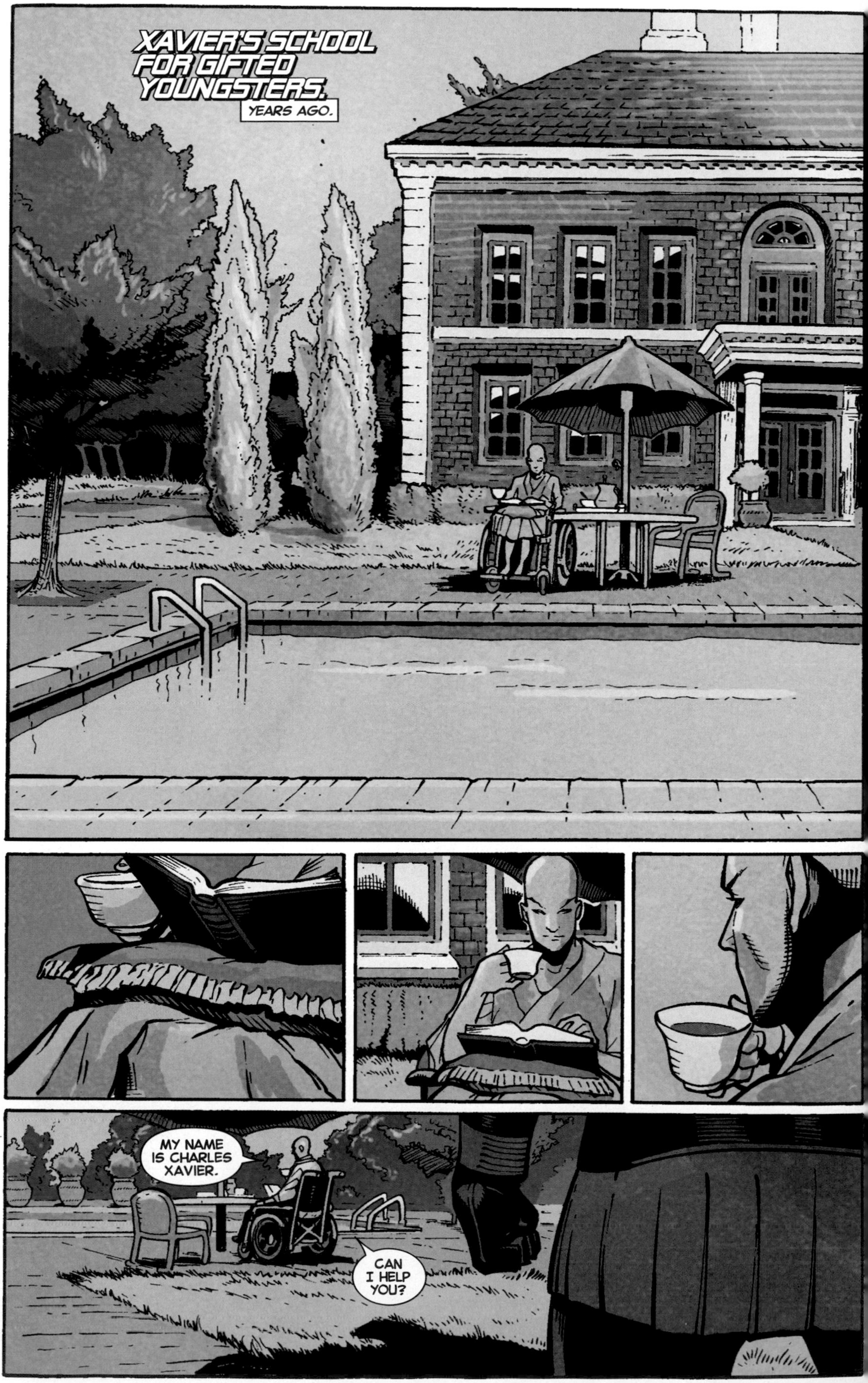
XAVIER'S SCHOOL FOR GIFTED YOUNGSTERS.
YEARS AGO.
MY NAME IS CHARLES XAVIER.
CAN I HELP YOU?

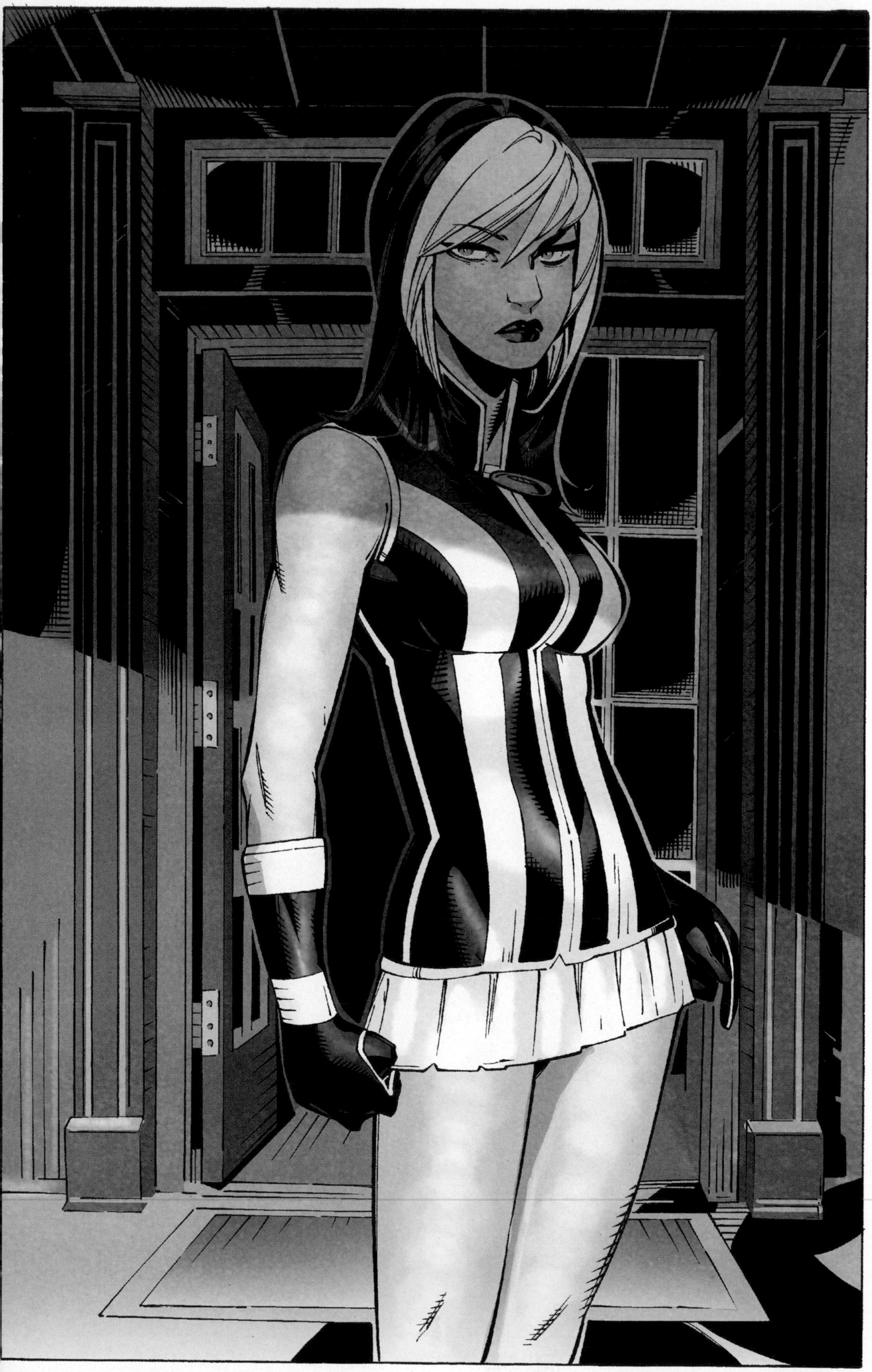

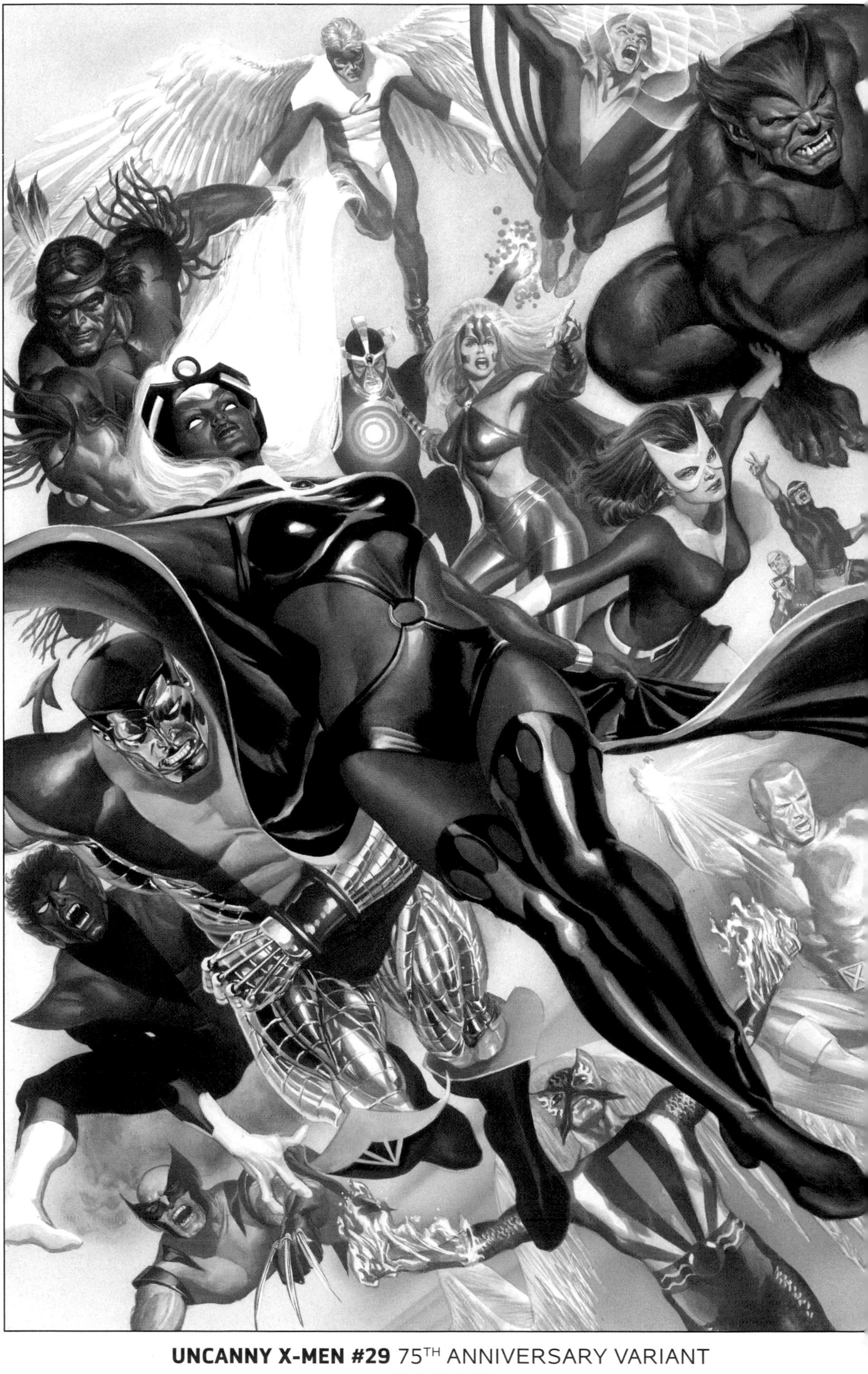

**UNCANNY X-MEN #29** 75TH ANNIVERSARY VARIANT
BY ALEX ROSS

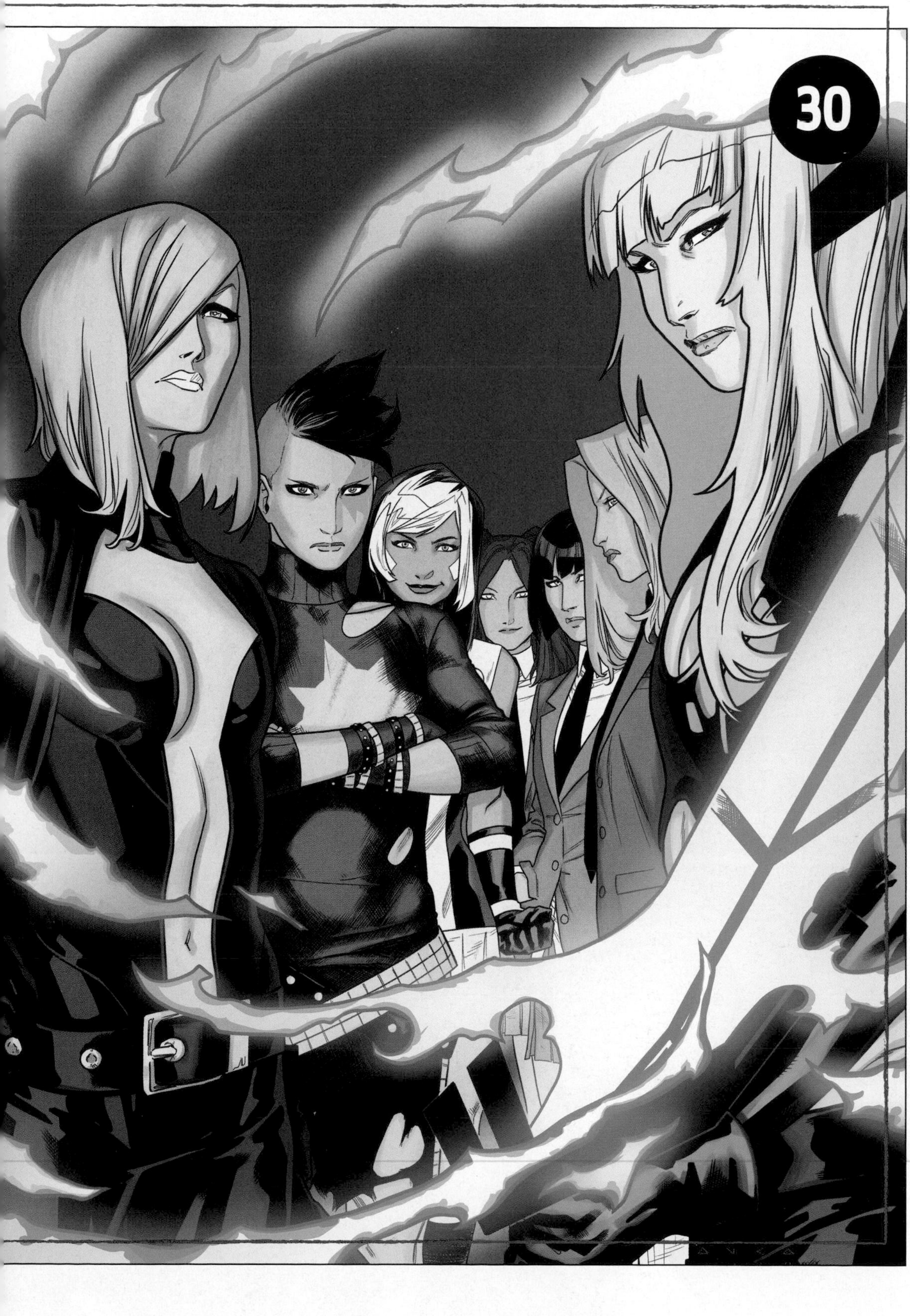
30

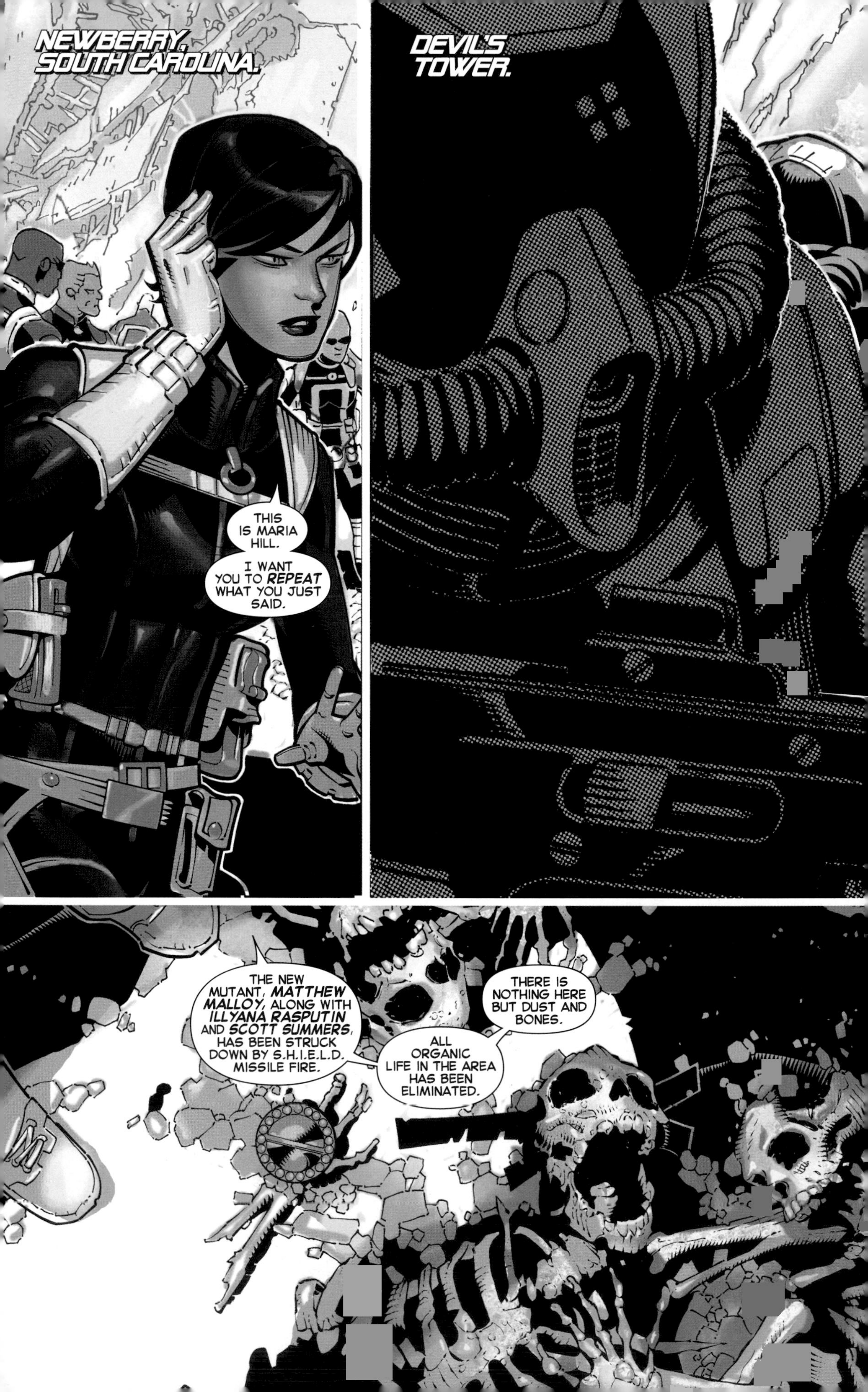
NEWBERRY, SOUTH CAROLINA.
THIS IS MARIA HILL.
I WANT YOU TO REPEAT WHAT YOU JUST SAID.
DEVIL'S TOWER.
THE NEW MUTANT, MATTHEW MALLOY, ALONG WITH ILLYANA RASPUTIN AND SCOTT SUMMERS, HAS BEEN STRUCK DOWN BY S.H.I.E.L.D. MISSILE FIRE.
ALL ORGANIC LIFE IN THE AREA HAS BEEN ELIMINATED.
THERE IS NOTHING HERE BUT DUST AND BONES.

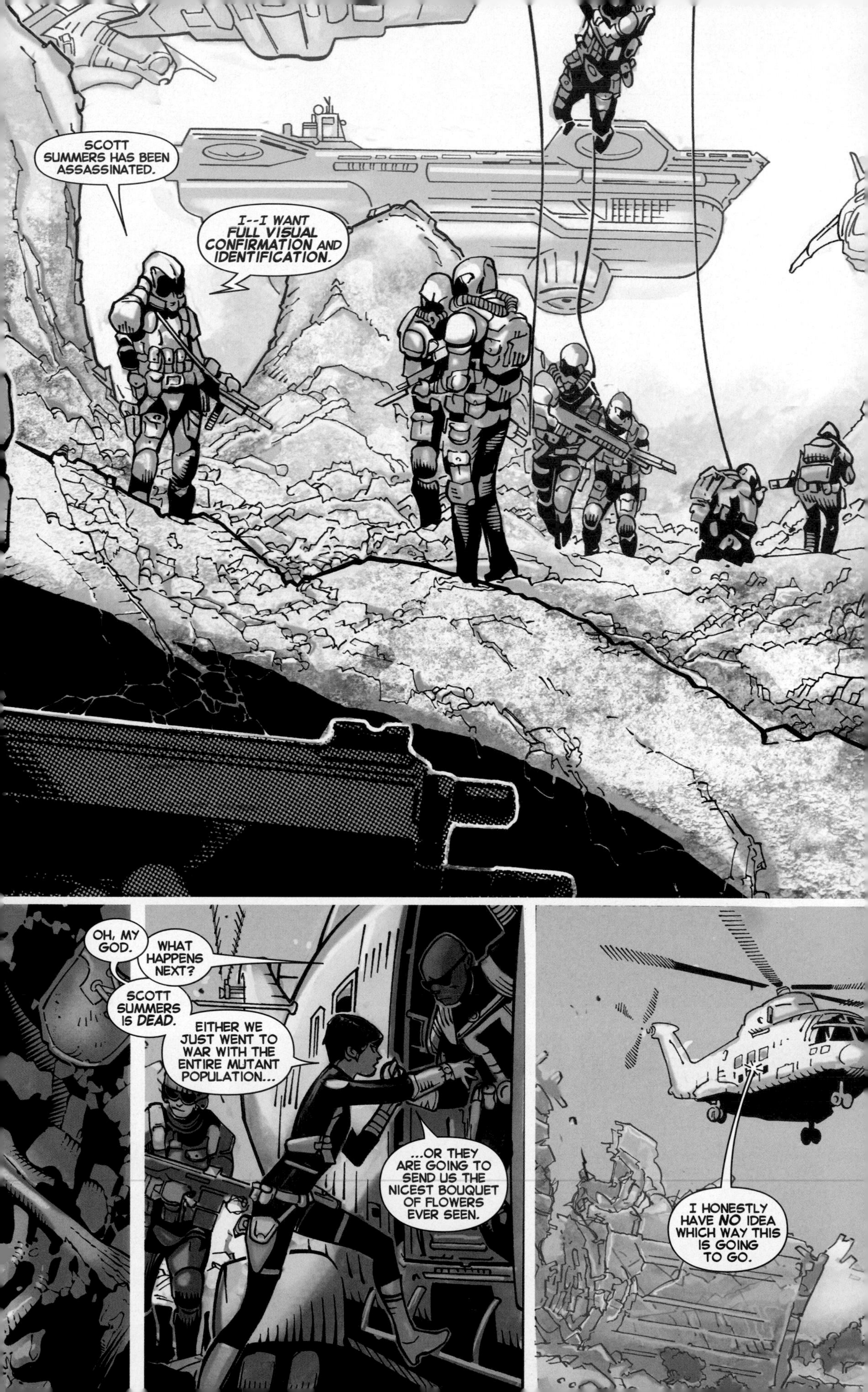
SCOTT SUMMERS HAS BEEN ASSASSINATED.
I--I WANT FULL VISUAL CONFIRMATION AND IDENTIFICATION.
OH, MY GOD.
WHAT HAPPENS NEXT?
SCOTT SUMMERS IS DEAD.
EITHER WE JUST WENT TO WAR WITH THE ENTIRE MUTANT POPULATION...
...OR THEY ARE GOING TO SEND US THE NICEST BOUQUET OF FLOWERS EVER SEEN.
I HONESTLY HAVE NO IDEA WHICH WAY THIS IS GOING TO GO.

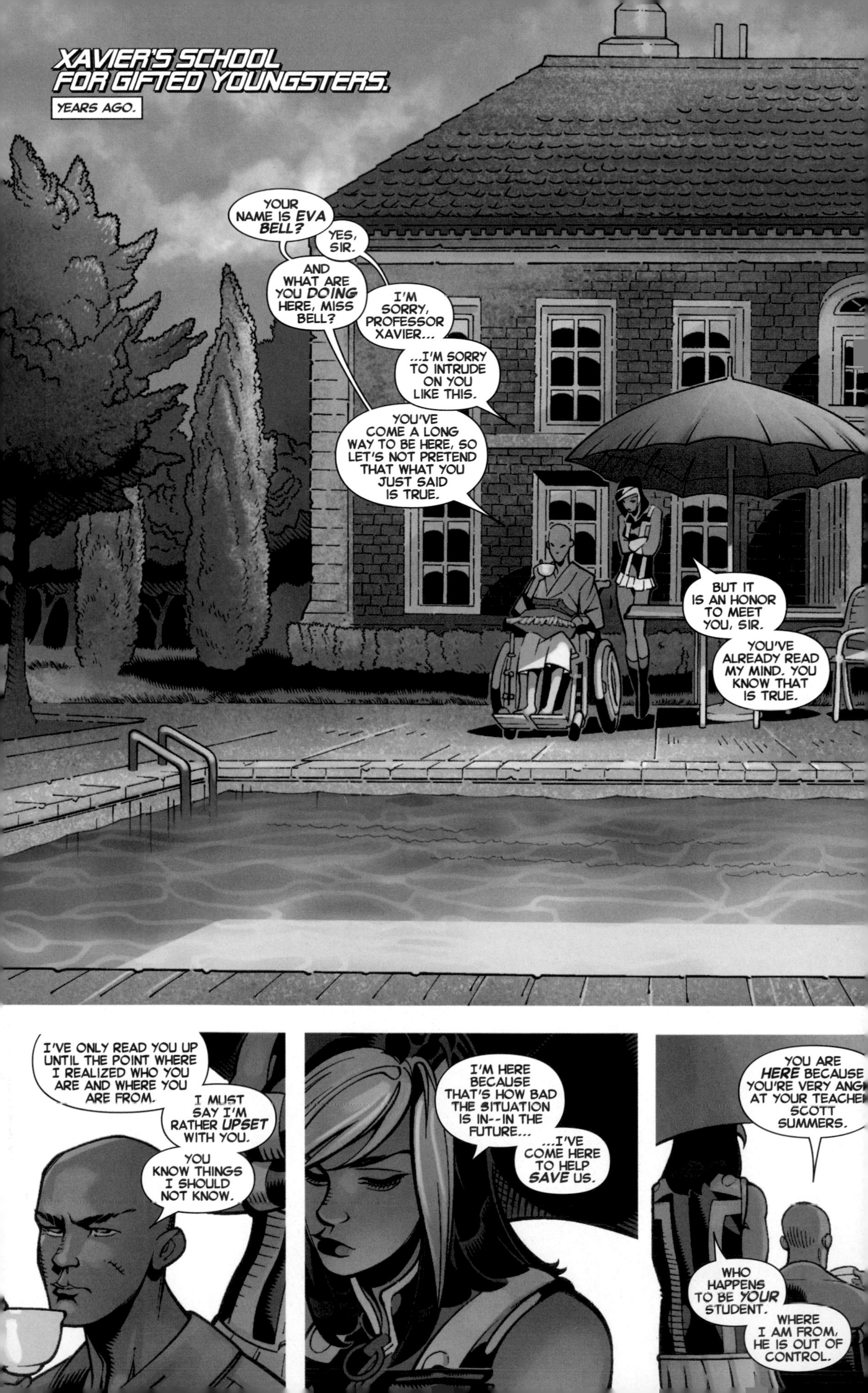
XAVIER'S SCHOOL FOR GIFTED YOUNGSTERS.
YEARS AGO.
YOUR NAME IS EVA BELL?
YES, SIR.
AND WHAT ARE YOU DOING HERE, MISS BELL?
I'M SORRY, PROFESSOR XAVIER...
...I'M SORRY TO INTRUDE ON YOU LIKE THIS.
YOU'VE COME A LONG WAY TO BE HERE, SO LET'S NOT PRETEND THAT WHAT YOU JUST SAID IS TRUE.
BUT IT IS AN HONOR TO MEET YOU, SIR.
YOU'VE ALREADY READ MY MIND. YOU KNOW THAT IS TRUE.
I'VE ONLY READ YOU UP UNTIL THE POINT WHERE I REALIZED WHO YOU ARE AND WHERE YOU ARE FROM.
I MUST SAY I'M RATHER UPSET WITH YOU.
YOU KNOW THINGS I SHOULD NOT KNOW.
I'M HERE BECAUSE THAT'S HOW BAD THE SITUATION IS IN--IN THE FUTURE...
...I'VE COME HERE TO HELP SAVE US.
YOU ARE HERE BECAUSE YOU'RE VERY ANG
AT YOUR TEACHE
SCOTT SUMMERS.
WHO HAPPENS TO BE YOUR STUDENT.
WHERE I AM FROM, HE IS OUT OF CONTROL.

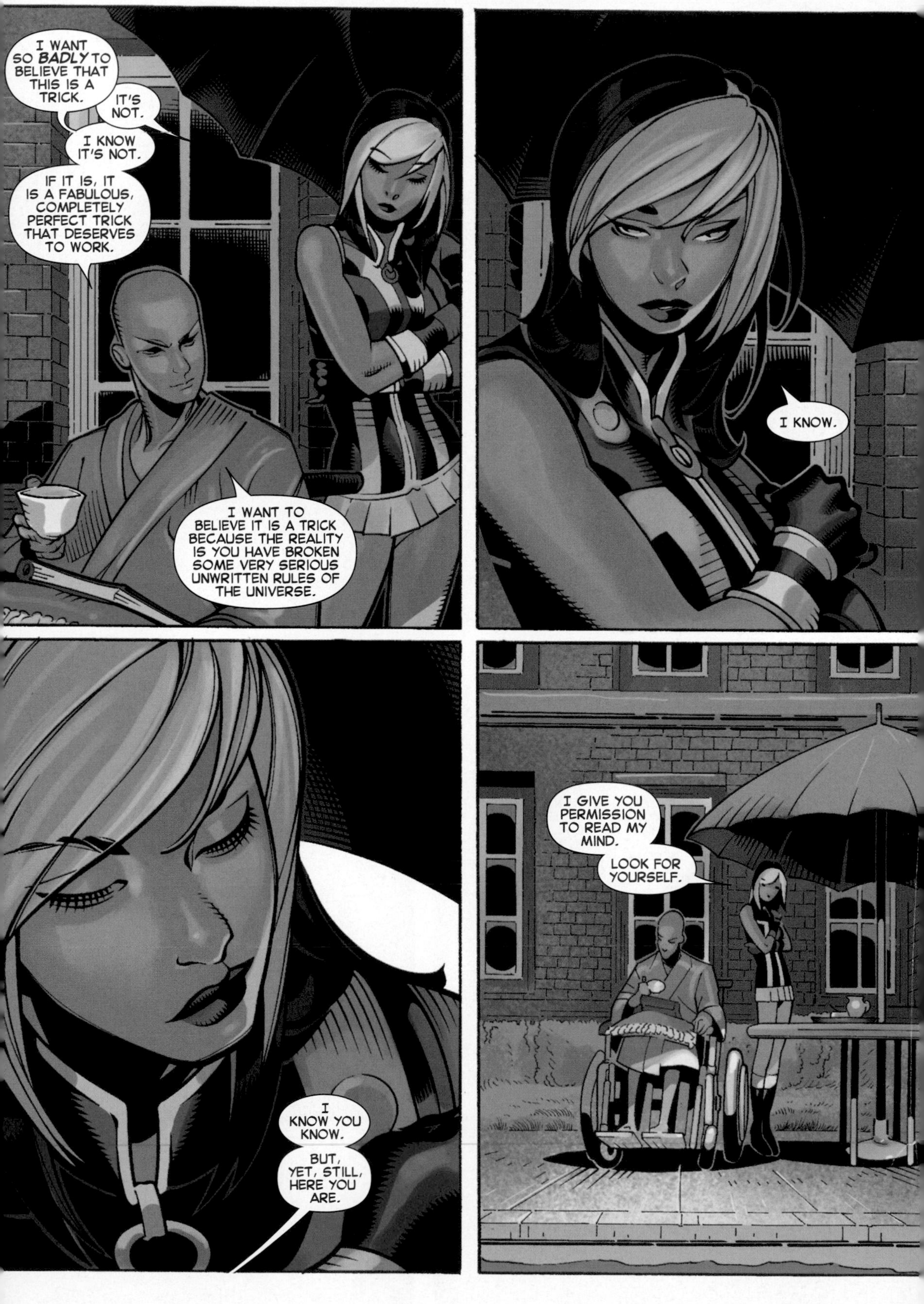
I WANT SO *BADLY* TO BELIEVE THAT THIS IS A TRICK.
IT'S NOT.
I KNOW IT'S NOT.
IF IT IS, IT IS A FABULOUS, COMPLETELY PERFECT TRICK THAT DESERVES TO WORK.
I WANT TO BELIEVE IT IS A TRICK BECAUSE THE REALITY IS YOU HAVE BROKEN SOME VERY SERIOUS UNWRITTEN RULES OF THE UNIVERSE.
I KNOW.
I KNOW YOU KNOW.
BUT, YET, STILL, HERE YOU ARE.
I GIVE YOU PERMISSION TO READ MY MIND.
LOOK FOR YOURSELF.

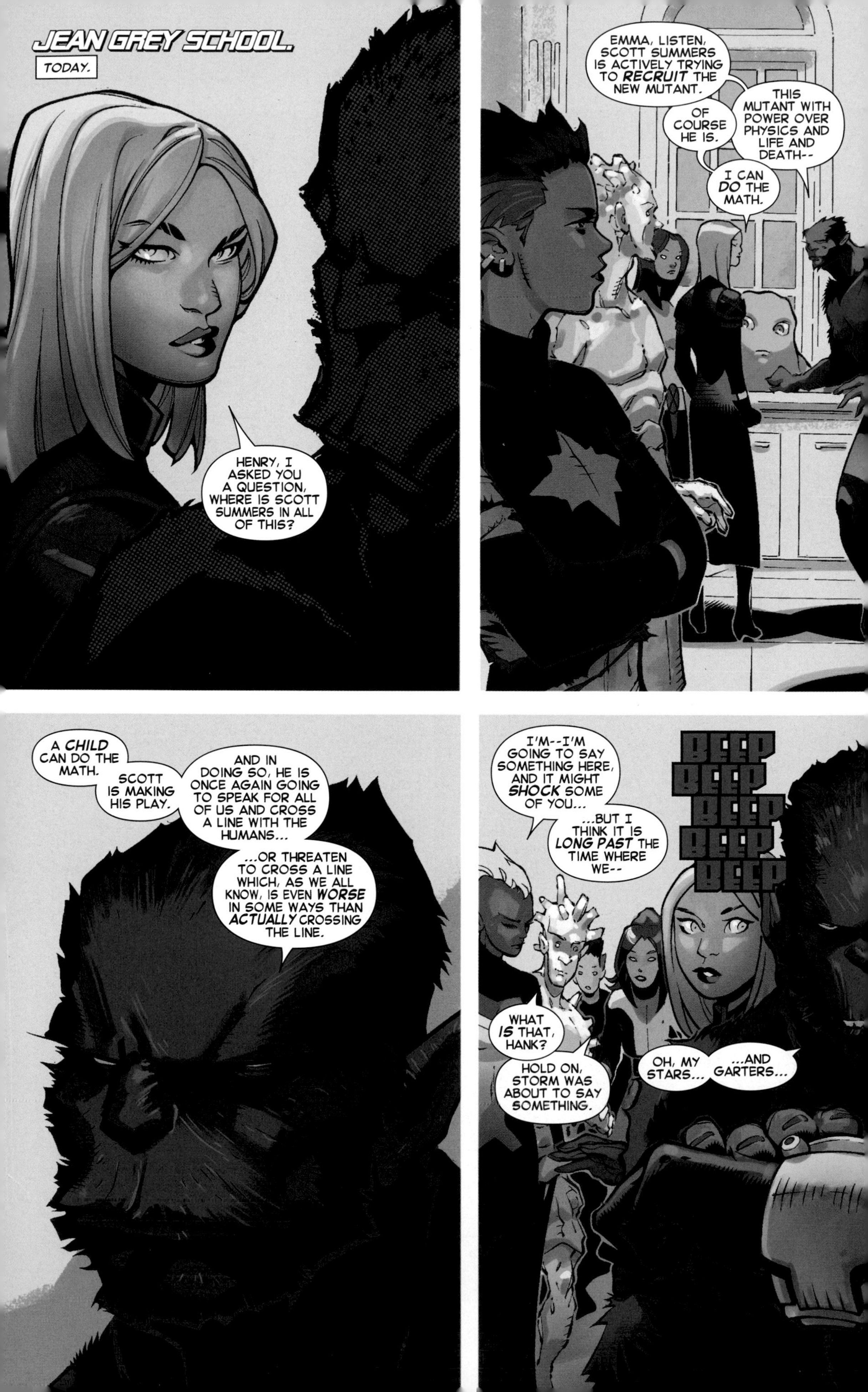
JEAN GREY SCHOOL.
TODAY.
HENRY, I ASKED YOU A QUESTION, WHERE IS SCOTT SUMMERS IN ALL OF THIS?
EMMA, LISTEN, SCOTT SUMMERS IS ACTIVELY TRYING TO RECRUIT THE NEW MUTANT.
OF COURSE HE IS.
THIS MUTANT WITH POWER OVER PHYSICS AND LIFE AND DEATH--
I CAN DO THE MATH.
A CHILD CAN DO THE MATH.
SCOTT IS MAKING HIS PLAY.
AND IN DOING SO, HE IS ONCE AGAIN GOING TO SPEAK FOR ALL OF US AND CROSS A LINE WITH THE HUMANS...
...OR THREATEN TO CROSS A LINE WHICH, AS WE ALL KNOW, IS EVEN WORSE IN SOME WAYS THAN ACTUALLY CROSSING THE LINE.
I'M--I'M GOING TO SAY SOMETHING HERE, AND IT MIGHT SHOCK SOME OF YOU...
...BUT I THINK IT IS LONG PAST THE TIME WHERE WE--
BEEP BEEP BEEP BEEP BEEP
WHAT IS THAT, HANK?
HOLD ON, STORM WAS ABOUT TO SAY SOMETHING.
OH, MY STARS...
...AND GARTERS...

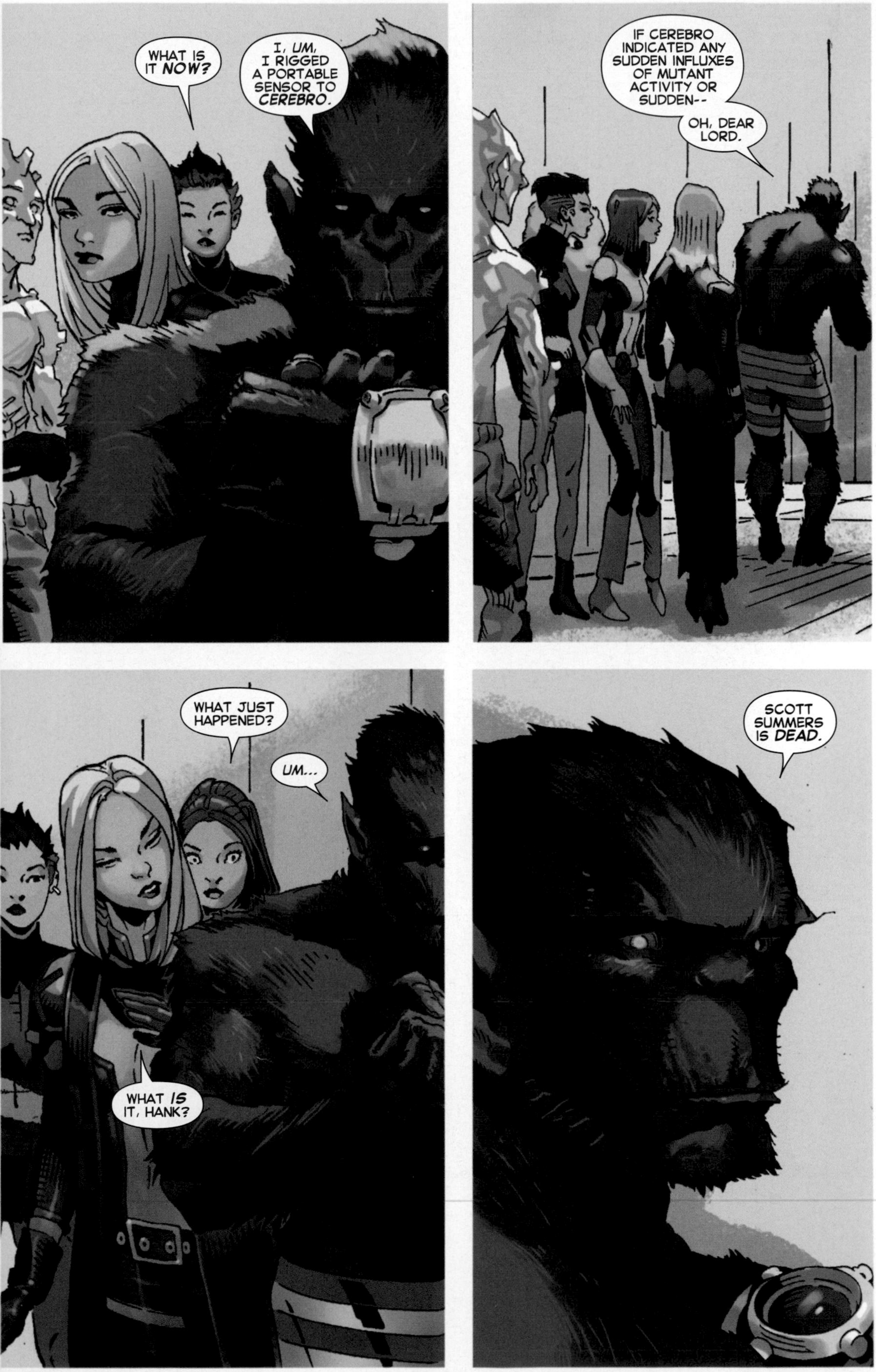
WHAT IS IT NOW?
I, UM, I RIGGED A PORTABLE SENSOR TO CEREBRO.
IF CEREBRO INDICATED ANY SUDDEN INFLUXES OF MUTANT ACTIVITY OR SUDDEN--
OH, DEAR LORD.
WHAT JUST HAPPENED?
UM...
WHAT IS IT, HANK?
SCOTT SUMMERS IS DEAD.

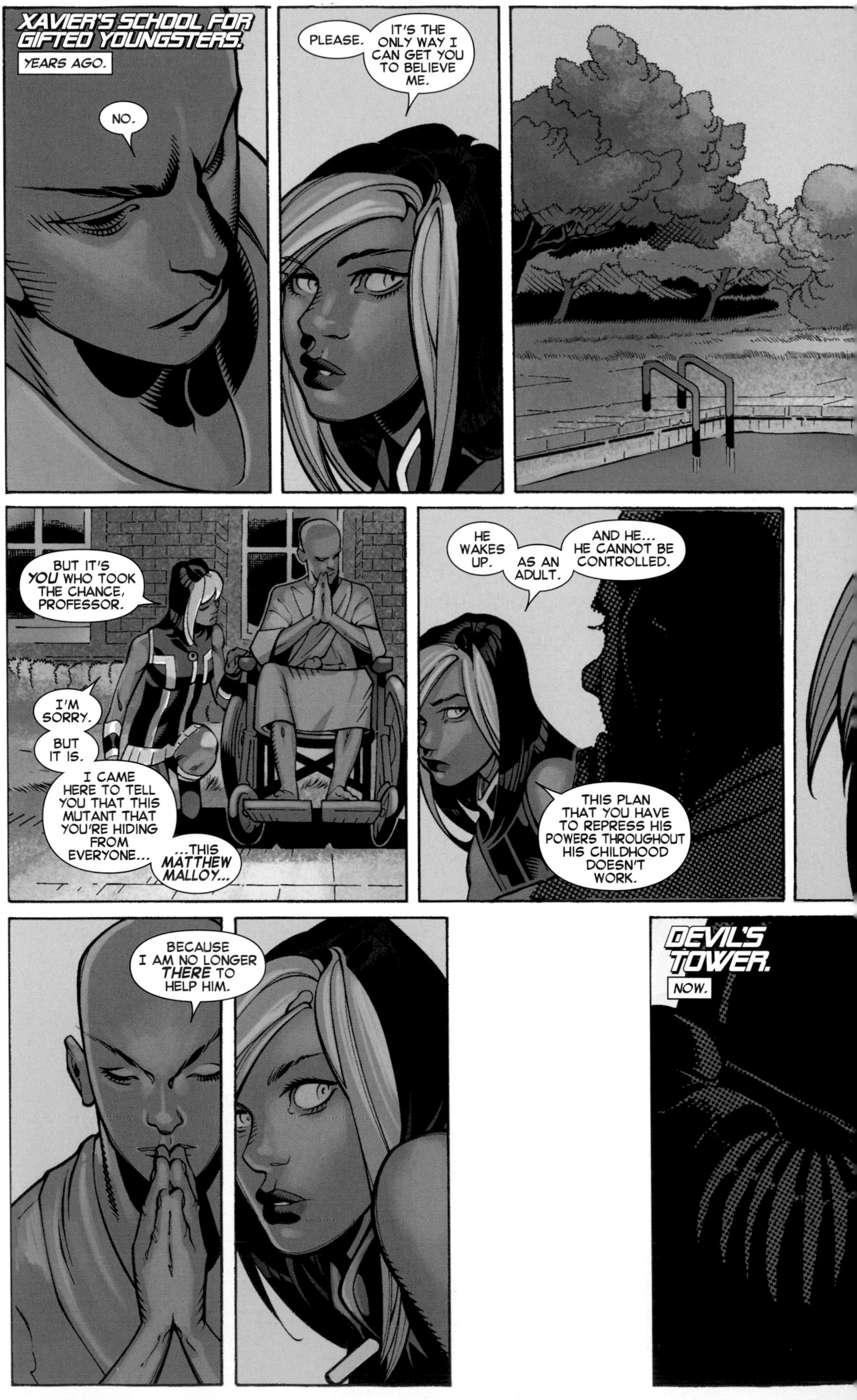
XAVIER'S SCHOOL FOR GIFTED YOUNGSTERS.
YEARS AGO.
NO.
PLEASE.
IT'S THE ONLY WAY I CAN GET YOU TO BELIEVE ME.
BUT IT'S YOU WHO TOOK THE CHANCE, PROFESSOR.
I'M SORRY.
BUT IT IS.
I CAME HERE TO TELL YOU THAT THIS MUTANT THAT YOU'RE HIDING FROM EVERYONE...
...THIS MATTHEW MALLOY...
HE WAKES UP.
AS AN ADULT.
AND HE... HE CANNOT BE CONTROLLED.
THIS PLAN THAT YOU HAVE TO REPRESS HIS POWERS THROUGHOUT HIS CHILDHOOD DOESN'T WORK.
BECAUSE I AM NO LONGER THERE TO HELP HIM.
DEVIL'S TOWER.
NOW.

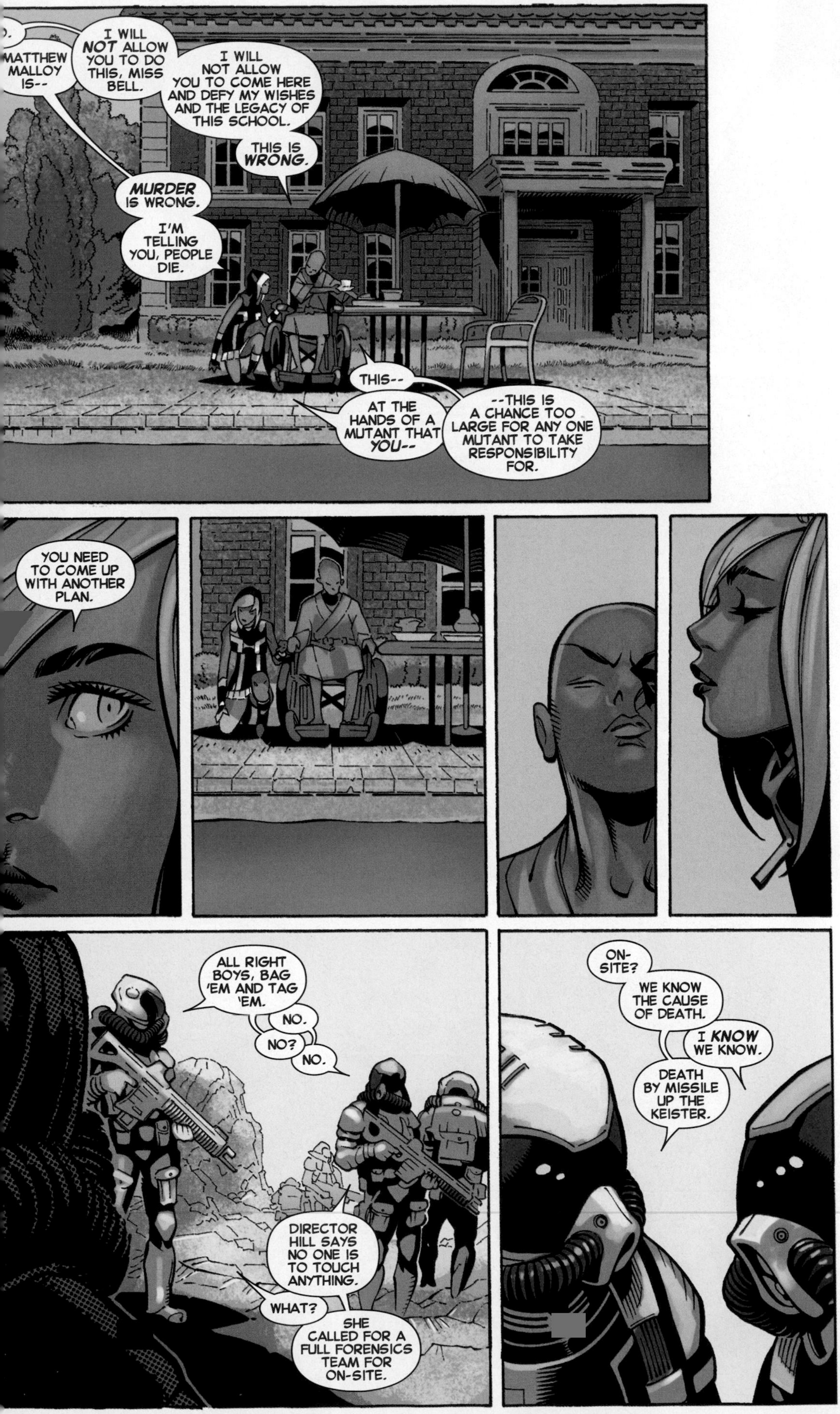
MATTHEW MALLOY IS--
I WILL NOT ALLOW YOU TO DO THIS, MISS BELL.
I WILL NOT ALLOW YOU TO COME HERE AND DEFY MY WISHES AND THE LEGACY OF THIS SCHOOL.
THIS IS WRONG.
MURDER IS WRONG.
I'M TELLING YOU, PEOPLE DIE.
AT THE HANDS OF A MUTANT THAT YOU--
THIS--
--THIS IS A CHANCE TOO LARGE FOR ANY ONE MUTANT TO TAKE RESPONSIBILITY FOR.
YOU NEED TO COME UP WITH ANOTHER PLAN.
ALL RIGHT BOYS, BAG 'EM AND TAG 'EM.
NO.
NO?
NO.
DIRECTOR HILL SAYS NO ONE IS TO TOUCH ANYTHING.
WHAT?
SHE CALLED FOR A FULL FORENSICS TEAM FOR ON-SITE.
ON-SITE?
WE KNOW THE CAUSE OF DEATH.
I KNOW WE KNOW.
DEATH BY MISSILE UP THE KEISTER.

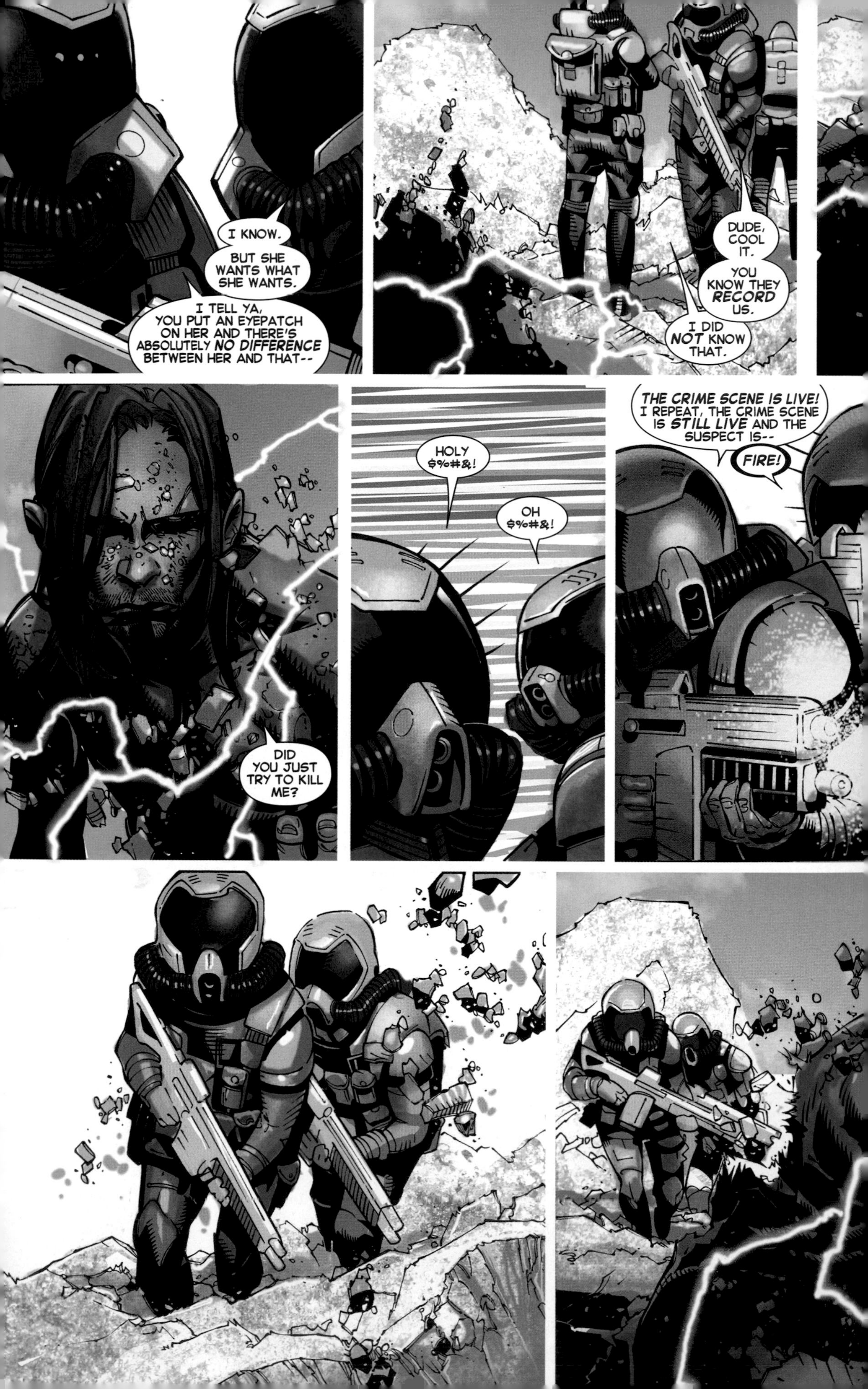
I KNOW.
BUT SHE WANTS WHAT SHE WANTS.
I TELL YA, YOU PUT AN EYEPATCH ON HER AND THERE'S ABSOLUTELY NO DIFFERENCE BETWEEN HER AND THAT--
DUDE, COOL IT.
YOU KNOW THEY RECORD US.
I DID NOT KNOW THAT.
DID YOU JUST TRY TO KILL ME?
HOLY $%#&!
OH $%#&!
THE CRIME SCENE IS LIVE! I REPEAT, THE CRIME SCENE IS STILL LIVE AND THE SUSPECT IS--
FIRE!

YOU DON'T THINK THAT S.H.I.E.L.D. RECORDS EVERYTHING WE SAY IN OUR ARMOR?

UH, NO.

WELL THEN, YOU'RE THE DUMBEST S.H.I.E.L.D. AGENT SINCE THE GUY WHO--

EXCUSE ME.

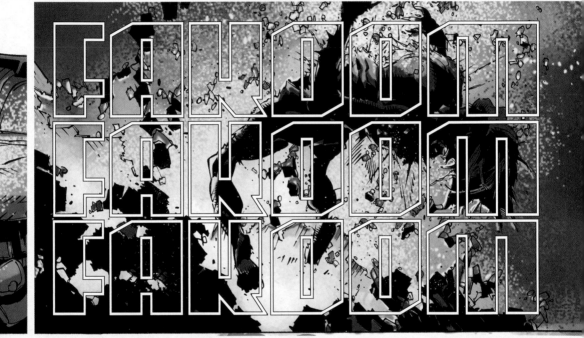

FAKOOM
FAKOOM
FAKOOM

OW.

THING IS...

...I DIDN'T KNOW I COULD DO ANY OF THIS.

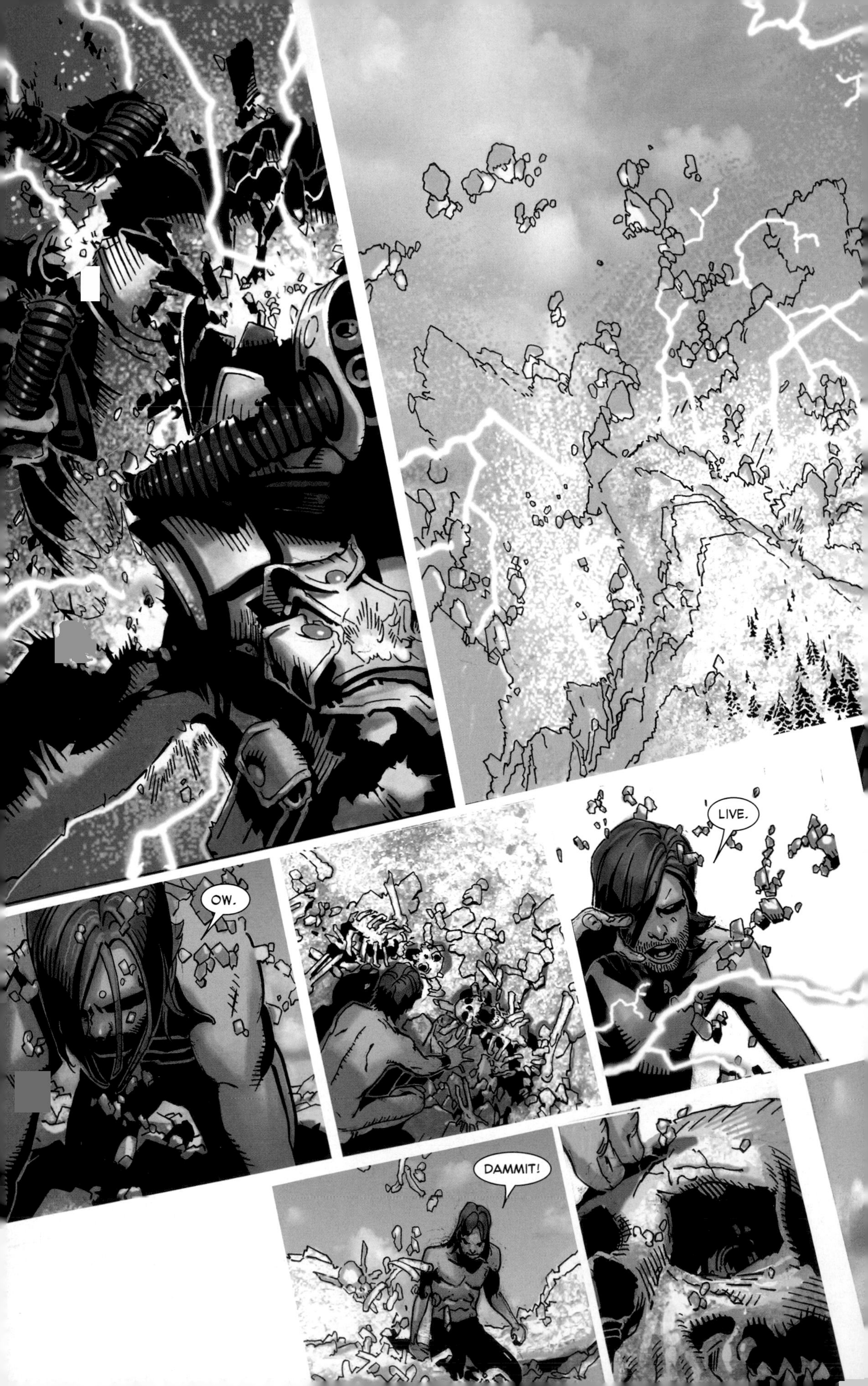

OW.
LIVE.
DAMMIT!

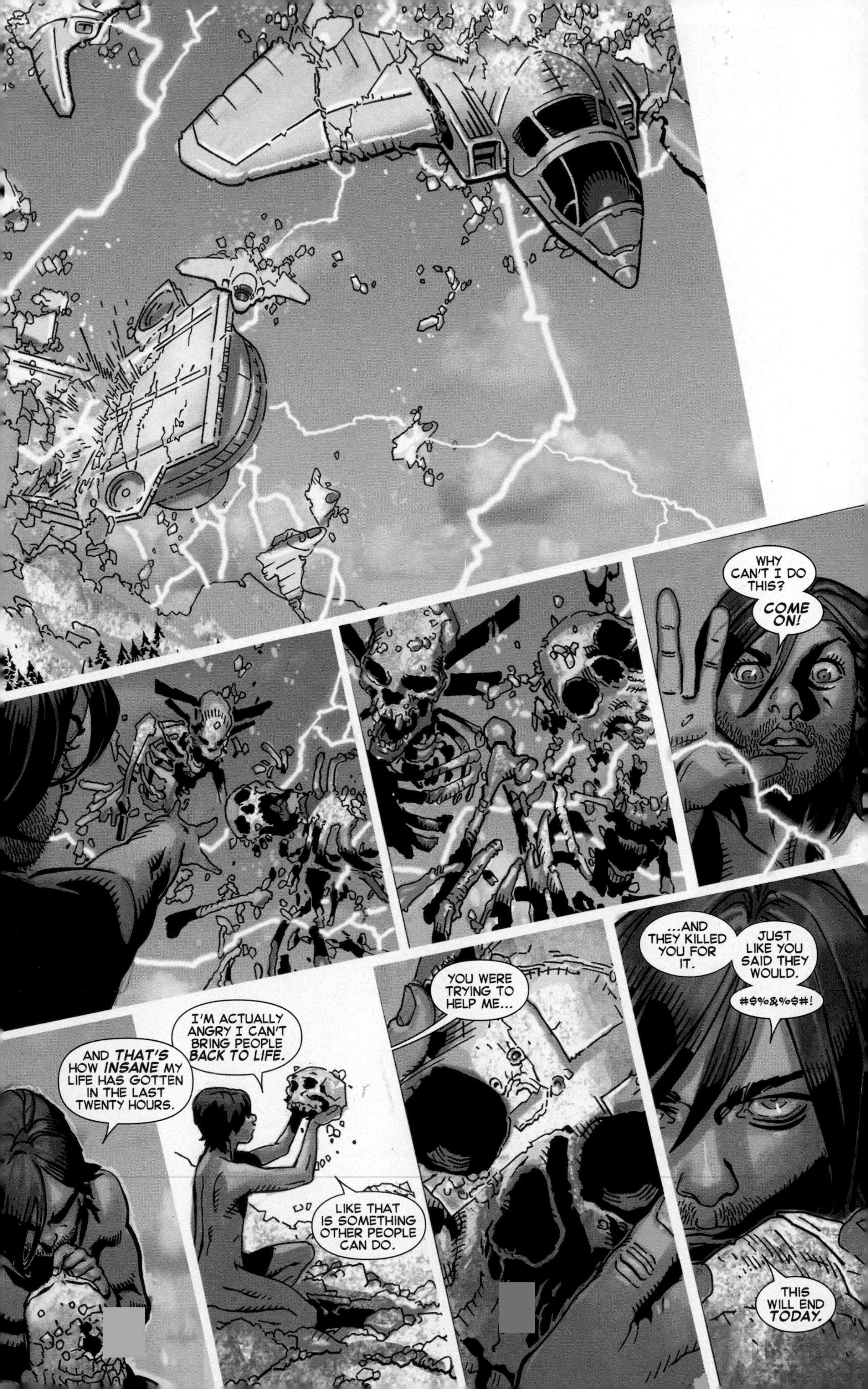
WHY CAN'T I DO THIS? COME ON!
AND THAT'S HOW INSANE MY LIFE HAS GOTTEN IN THE LAST TWENTY HOURS.
I'M ACTUALLY ANGRY I CAN'T BRING PEOPLE BACK TO LIFE.
LIKE THAT IS SOMETHING OTHER PEOPLE CAN DO.
YOU WERE TRYING TO HELP ME...
...AND THEY KILLED YOU FOR IT.
JUST LIKE YOU SAID THEY WOULD.
#$%&%$#!
THIS WILL END TODAY.

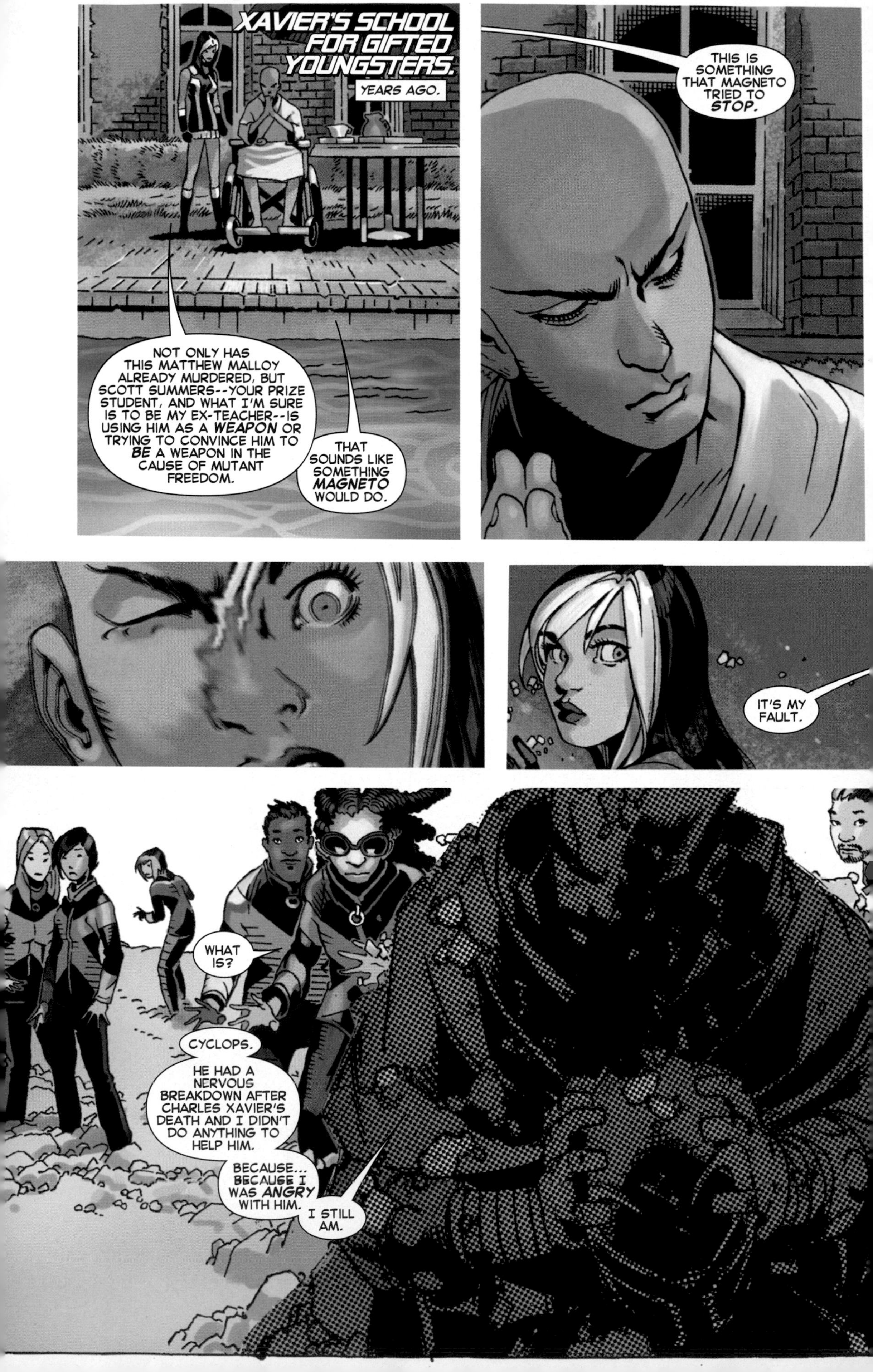
XAVIER'S SCHOOL FOR GIFTED YOUNGSTERS.
YEARS AGO.
NOT ONLY HAS THIS MATTHEW MALLOY ALREADY MURDERED, BUT SCOTT SUMMERS--YOUR PRIZE STUDENT, AND WHAT I'M SURE IS TO BE MY EX-TEACHER--IS USING HIM AS A WEAPON OR TRYING TO CONVINCE HIM TO BE A WEAPON IN THE CAUSE OF MUTANT FREEDOM.
THAT SOUNDS LIKE SOMETHING MAGNETO WOULD DO.
THIS IS SOMETHING THAT MAGNETO TRIED TO STOP.
IT'S MY FAULT.
WHAT IS?
CYCLOPS.
HE HAD A NERVOUS BREAKDOWN AFTER CHARLES XAVIER'S DEATH AND I DIDN'T DO ANYTHING TO HELP HIM.
BECAUSE... BECAUSE I WAS ANGRY WITH HIM.
I STILL AM.

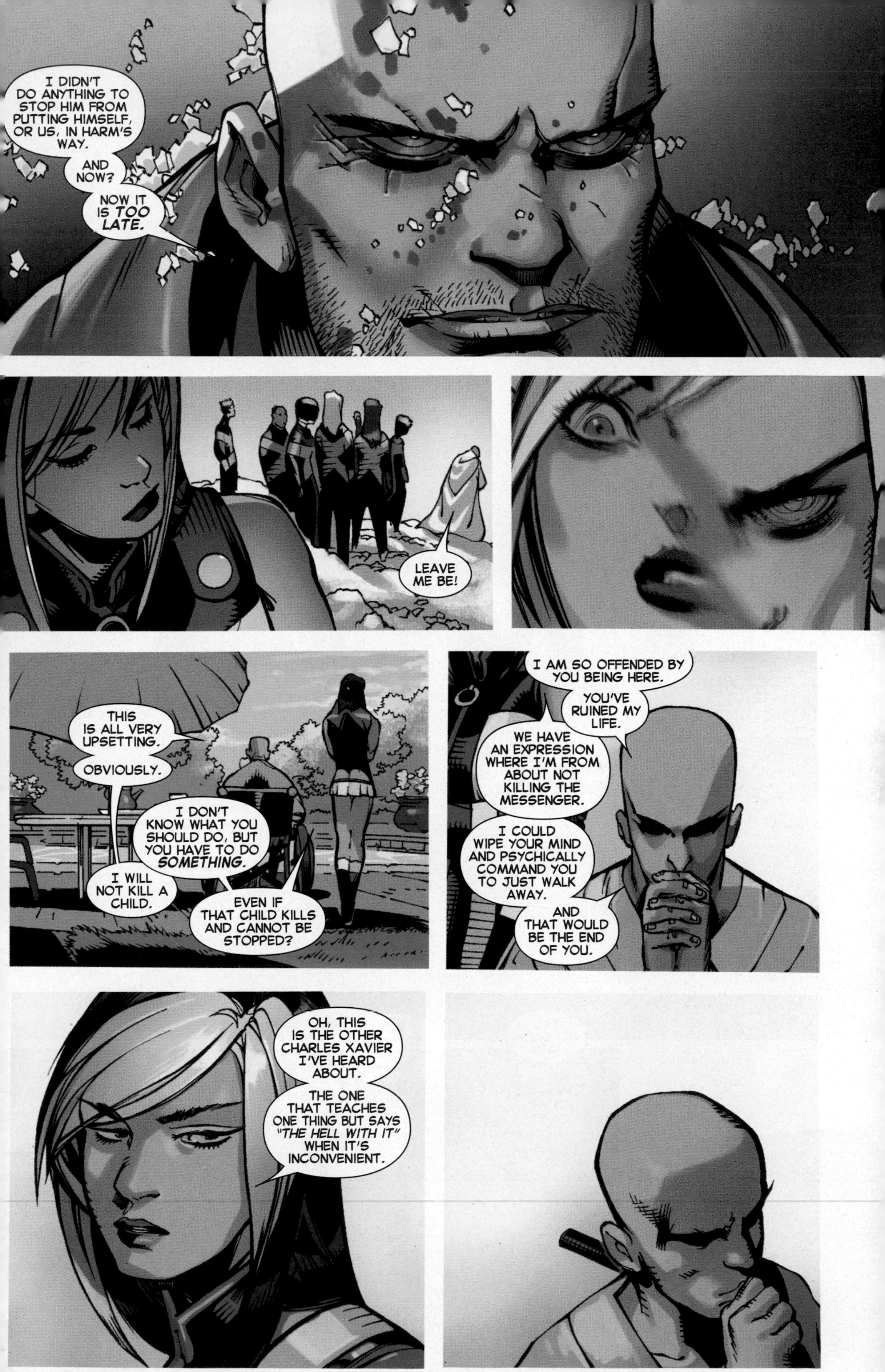

I DIDN'T DO ANYTHING TO STOP HIM FROM PUTTING HIMSELF, OR US, IN HARM'S WAY.
AND NOW?
NOW IT IS TOO LATE.
LEAVE ME BE!
THIS IS ALL VERY UPSETTING.
OBVIOUSLY.
I DON'T KNOW WHAT YOU SHOULD DO, BUT YOU HAVE TO DO SOMETHING.
I WILL NOT KILL A CHILD.
EVEN IF THAT CHILD KILLS AND CANNOT BE STOPPED?
I AM SO OFFENDED BY YOU BEING HERE.
YOU'VE RUINED MY LIFE.
WE HAVE AN EXPRESSION WHERE I'M FROM ABOUT NOT KILLING THE MESSENGER.
I COULD WIPE YOUR MIND AND PSYCHICALLY COMMAND YOU TO JUST WALK AWAY.
AND THAT WOULD BE THE END OF YOU.
OH, THIS IS THE OTHER CHARLES XAVIER I'VE HEARD ABOUT.
THE ONE THAT TEACHES ONE THING BUT SAYS "THE HELL WITH IT" WHEN IT'S INCONVENIENT.

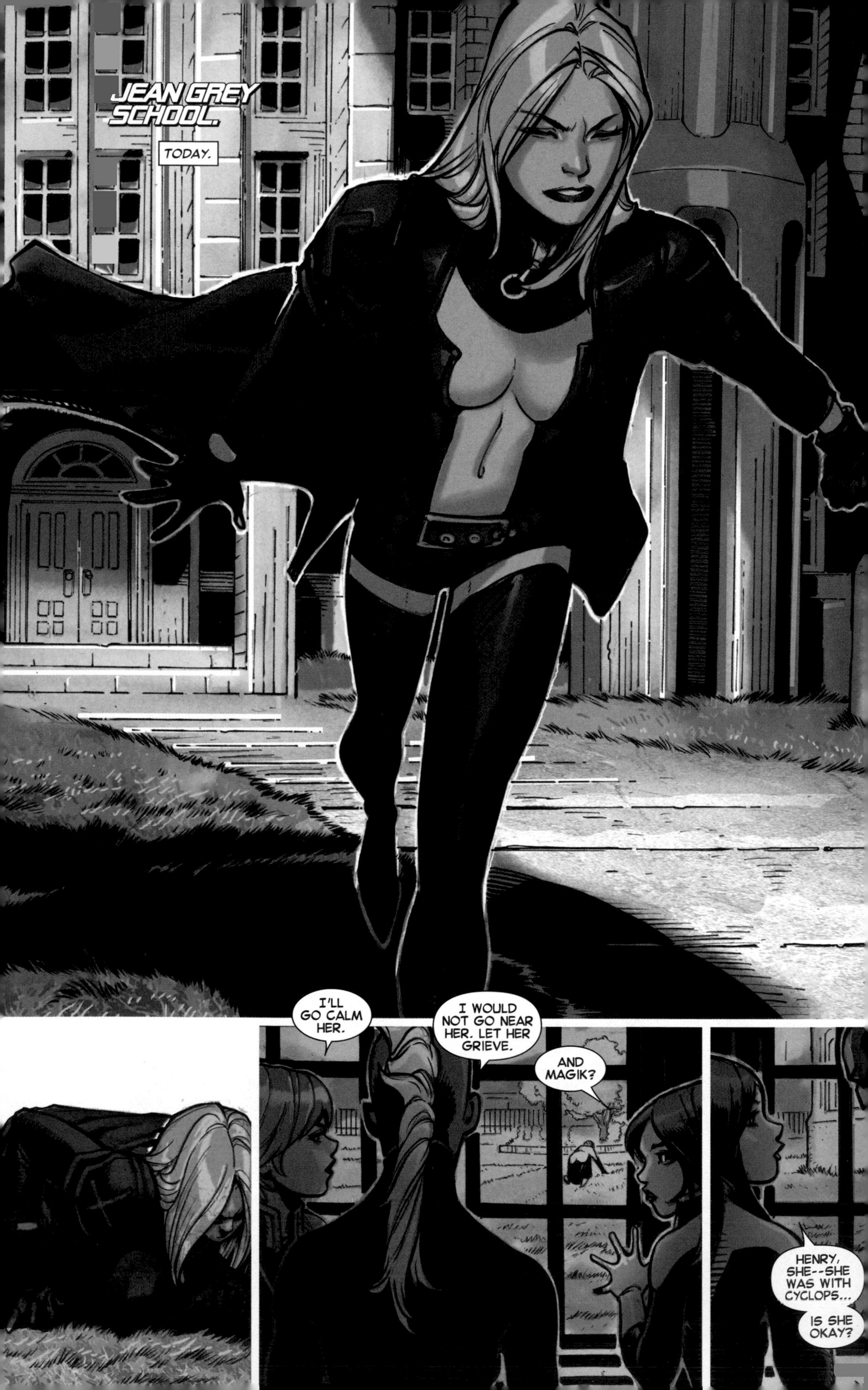
JEAN GREY SCHOOL.
TODAY.
I'LL GO CALM HER.
I WOULD NOT GO NEAR HER. LET HER GRIEVE.
AND MAGIK?
HENRY, SHE--SHE WAS WITH CYCLOPS...
IS SHE OKAY?

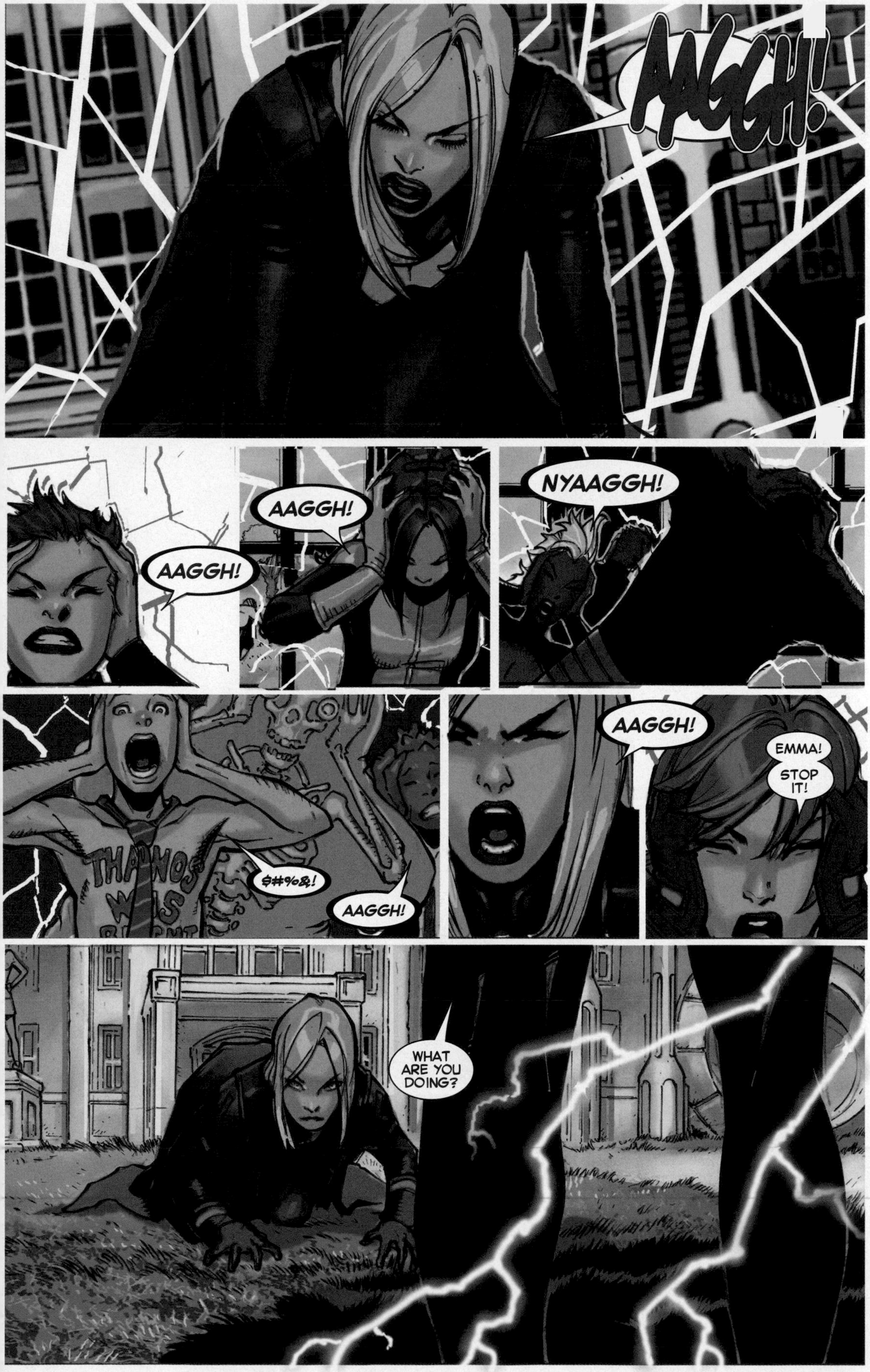
AAGGH!
AAGGH!
AAGGH!
NYAAGGH!
$#%&!
AAGGH!
AAGGH!
EMMA!
STOP IT!
WHAT ARE YOU DOING?

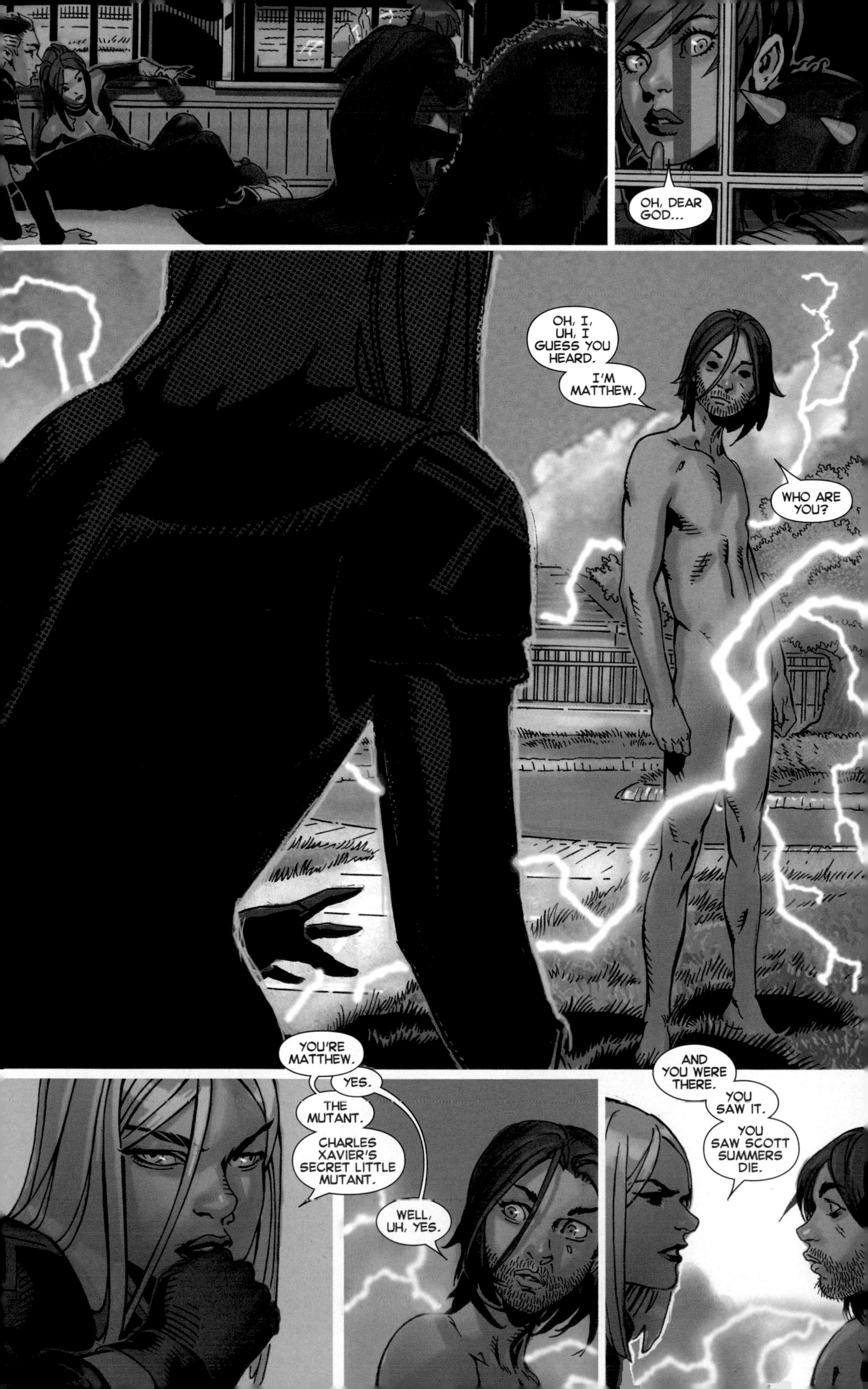
OH, DEAR GOD...
OH, I, UH, I GUESS YOU HEARD.
I'M MATTHEW.
WHO ARE YOU?
YOU'RE MATTHEW.
YES.
THE MUTANT.
CHARLES XAVIER'S SECRET LITTLE MUTANT.
WELL, UH, YES.
AND YOU WERE THERE.
YOU SAW IT.
YOU SAW SCOTT SUMMERS DIE.

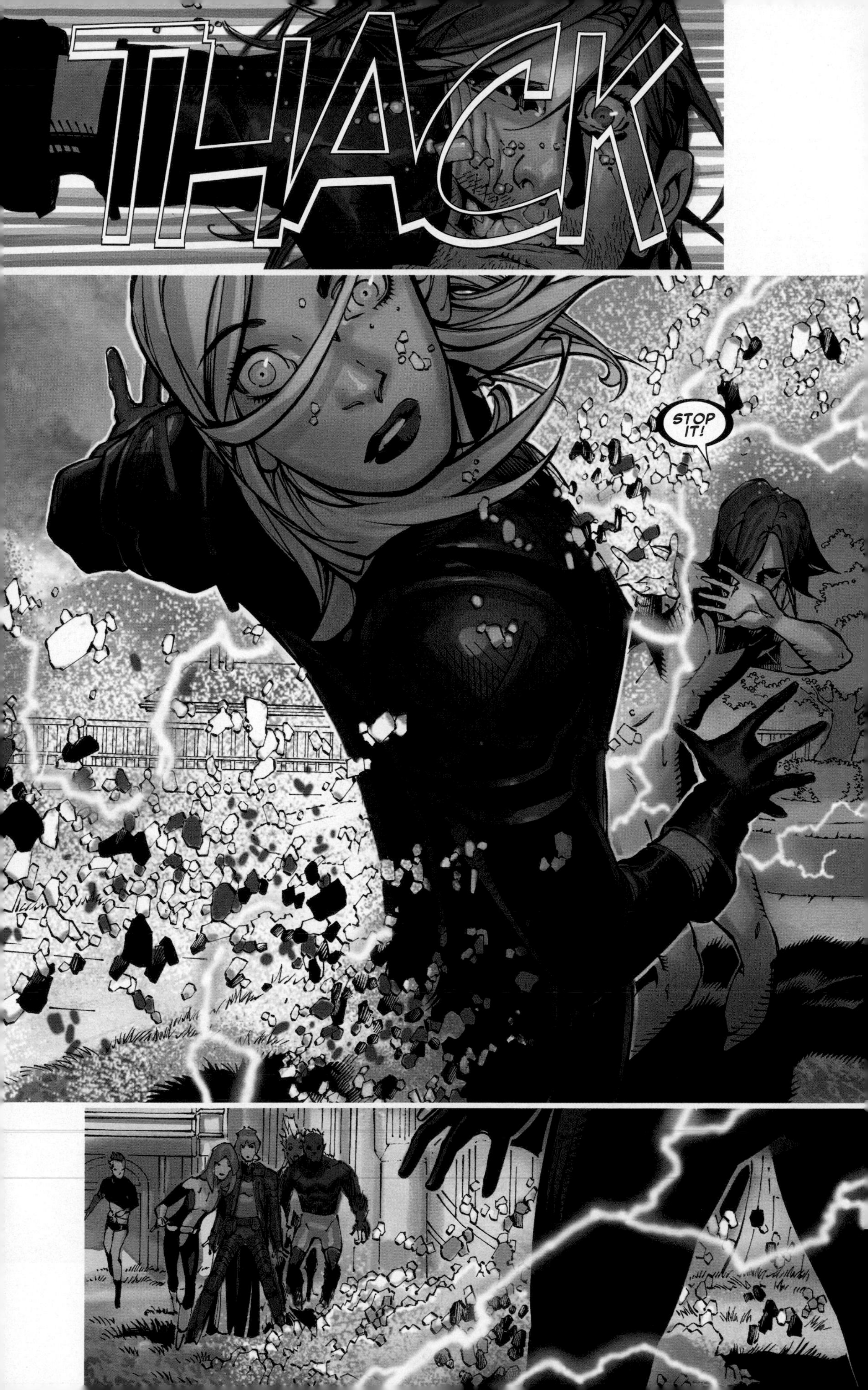
THACK
STOP IT!

I...I DIDN'T MEAN THAT.

SHE WAS GOING TO KILL ME.

I...I CAN'T BRING HER BACK.

WHO WAS SHE?

## THE NEW XAVIER SCHOOL.

TODAY.

HAS ANYONE SEEN EVA?

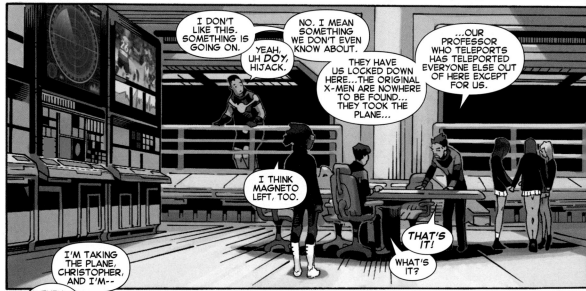

I DON'T LIKE THIS. SOMETHING IS GOING ON.

YEAH, UH *DOY*, HIJACK.

NO. I MEAN SOMETHING WE DON'T EVEN KNOW ABOUT.

THEY HAVE US LOCKED DOWN HERE...THE ORIGINAL X-MEN ARE NOWHERE TO BE FOUND... THEY TOOK THE PLANE...

...OUR PROFESSOR WHO TELEPORTS HAS TELEPORTED EVERYONE ELSE OUT OF HERE EXCEPT FOR US.

I THINK MAGNETO LEFT, TOO.

THAT'S IT!

WHAT'S IT?

I'M TAKING THE PLANE, CHRISTOPHER, AND I'M--

THEY TOOK THE PLANE.

I'M A MUTANT THAT CAN *CONTROL* MACHINES.

THERE MUST BE SOMETHING AROUND HERE I CAN HIJACK.

LADIES?

UM?

I THINK THEY ARE BUSY IN THEIR HIVE-MIND THING AND NOT TALKING TO US?

I DON'T BLAME THEM.

AAAAGGHH!

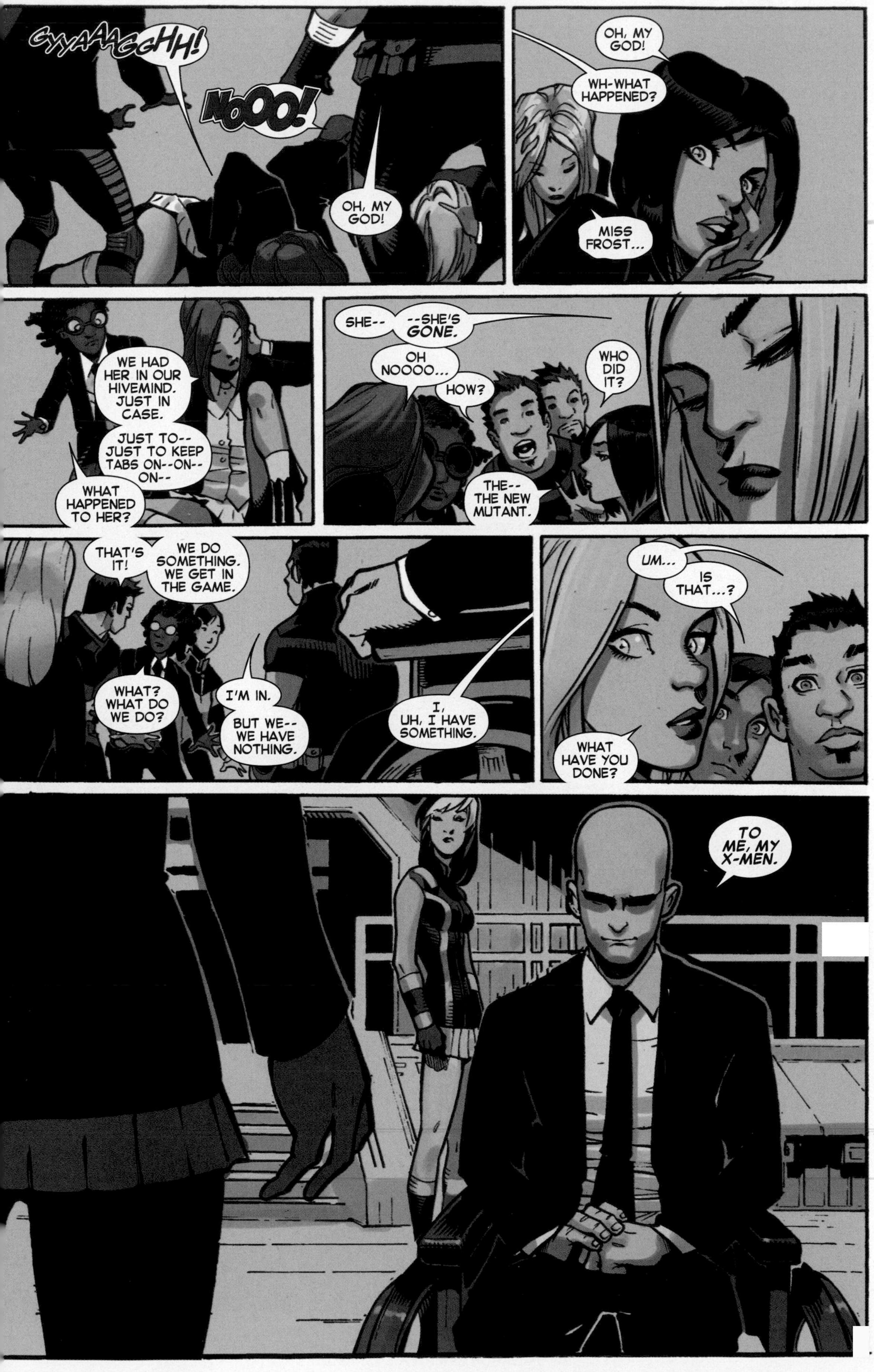
GYYAAAGGHH!
NOOO!
OH, MY GOD!
OH, MY GOD!
WH-WHAT HAPPENED?
MISS FROST...
WE HAD HER IN OUR HIVEMIND. JUST IN CASE.
JUST TO-- JUST TO KEEP TABS ON--ON-- ON--
WHAT HAPPENED TO HER?
SHE--
--SHE'S GONE.
OH NOOOO...
HOW?
WHO DID IT?
THE-- THE NEW MUTANT.
THAT'S IT!
WE DO SOMETHING. WE GET IN THE GAME.
WHAT? WHAT DO WE DO?
I'M IN.
BUT WE-- WE HAVE NOTHING.
I, UH, I HAVE SOMETHING.
UM...
IS THAT...?
WHAT HAVE YOU DONE?
TO ME, MY X-MEN.

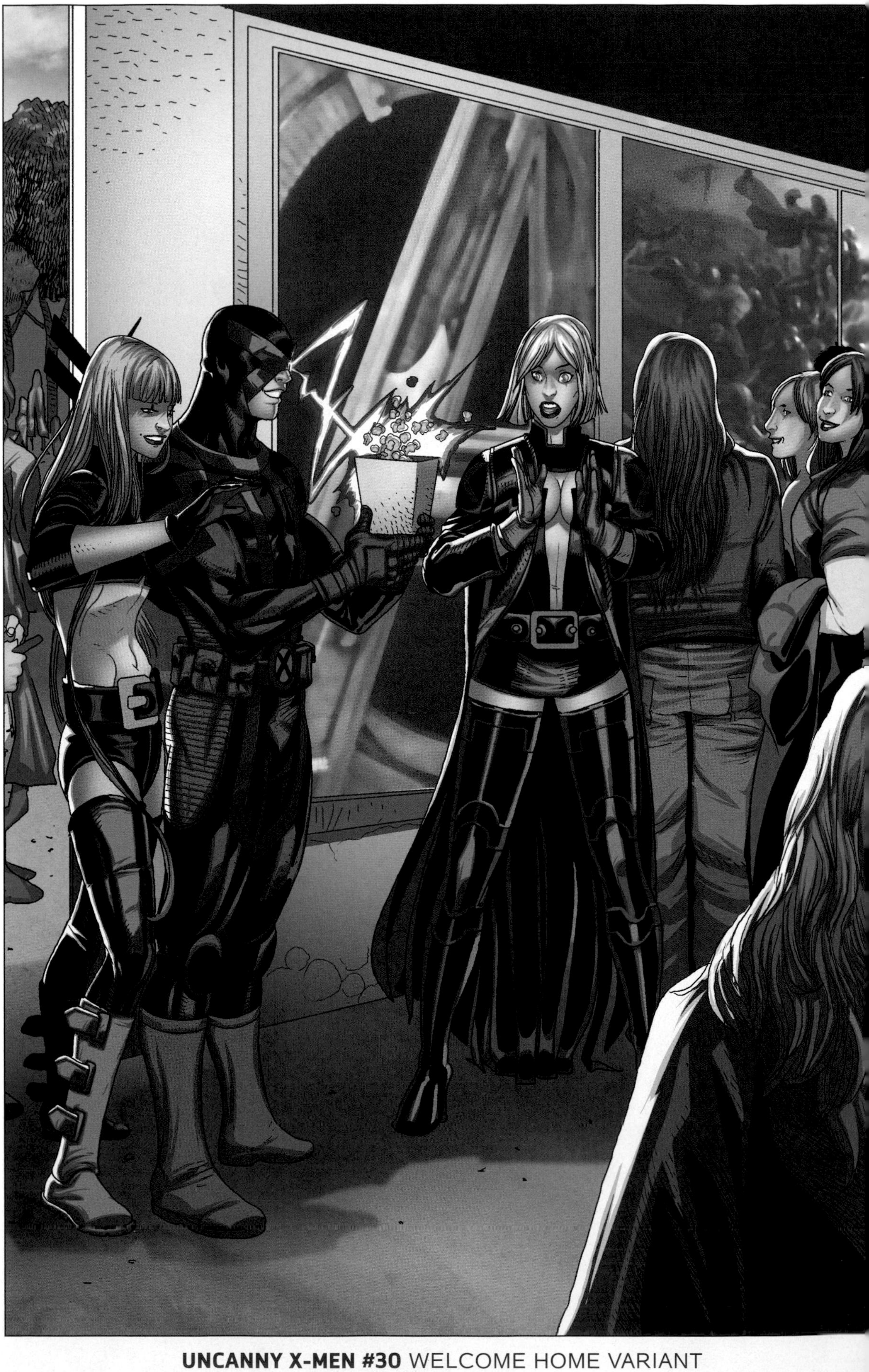

**UNCANNY X-MEN #30** WELCOME HOME VARIANT
BY SALVADOR LARROCA & ISRAEL SILVA

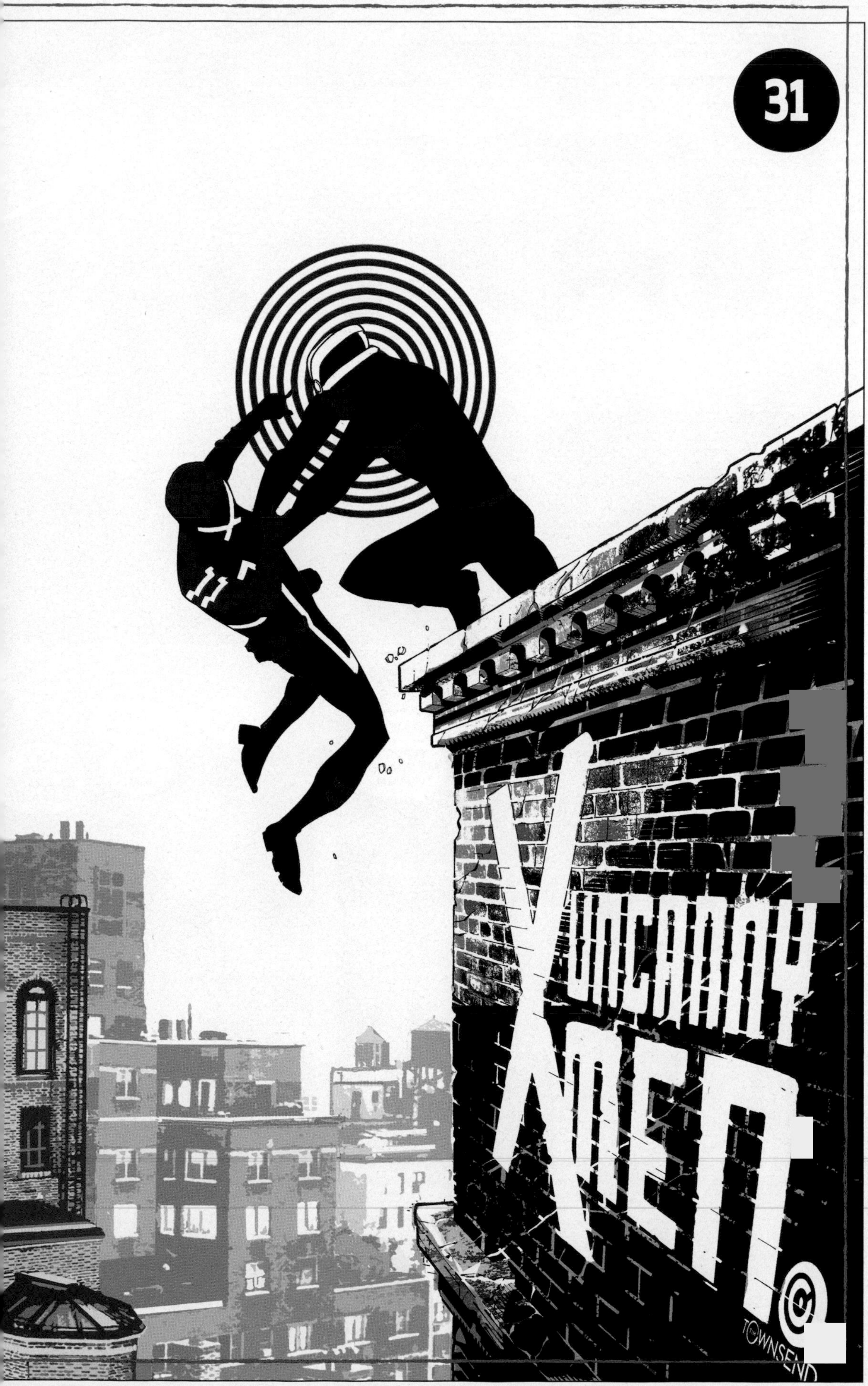
31
UNCANNY
X-MEN
TOWNSEND

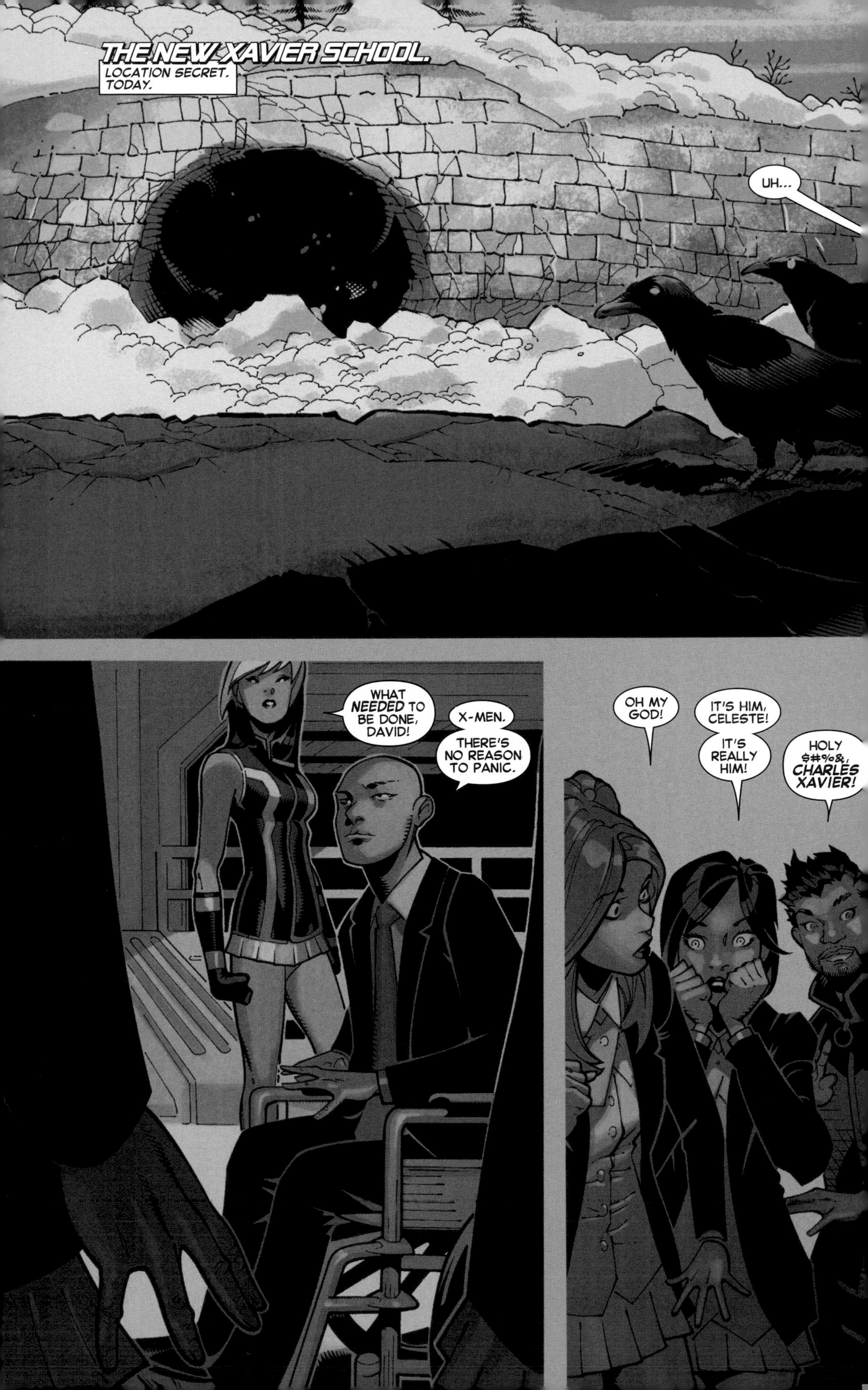

THE NEW XAVIER SCHOOL.
LOCATION SECRET. TODAY.
UH...
WHAT NEEDED TO BE DONE, DAVID!
X-MEN.
THERE'S NO REASON TO PANIC.
OH MY GOD!
IT'S HIM, CELESTE!
IT'S REALLY HIM!
HOLY $#%&, CHARLES XAVIER!

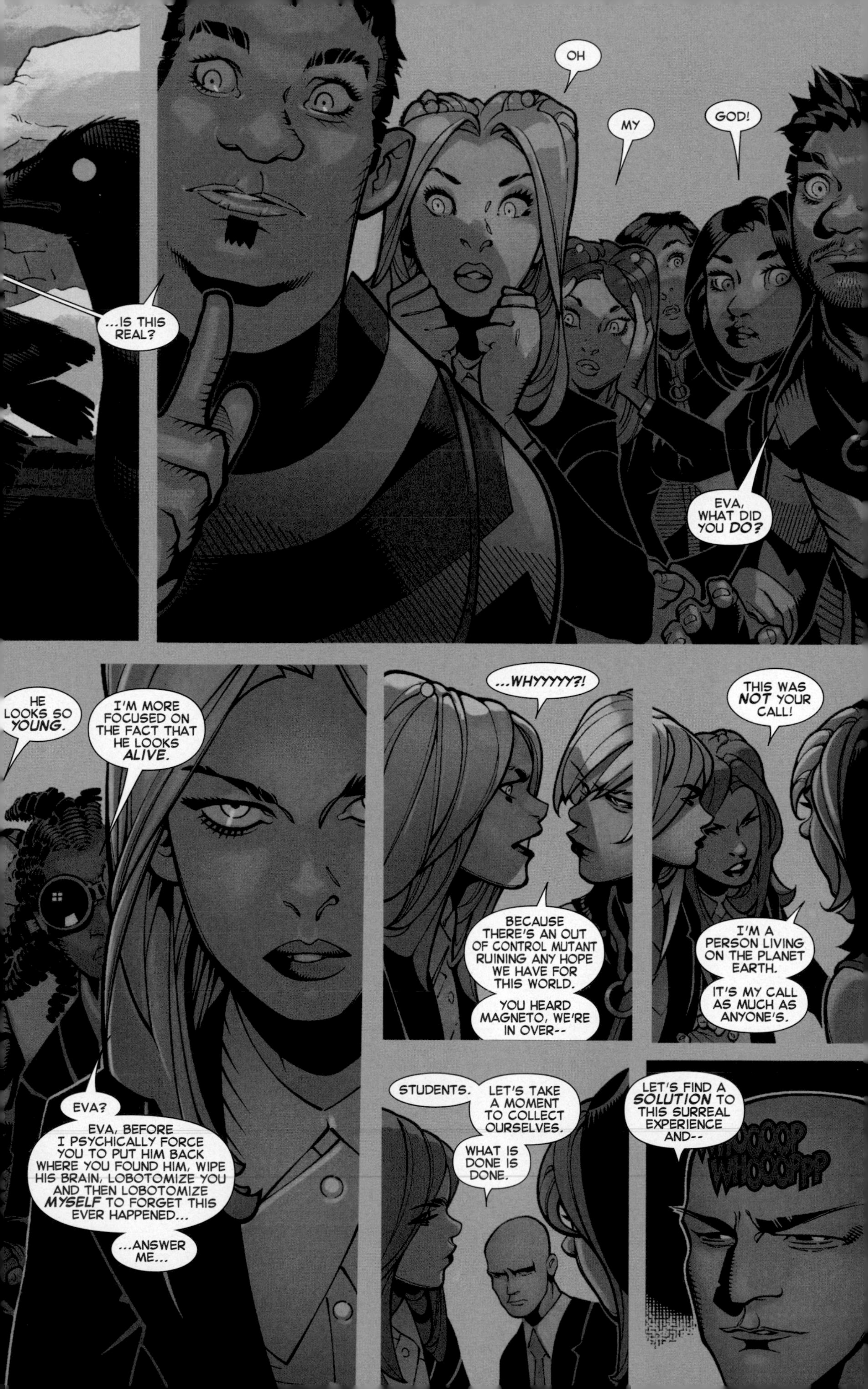

OH
MY
GOD!
...IS THIS REAL?
EVA, WHAT DID YOU DO?
HE LOOKS SO YOUNG.
I'M MORE FOCUSED ON THE FACT THAT HE LOOKS ALIVE.
EVA?
EVA, BEFORE I PSYCHICALLY FORCE YOU TO PUT HIM BACK WHERE YOU FOUND HIM, WIPE HIS BRAIN, LOBOTOMIZE YOU AND THEN LOBOTOMIZE MYSELF TO FORGET THIS EVER HAPPENED...
...ANSWER ME...
...WHYYYYY?!
BECAUSE THERE'S AN OUT OF CONTROL MUTANT RUINING ANY HOPE WE HAVE FOR THIS WORLD.
YOU HEARD MAGNETO, WE'RE IN OVER--
THIS WAS NOT YOUR CALL!
I'M A PERSON LIVING ON THE PLANET EARTH.
IT'S MY CALL AS MUCH AS ANYONE'S.
STUDENTS.
LET'S TAKE A MOMENT TO COLLECT OURSELVES.
WHAT IS DONE IS DONE.
LET'S FIND A SOLUTION TO THIS SURREAL EXPERIENCE AND--
WHOOOP WHOOOP

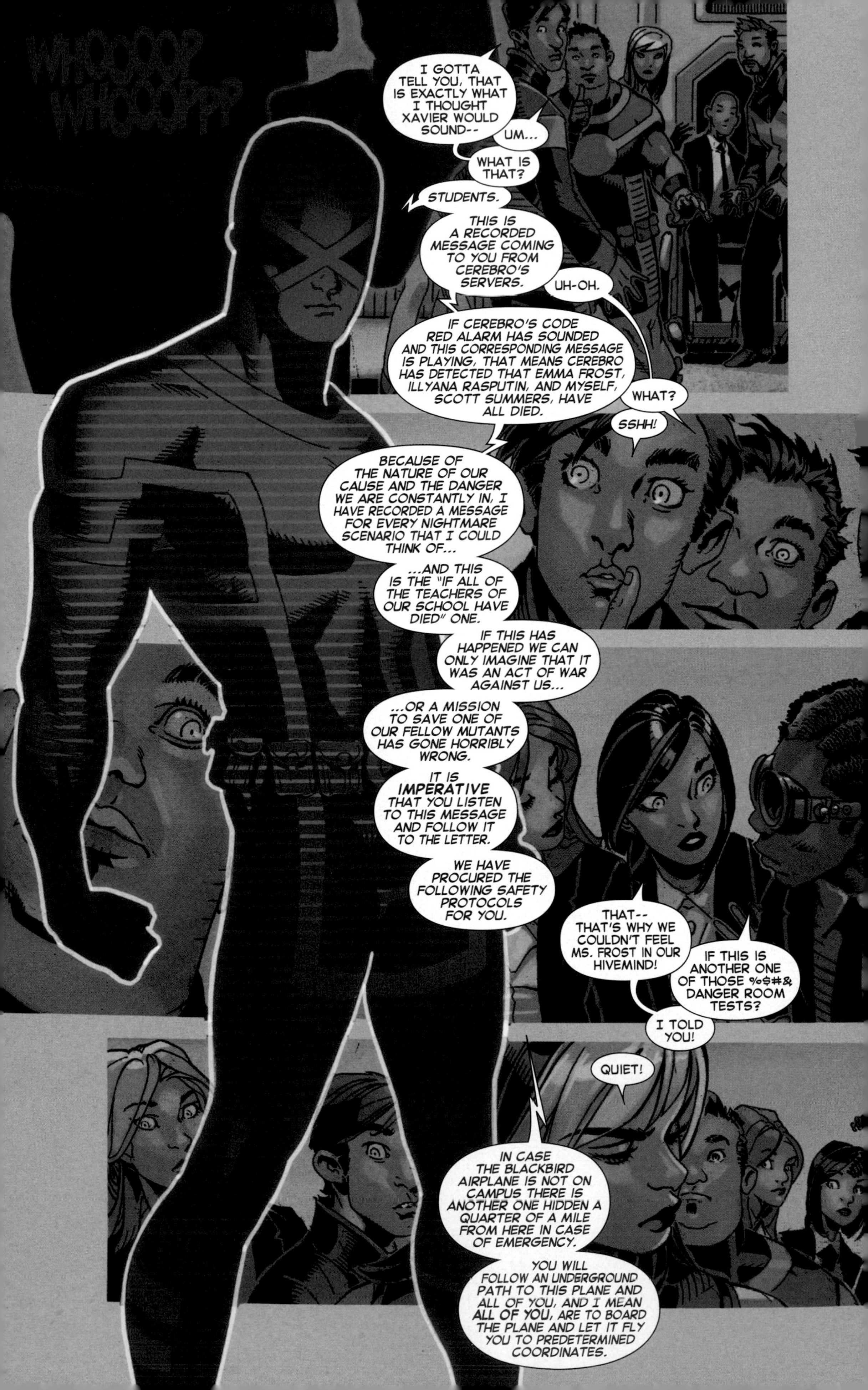
I GOTTA TELL YOU, THAT IS EXACTLY WHAT I THOUGHT XAVIER WOULD SOUND--
UM...
WHAT IS THAT?
STUDENTS.
THIS IS A RECORDED MESSAGE COMING TO YOU FROM CEREBRO'S SERVERS.
UH-OH.
IF CEREBRO'S CODE RED ALARM HAS SOUNDED AND THIS CORRESPONDING MESSAGE IS PLAYING, THAT MEANS CEREBRO HAS DETECTED THAT EMMA FROST, ILLYANA RASPUTIN, AND MYSELF, SCOTT SUMMERS, HAVE ALL DIED.
WHAT?
SSHH!
BECAUSE OF THE NATURE OF OUR CAUSE AND THE DANGER WE ARE CONSTANTLY IN, I HAVE RECORDED A MESSAGE FOR EVERY NIGHTMARE SCENARIO THAT I COULD THINK OF...
...AND THIS IS THE "IF ALL OF THE TEACHERS OF OUR SCHOOL HAVE DIED" ONE.
IF THIS HAS HAPPENED WE CAN ONLY IMAGINE THAT IT WAS AN ACT OF WAR AGAINST US...
...OR A MISSION TO SAVE ONE OF OUR FELLOW MUTANTS HAS GONE HORRIBLY WRONG.
IT IS IMPERATIVE THAT YOU LISTEN TO THIS MESSAGE AND FOLLOW IT TO THE LETTER.
WE HAVE PROCURED THE FOLLOWING SAFETY PROTOCOLS FOR YOU.
THAT-- THAT'S WHY WE COULDN'T FEEL MS. FROST IN OUR HIVEMIND!
IF THIS IS ANOTHER ONE OF THOSE %$#& DANGER ROOM TESTS?
I TOLD YOU!
QUIET!
IN CASE THE BLACKBIRD AIRPLANE IS NOT ON CAMPUS THERE IS ANOTHER ONE HIDDEN A QUARTER OF A MILE FROM HERE IN CASE OF EMERGENCY.
YOU WILL FOLLOW AN UNDERGROUND PATH TO THIS PLANE AND ALL OF YOU, AND I MEAN ALL OF YOU, ARE TO BOARD THE PLANE AND LET IT FLY YOU TO PREDETERMINED COORDINATES.

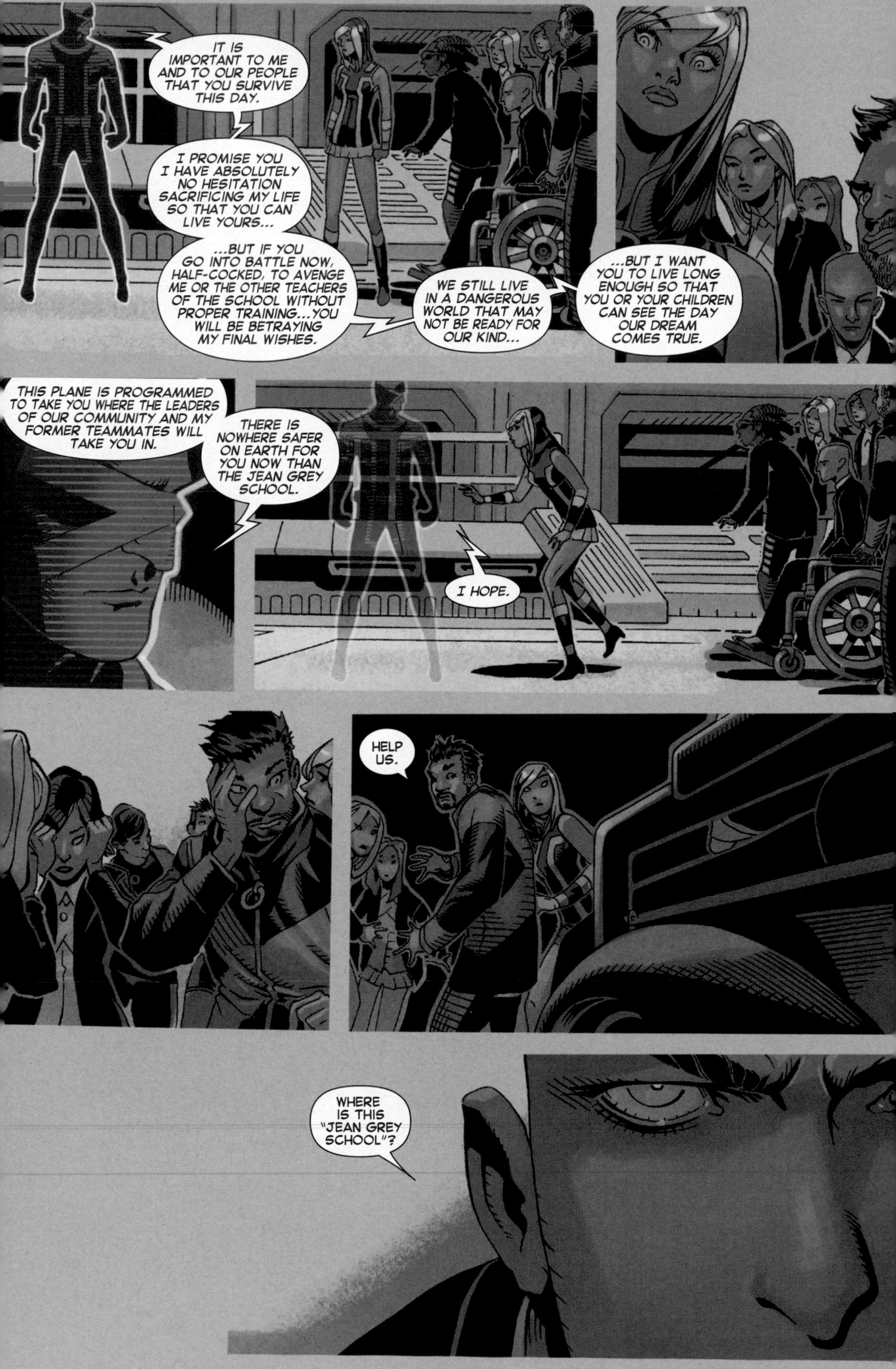
IT IS IMPORTANT TO ME AND TO OUR PEOPLE THAT YOU SURVIVE THIS DAY.
I PROMISE YOU I HAVE ABSOLUTELY NO HESITATION SACRIFICING MY LIFE SO THAT YOU CAN LIVE YOURS...
...BUT IF YOU GO INTO BATTLE NOW, HALF-COCKED, TO AVENGE ME OR THE OTHER TEACHERS OF THE SCHOOL WITHOUT PROPER TRAINING...YOU WILL BE BETRAYING MY FINAL WISHES.
WE STILL LIVE IN A DANGEROUS WORLD THAT MAY NOT BE READY FOR OUR KIND...
...BUT I WANT YOU TO LIVE LONG ENOUGH SO THAT YOU OR YOUR CHILDREN CAN SEE THE DAY OUR DREAM COMES TRUE.
THIS PLANE IS PROGRAMMED TO TAKE YOU WHERE THE LEADERS OF OUR COMMUNITY AND MY FORMER TEAMMATES WILL TAKE YOU IN.
THERE IS NOWHERE SAFER ON EARTH FOR YOU NOW THAN THE JEAN GREY SCHOOL.
I HOPE.
HELP US.
WHERE IS THIS "JEAN GREY SCHOOL"?

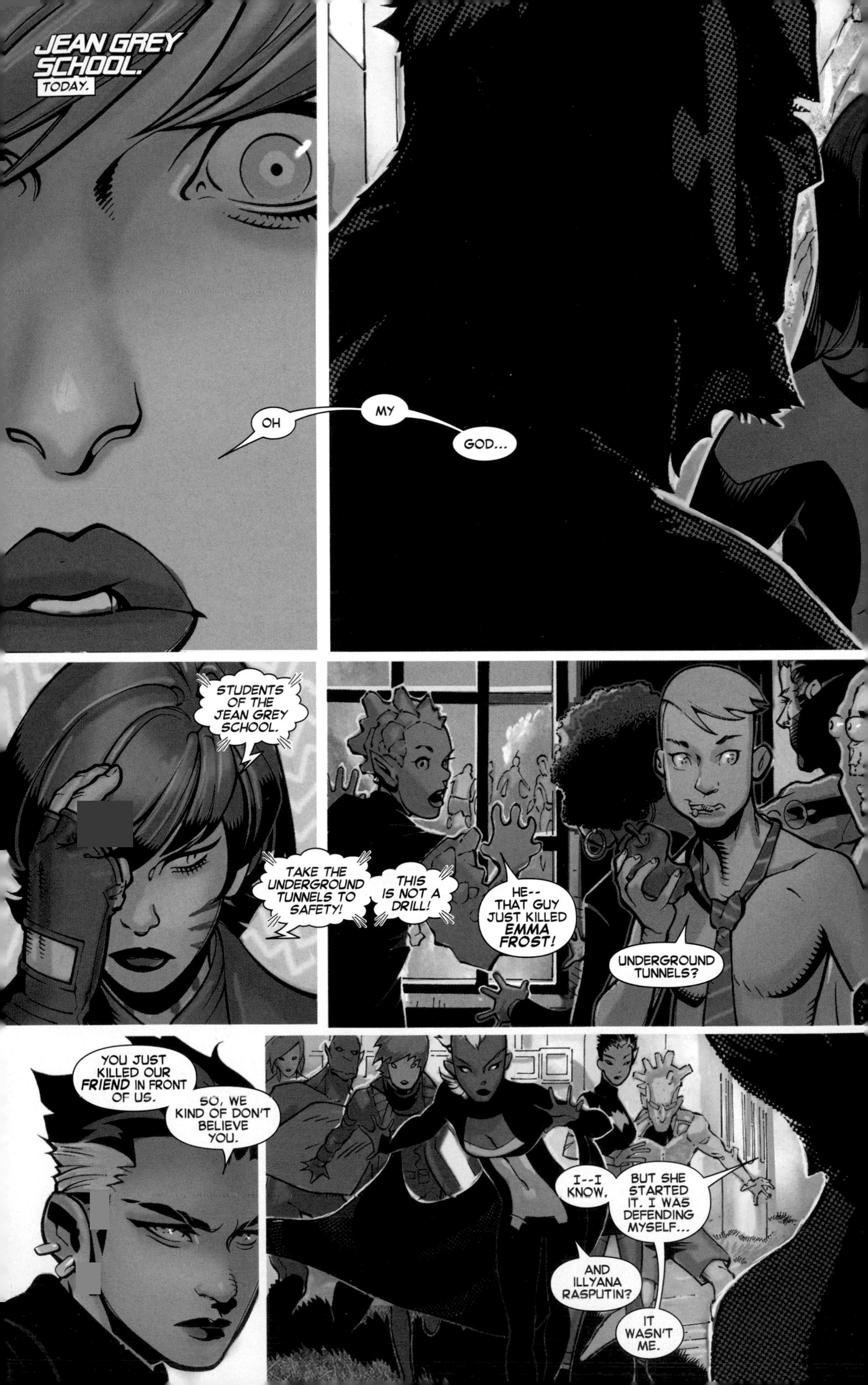

JEAN GREY SCHOOL.
TODAY.
OH
MY
GOD...
STUDENTS OF THE JEAN GREY SCHOOL.
TAKE THE UNDERGROUND TUNNELS TO SAFETY!
THIS IS NOT A DRILL!
HE-- THAT GUY JUST KILLED EMMA FROST!
UNDERGROUND TUNNELS?
YOU JUST KILLED OUR FRIEND IN FRONT OF US.
SO, WE KIND OF DON'T BELIEVE YOU.
I--I KNOW.
BUT SHE STARTED IT. I WAS DEFENDING MYSELF...
AND ILLYANA RASPUTIN?
IT WASN'T ME.

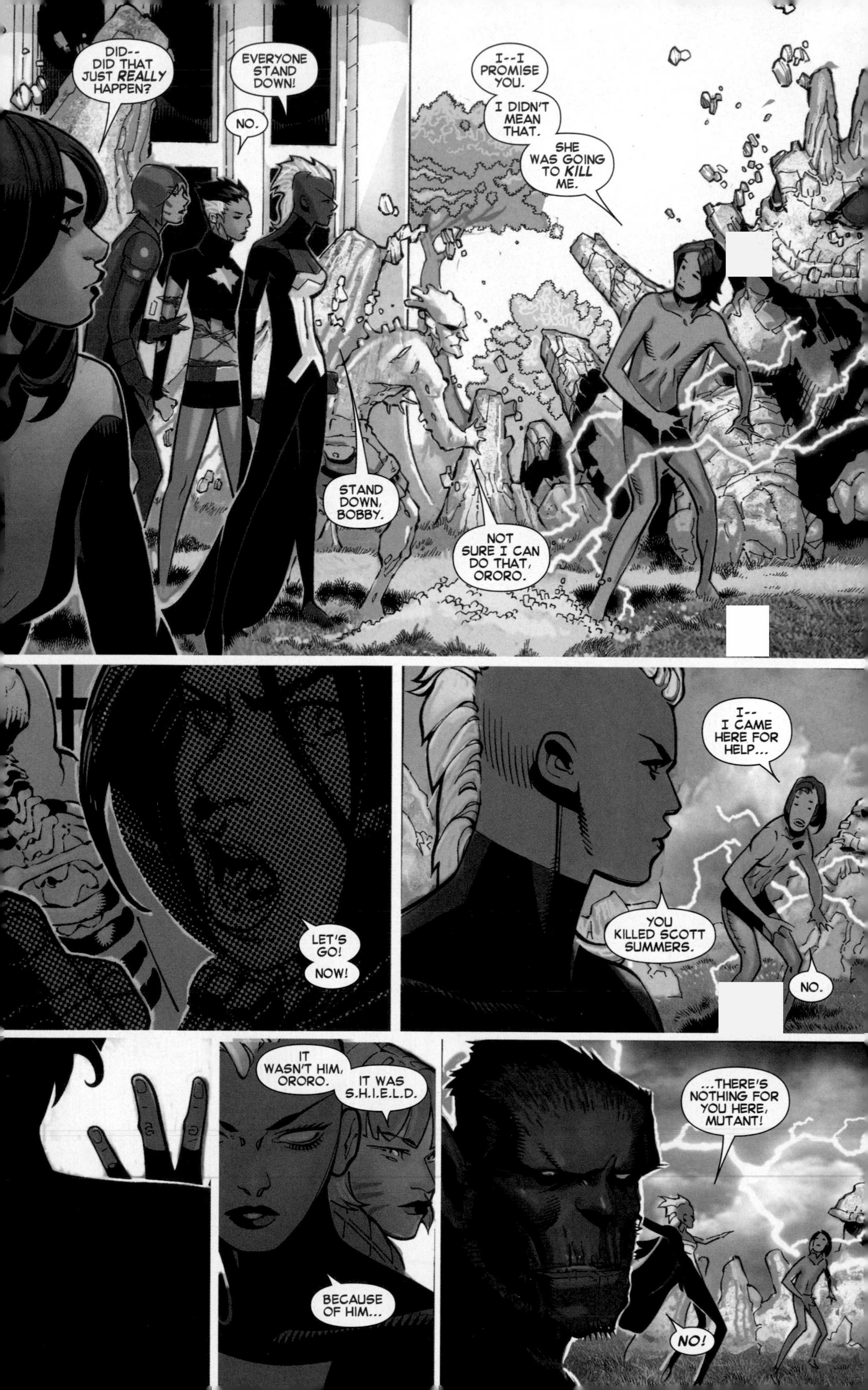
DID-- DID THAT JUST REALLY HAPPEN?
EVERYONE STAND DOWN!
NO.
I--I PROMISE YOU.
I DIDN'T MEAN THAT.
SHE WAS GOING TO KILL ME.
STAND DOWN, BOBBY.
NOT SURE I CAN DO THAT, ORORO.
LET'S GO!
NOW!
I-- I CAME HERE FOR HELP...
YOU KILLED SCOTT SUMMERS.
NO.
IT WASN'T HIM, ORORO.
IT WAS S.H.I.E.L.D.
BECAUSE OF HIM...
...THERE'S NOTHING FOR YOU HERE, MUTANT!
NO!

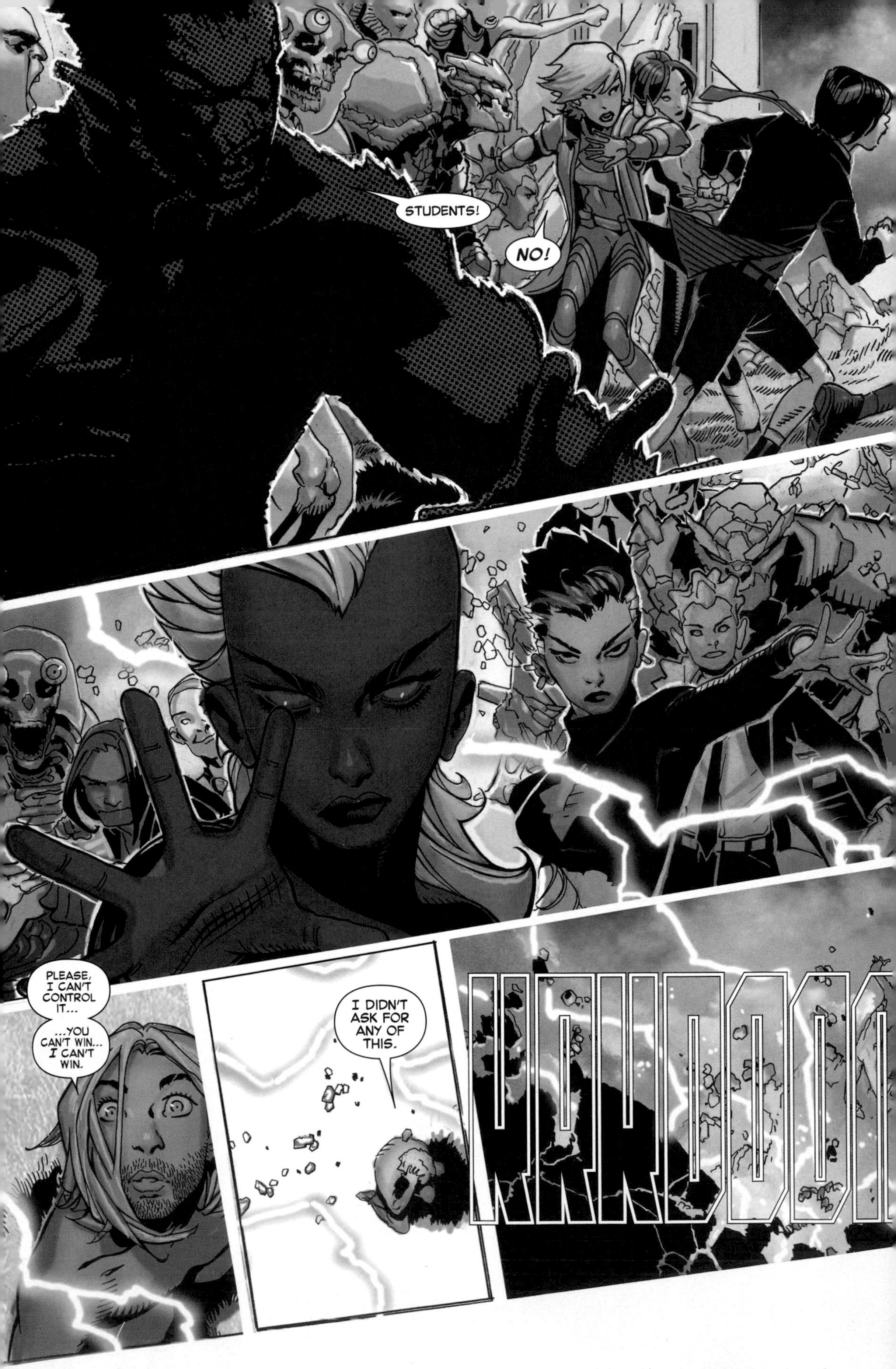
STUDENTS!
NO!
PLEASE, I CAN'T CONTROL IT...
...YOU CAN'T WIN... I CAN'T WIN.
I DIDN'T ASK FOR ANY OF THIS.

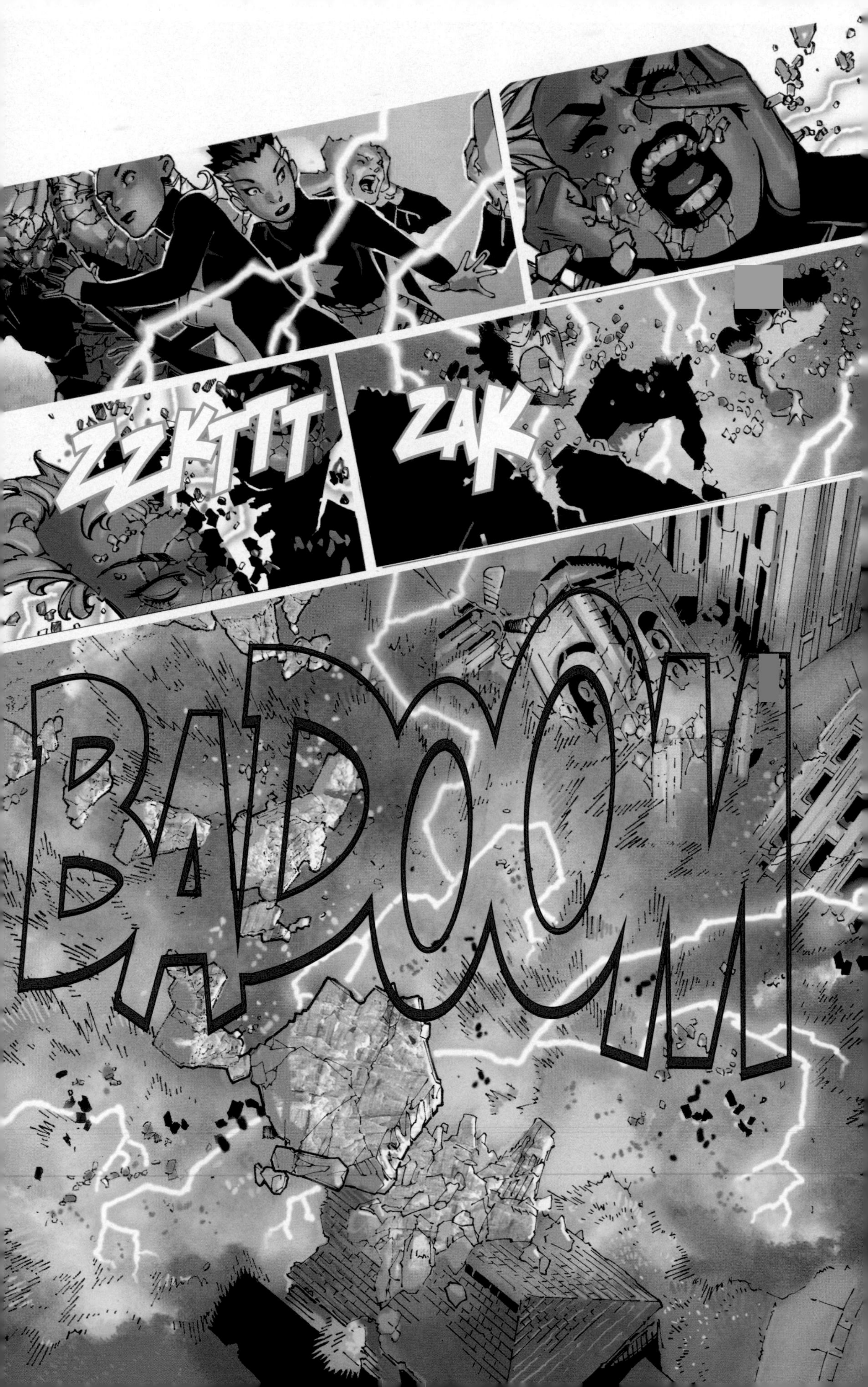
ZZKTTT
ZAK
BADOOM

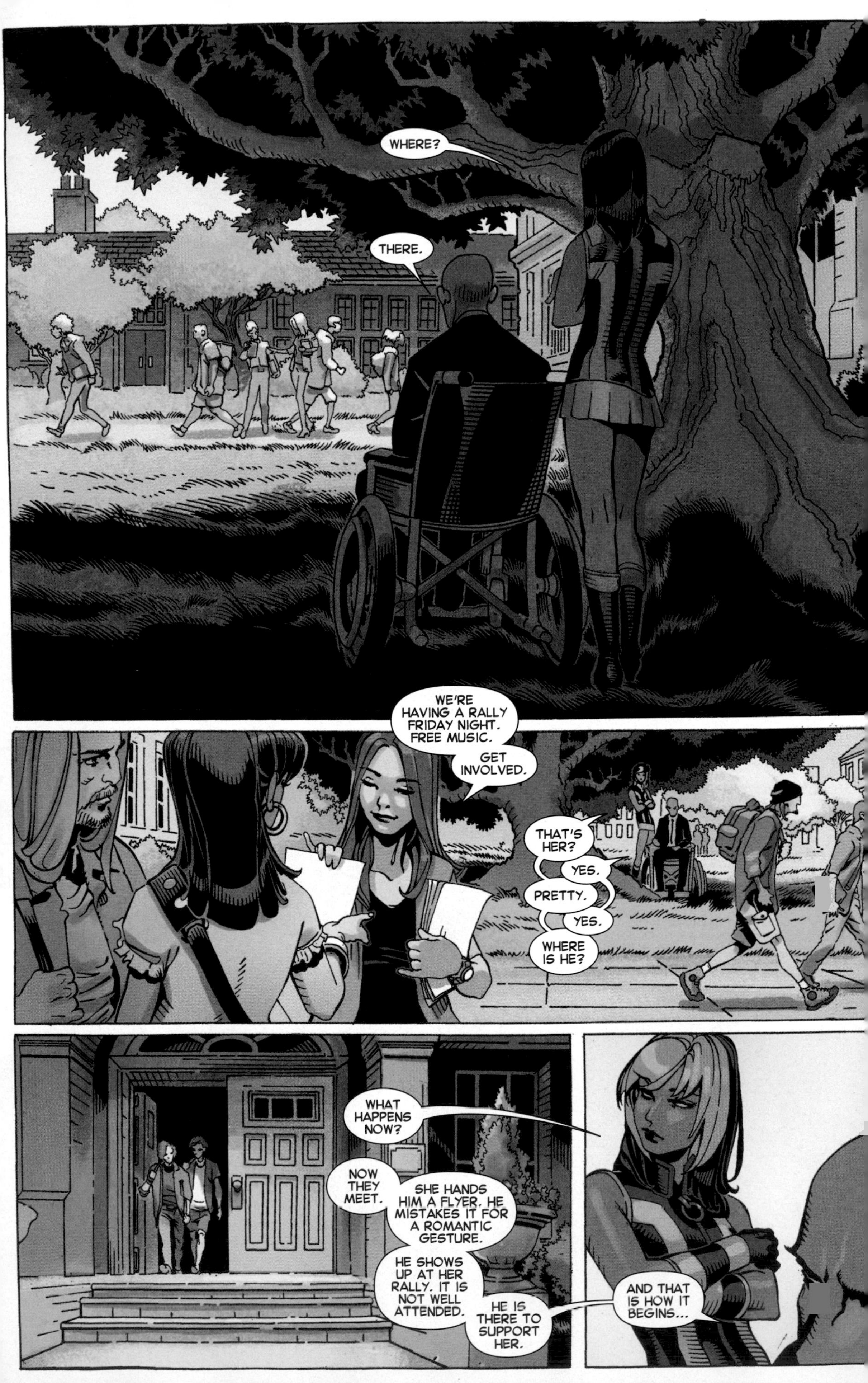

WHERE?
THERE.
WE'RE HAVING A RALLY FRIDAY NIGHT. FREE MUSIC.
GET INVOLVED.
THAT'S HER?
YES.
PRETTY.
YES.
WHERE IS HE?
WHAT HAPPENS NOW?
NOW THEY MEET.
SHE HANDS HIM A FLYER. HE MISTAKES IT FOR A ROMANTIC GESTURE.
HE SHOWS UP AT HER RALLY. IT IS NOT WELL ATTENDED.
HE IS THERE TO SUPPORT HER.
AND THAT IS HOW IT BEGINS...

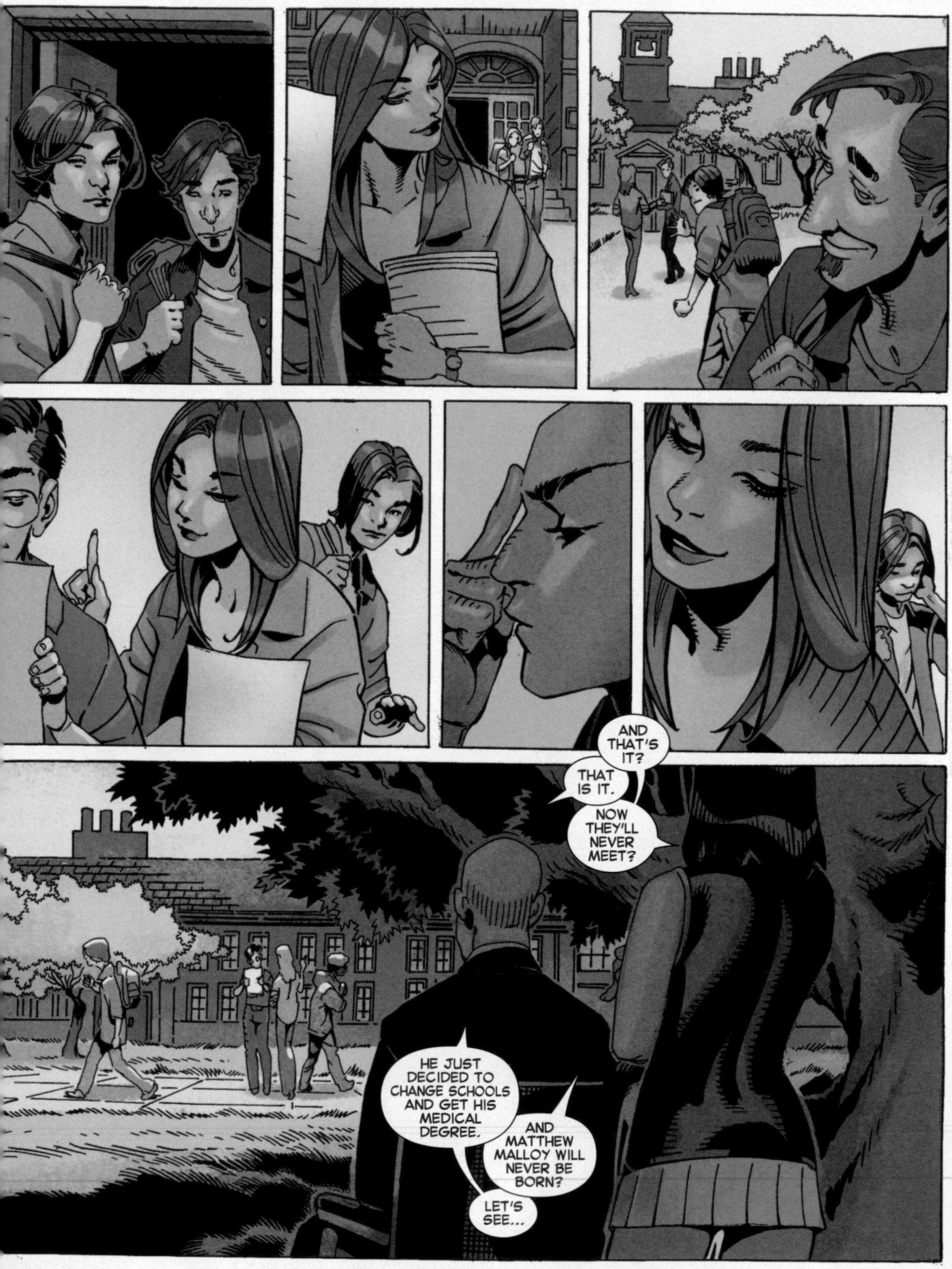
AND THAT'S IT?
THAT IS IT.
NOW THEY'LL NEVER MEET?
HE JUST DECIDED TO CHANGE SCHOOLS AND GET HIS MEDICAL DEGREE.
AND MATTHEW MALLOY WILL NEVER BE BORN?
LET'S SEE...

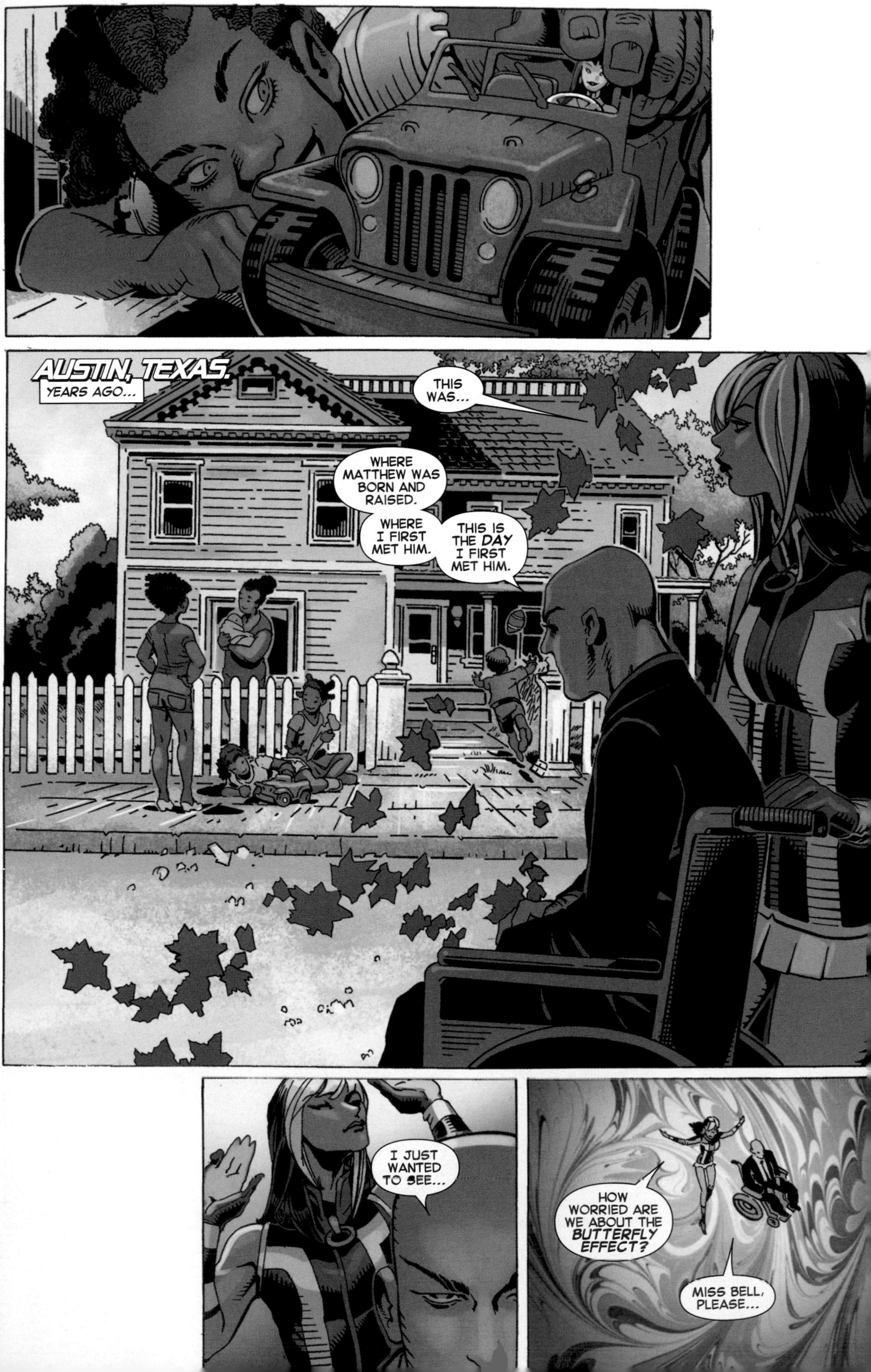
AUSTIN, TEXAS.
YEARS AGO...
THIS WAS...
WHERE MATTHEW WAS BORN AND RAISED.
WHERE I FIRST MET HIM.
THIS IS THE DAY I FIRST MET HIM.
I JUST WANTED TO SEE...
HOW WORRIED ARE WE ABOUT THE BUTTERFLY EFFECT?
MISS BELL, PLEASE...

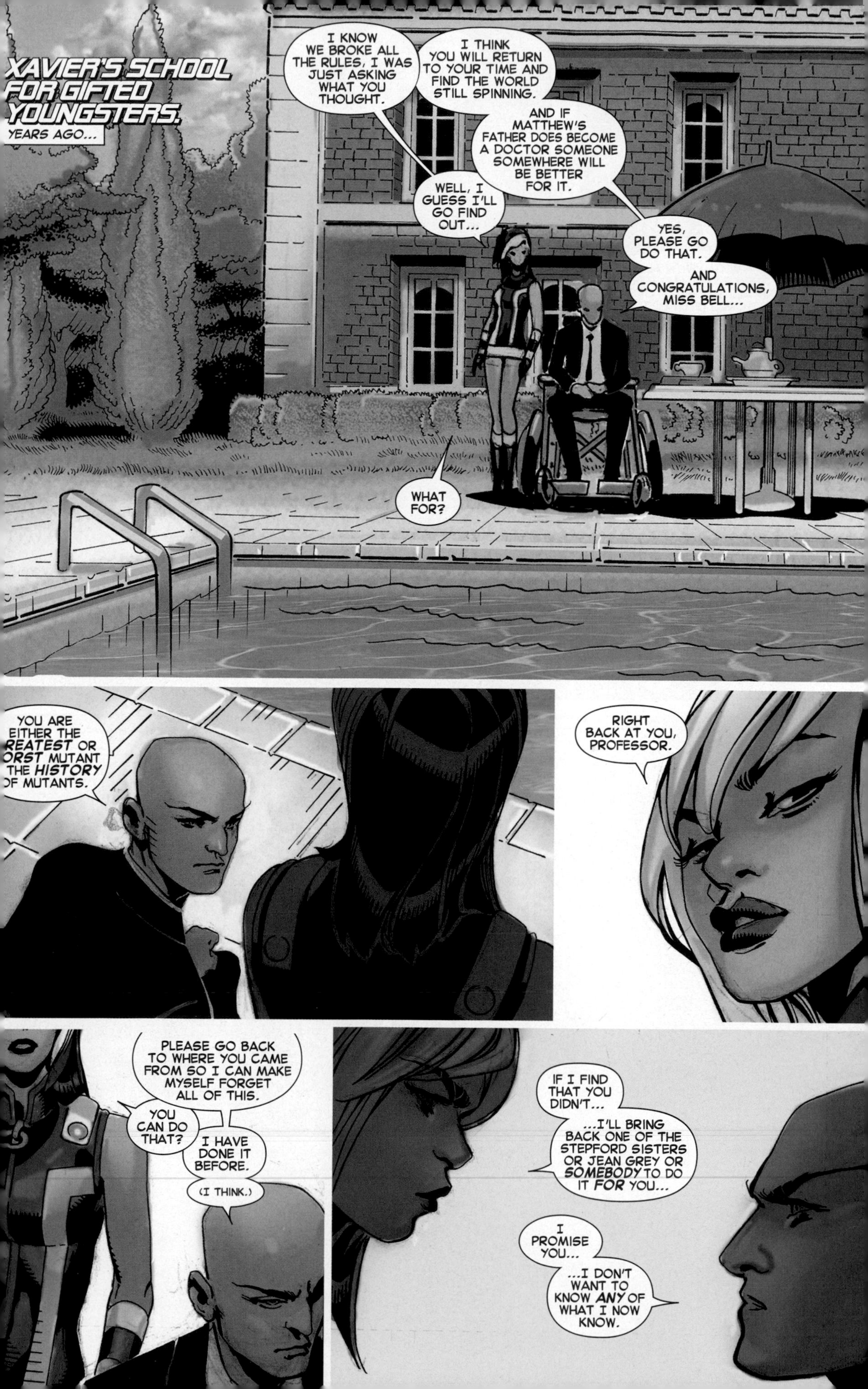
XAVIER'S SCHOOL FOR GIFTED YOUNGSTERS.
YEARS AGO...
I KNOW WE BROKE ALL THE RULES, I WAS JUST ASKING WHAT YOU THOUGHT.
I THINK YOU WILL RETURN TO YOUR TIME AND FIND THE WORLD STILL SPINNING.
AND IF MATTHEW'S FATHER DOES BECOME A DOCTOR SOMEONE SOMEWHERE WILL BE BETTER FOR IT.
WELL, I GUESS I'LL GO FIND OUT...
YES, PLEASE GO DO THAT.
AND CONGRATULATIONS, MISS BELL...
WHAT FOR?
YOU ARE EITHER THE REATEST OR ORST MUTANT THE HISTORY OF MUTANTS.
RIGHT BACK AT YOU, PROFESSOR.
PLEASE GO BACK TO WHERE YOU CAME FROM SO I CAN MAKE MYSELF FORGET ALL OF THIS.
YOU CAN DO THAT?
I HAVE DONE IT BEFORE.
(I THINK.)
IF I FIND THAT YOU DIDN'T...
...I'LL BRING BACK ONE OF THE STEPFORD SISTERS OR JEAN GREY OR SOMEBODY TO DO IT FOR YOU...
I PROMISE YOU...
...I DON'T WANT TO KNOW ANY OF WHAT I NOW KNOW.

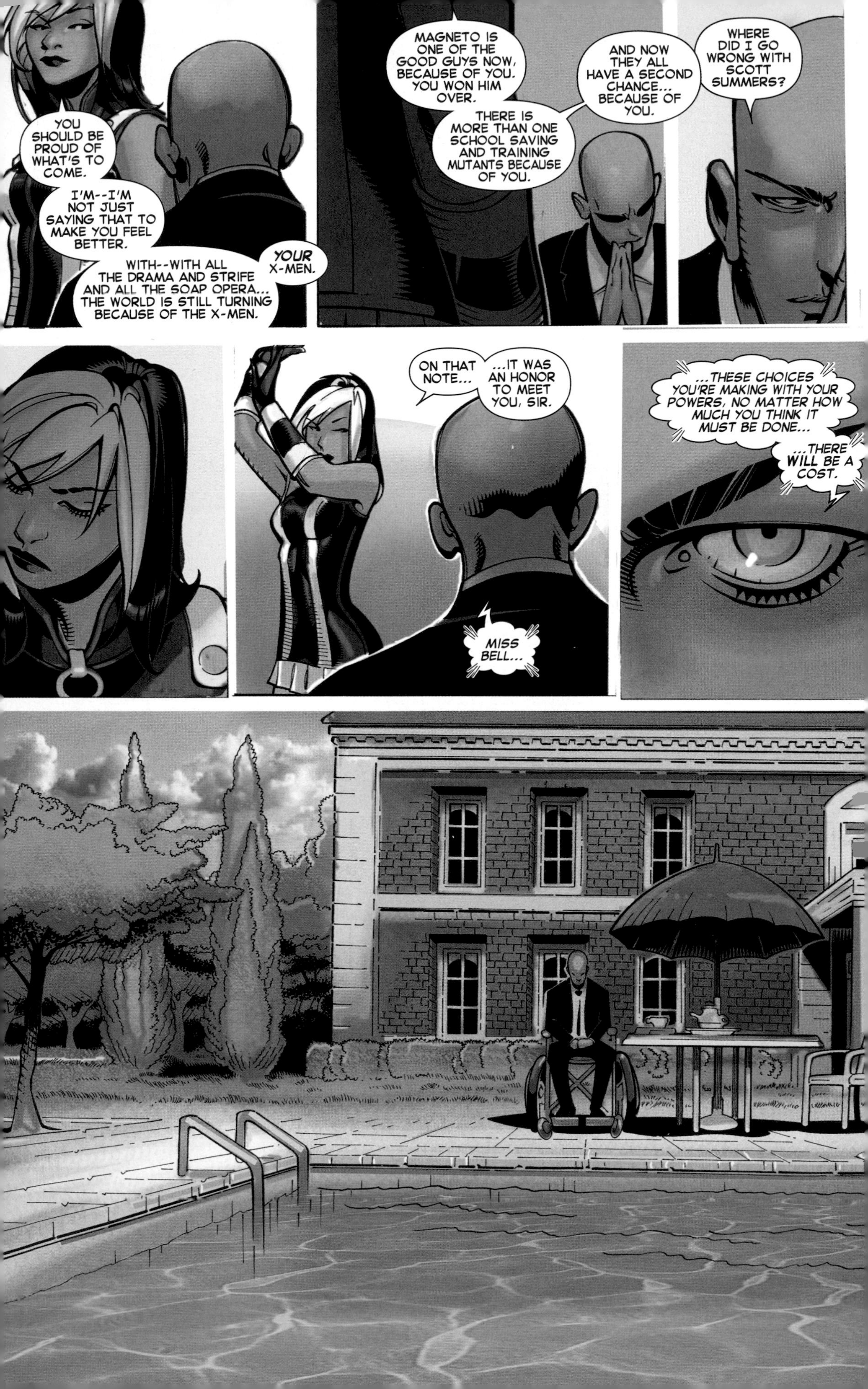

YOU SHOULD BE PROUD OF WHAT'S TO COME.
I'M--I'M NOT JUST SAYING THAT TO MAKE YOU FEEL BETTER.
WITH--WITH ALL THE DRAMA AND STRIFE AND ALL THE SOAP OPERA... THE WORLD IS STILL TURNING BECAUSE OF THE X-MEN.
YOUR X-MEN.
MAGNETO IS ONE OF THE GOOD GUYS NOW, BECAUSE OF YOU. YOU WON HIM OVER.
THERE IS MORE THAN ONE SCHOOL SAVING AND TRAINING MUTANTS BECAUSE OF YOU.
AND NOW THEY ALL HAVE A SECOND CHANCE... BECAUSE OF YOU.
WHERE DID I GO WRONG WITH SCOTT SUMMERS?
ON THAT NOTE...
...IT WAS AN HONOR TO MEET YOU, SIR.
MISS BELL...
...THESE CHOICES YOU'RE MAKING WITH YOUR POWERS, NO MATTER HOW MUCH YOU THINK IT MUST BE DONE...
...THERE WILL BE A COST.

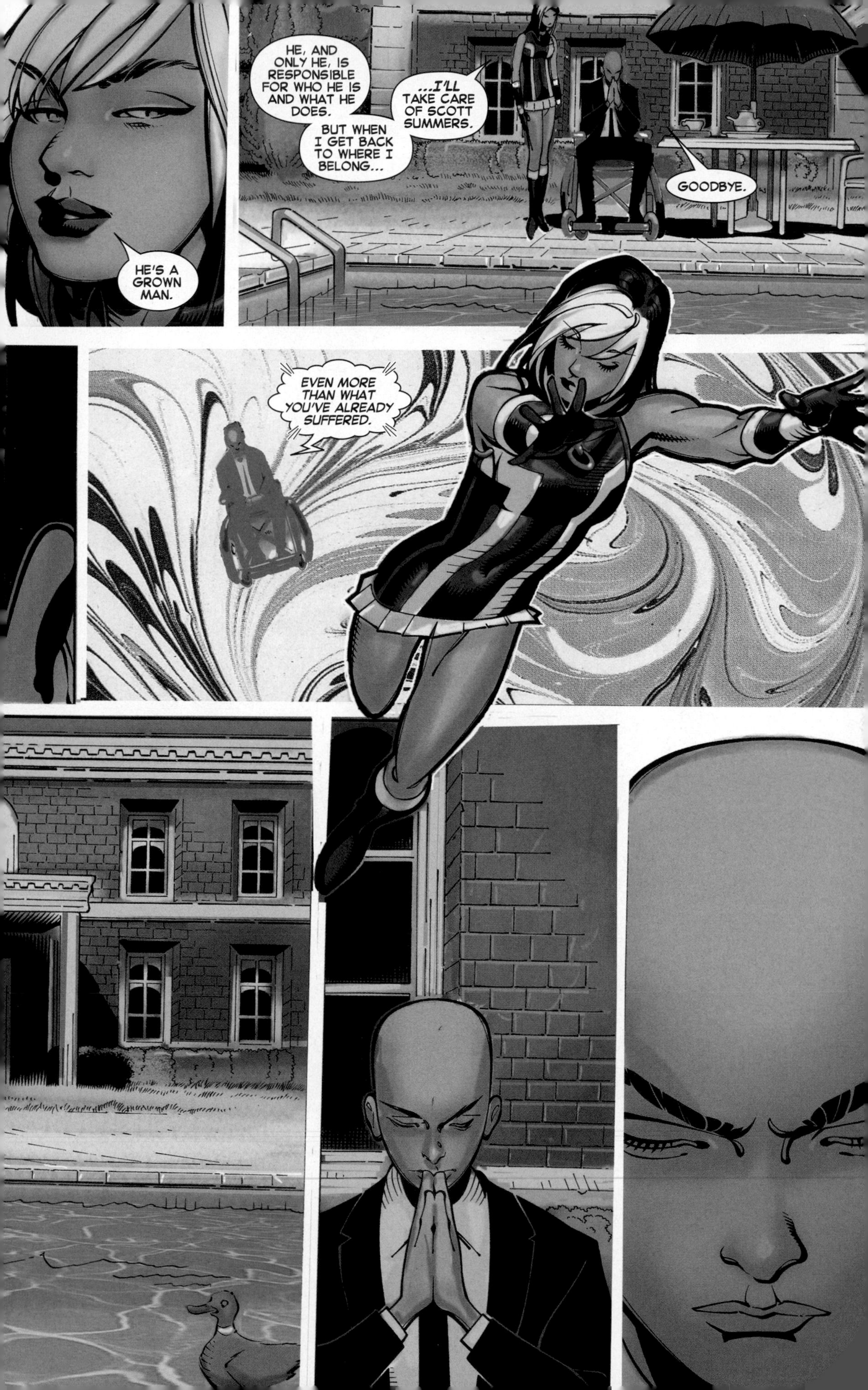
HE'S A GROWN MAN.
HE, AND ONLY HE, IS RESPONSIBLE FOR WHO HE IS AND WHAT HE DOES.
BUT WHEN I GET BACK TO WHERE I BELONG...
...I'LL TAKE CARE OF SCOTT SUMMERS.
GOODBYE.
EVEN MORE THAN WHAT YOU'VE ALREADY SUFFERED.

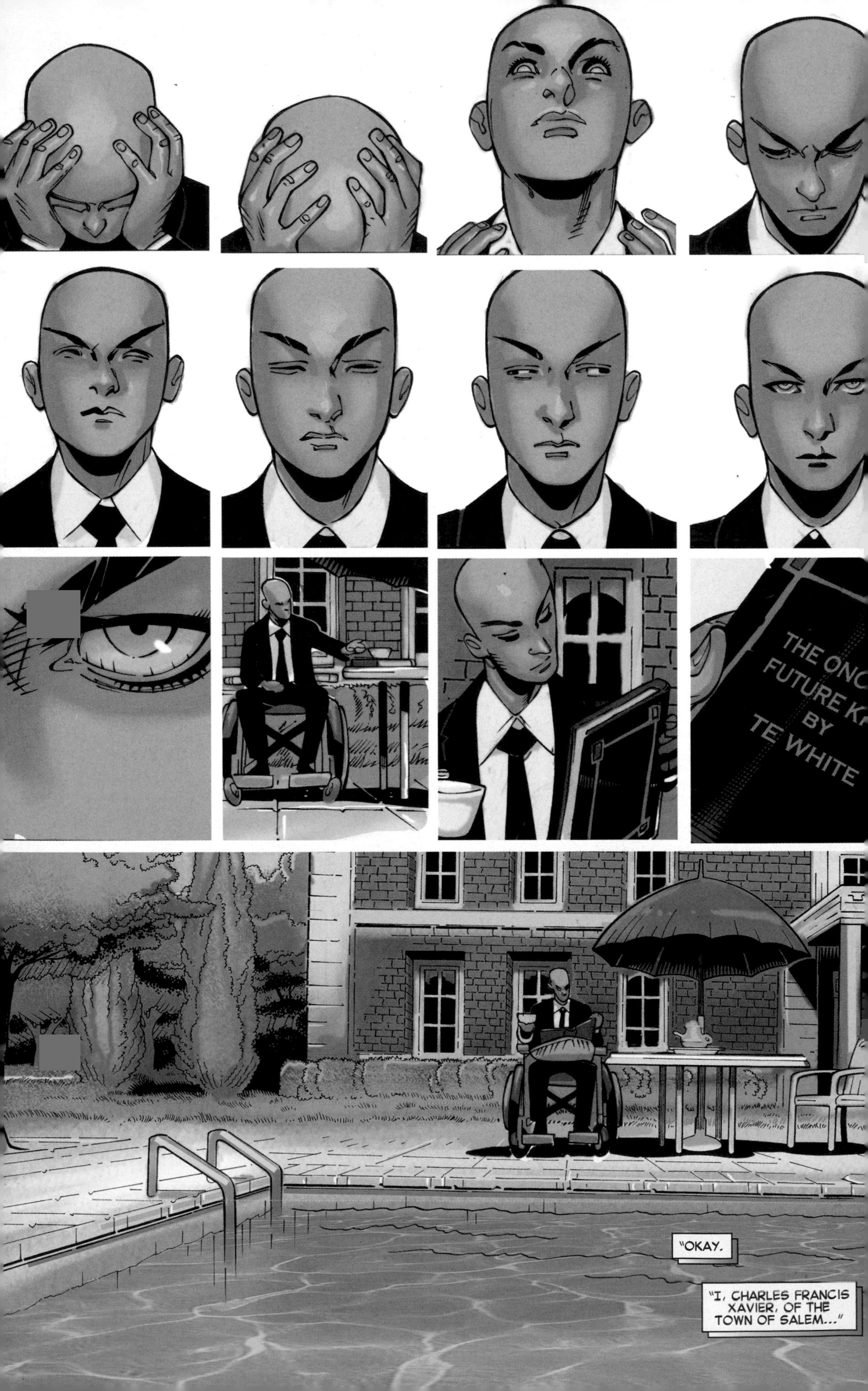
THE ONC
FUTURE K
BY
TE WHITE
"OKAY.
"I, CHARLES FRANCIS XAVIER, OF THE TOWN OF SALEM..."

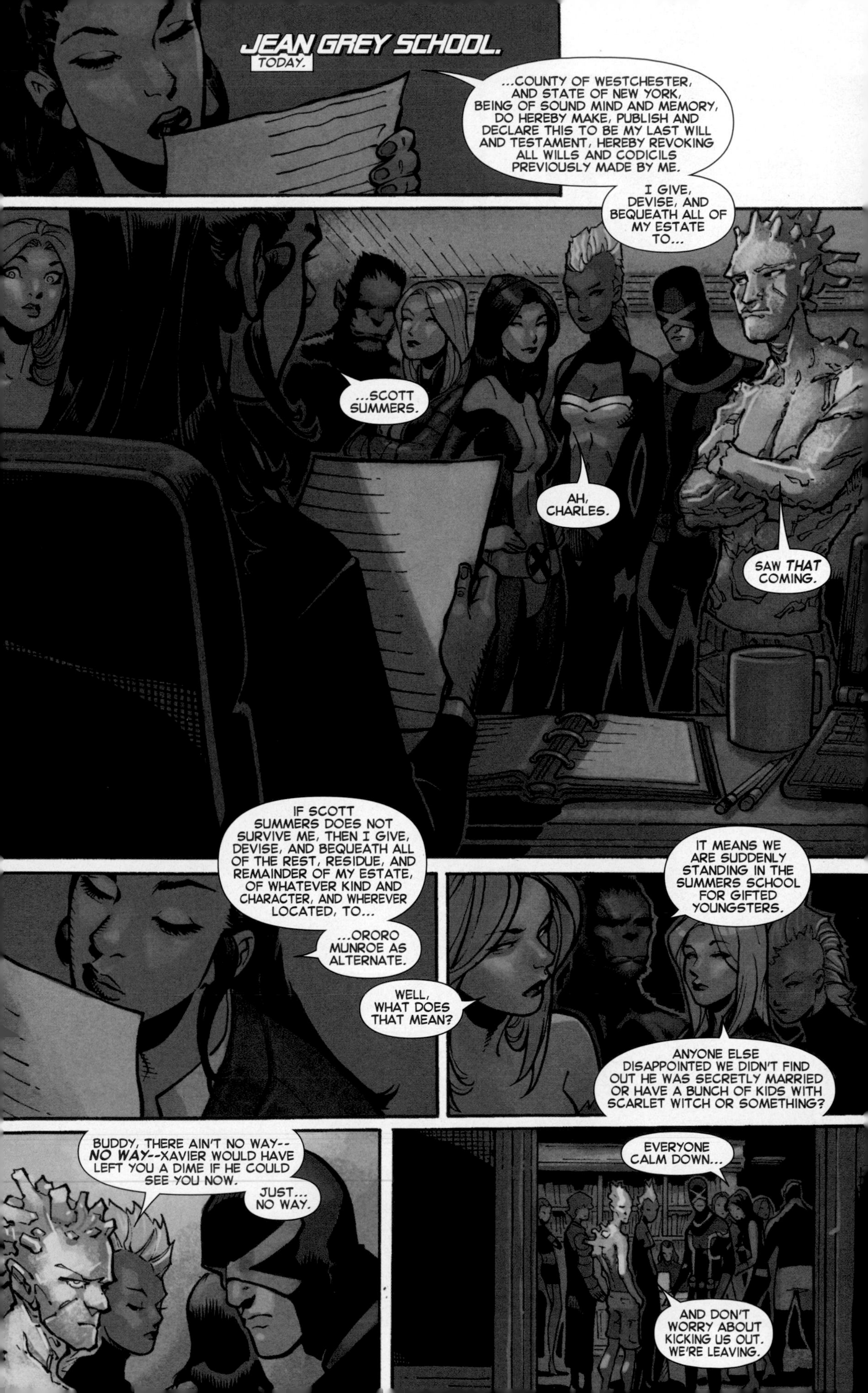
JEAN GREY SCHOOL.
TODAY.
...COUNTY OF WESTCHESTER, AND STATE OF NEW YORK, BEING OF SOUND MIND AND MEMORY, DO HEREBY MAKE, PUBLISH AND DECLARE THIS TO BE MY LAST WILL AND TESTAMENT, HEREBY REVOKING ALL WILLS AND CODICILS PREVIOUSLY MADE BY ME.
I GIVE, DEVISE, AND BEQUEATH ALL OF MY ESTATE TO...
...SCOTT SUMMERS.
AH, CHARLES.
SAW THAT COMING.
IF SCOTT SUMMERS DOES NOT SURVIVE ME, THEN I GIVE, DEVISE, AND BEQUEATH ALL OF THE REST, RESIDUE, AND REMAINDER OF MY ESTATE, OF WHATEVER KIND AND CHARACTER, AND WHEREVER LOCATED, TO...
...ORORO MUNROE AS ALTERNATE.
WELL, WHAT DOES THAT MEAN?
IT MEANS WE ARE SUDDENLY STANDING IN THE SUMMERS SCHOOL FOR GIFTED YOUNGSTERS.
ANYONE ELSE DISAPPOINTED WE DIDN'T FIND OUT HE WAS SECRETLY MARRIED OR HAVE A BUNCH OF KIDS WITH SCARLET WITCH OR SOMETHING?
BUDDY, THERE AIN'T NO WAY-- NO WAY--XAVIER WOULD HAVE LEFT YOU A DIME IF HE COULD SEE YOU NOW.
JUST... NO WAY.
EVERYONE CALM DOWN...
AND DON'T WORRY ABOUT KICKING US OUT. WE'RE LEAVING.

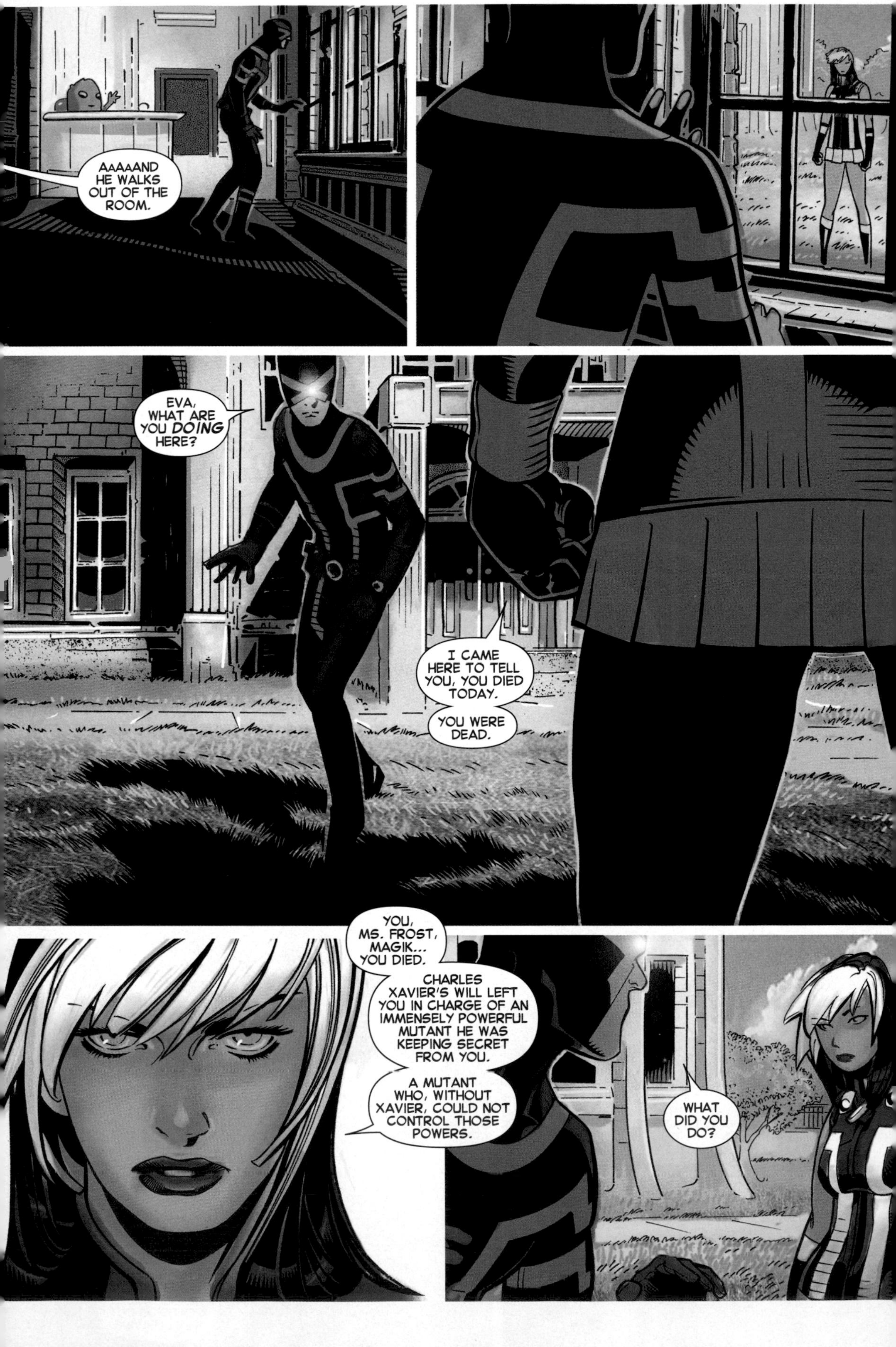

AAAAAND HE WALKS OUT OF THE ROOM.
EVA, WHAT ARE YOU *DOING* HERE?
I CAME HERE TO TELL YOU, YOU DIED TODAY.
YOU WERE DEAD.
YOU, MS. FROST, MAGIK... YOU DIED.
CHARLES XAVIER'S WILL LEFT YOU IN CHARGE OF AN IMMENSELY POWERFUL MUTANT HE WAS KEEPING SECRET FROM YOU.
A MUTANT WHO, WITHOUT XAVIER, COULD NOT CONTROL THOSE POWERS.
WHAT DID YOU DO?

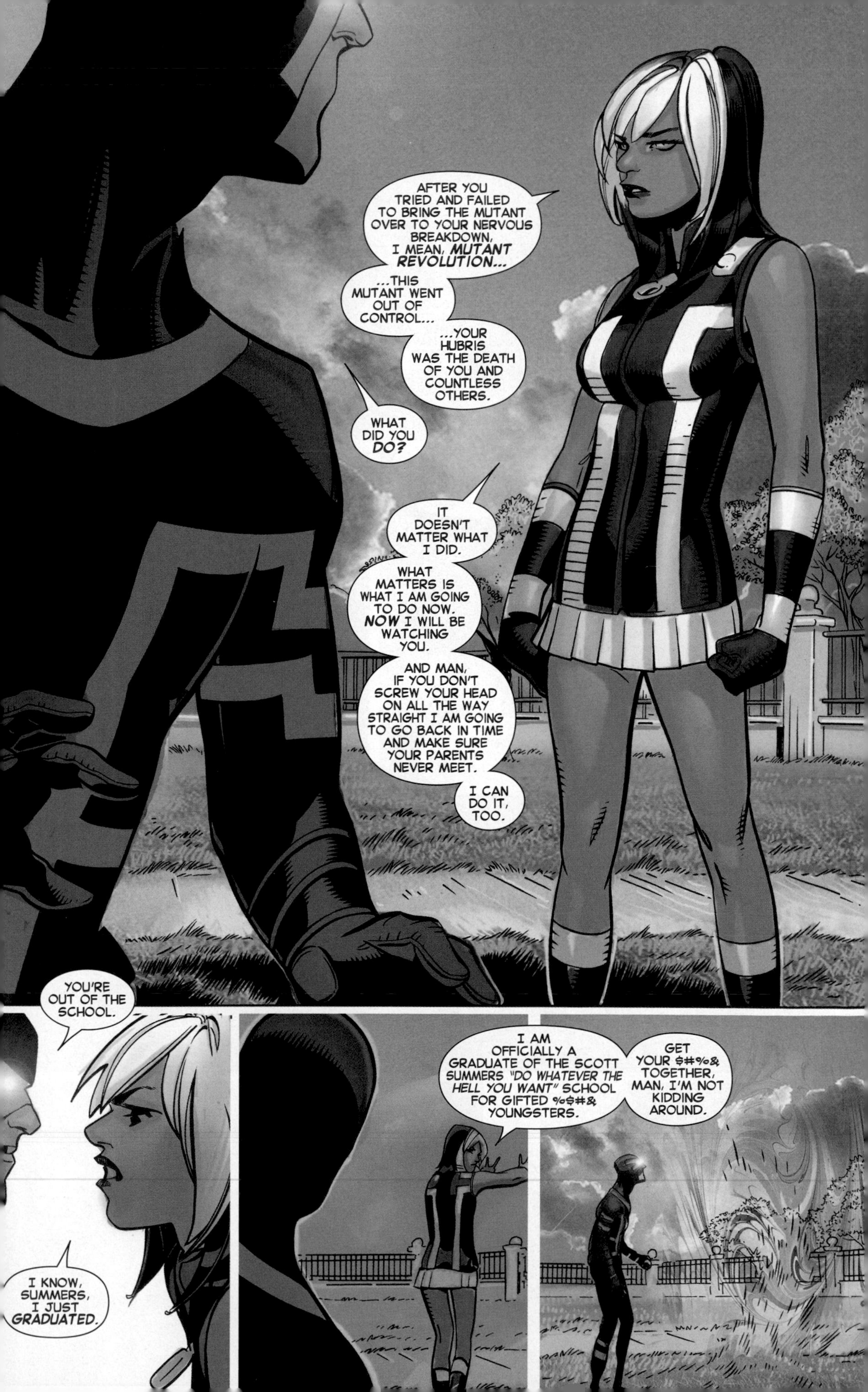

AFTER YOU TRIED AND FAILED TO BRING THE MUTANT OVER TO YOUR NERVOUS BREAKDOWN, I MEAN, *MUTANT REVOLUTION...*
...THIS MUTANT WENT OUT OF CONTROL...
...YOUR HUBRIS WAS THE DEATH OF YOU AND COUNTLESS OTHERS.
WHAT DID YOU *DO?*
IT DOESN'T MATTER WHAT I DID.
WHAT MATTERS IS WHAT I AM GOING TO DO NOW. *NOW* I WILL BE WATCHING YOU.
AND MAN, IF YOU DON'T SCREW YOUR HEAD ON ALL THE WAY STRAIGHT I AM GOING TO GO BACK IN TIME AND MAKE SURE YOUR PARENTS NEVER MEET.
I CAN DO IT, TOO.
YOU'RE OUT OF THE SCHOOL.
I KNOW, SUMMERS, I JUST *GRADUATED.*
I AM OFFICIALLY A GRADUATE OF THE SCOTT SUMMERS *"DO WHATEVER THE HELL YOU WANT"* SCHOOL FOR GIFTED %$#& YOUNGSTERS.
GET YOUR $#%& TOGETHER, MAN, I'M NOT KIDDING AROUND.

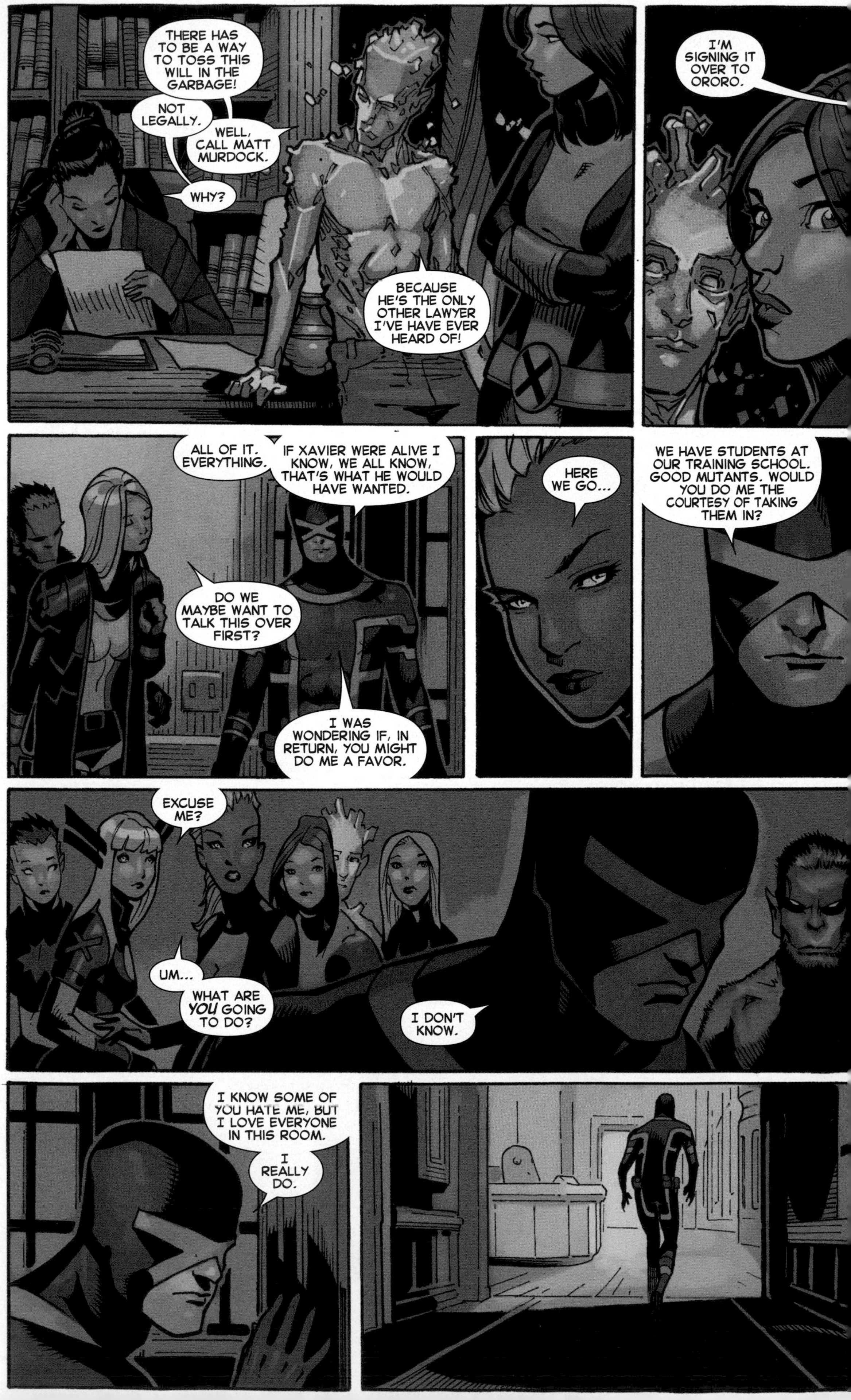
THERE HAS TO BE A WAY TO TOSS THIS WILL IN THE GARBAGE!
NOT LEGALLY.
WELL, CALL MATT MURDOCK.
WHY?
BECAUSE HE'S THE ONLY OTHER LAWYER I'VE HAVE EVER HEARD OF!
I'M SIGNING IT OVER TO ORORO.
ALL OF IT. EVERYTHING.
IF XAVIER WERE ALIVE I KNOW, WE ALL KNOW, THAT'S WHAT HE WOULD HAVE WANTED.
DO WE MAYBE WANT TO TALK THIS OVER FIRST?
I WAS WONDERING IF, IN RETURN, YOU MIGHT DO ME A FAVOR.
HERE WE GO...
WE HAVE STUDENTS AT OUR TRAINING SCHOOL. GOOD MUTANTS. WOULD YOU DO ME THE COURTESY OF TAKING THEM IN?
EXCUSE ME?
UM...
WHAT ARE *YOU* GOING TO DO?
I DON'T KNOW.
I KNOW SOME OF YOU HATE ME, BUT I LOVE EVERYONE IN THIS ROOM.
I REALLY DO.

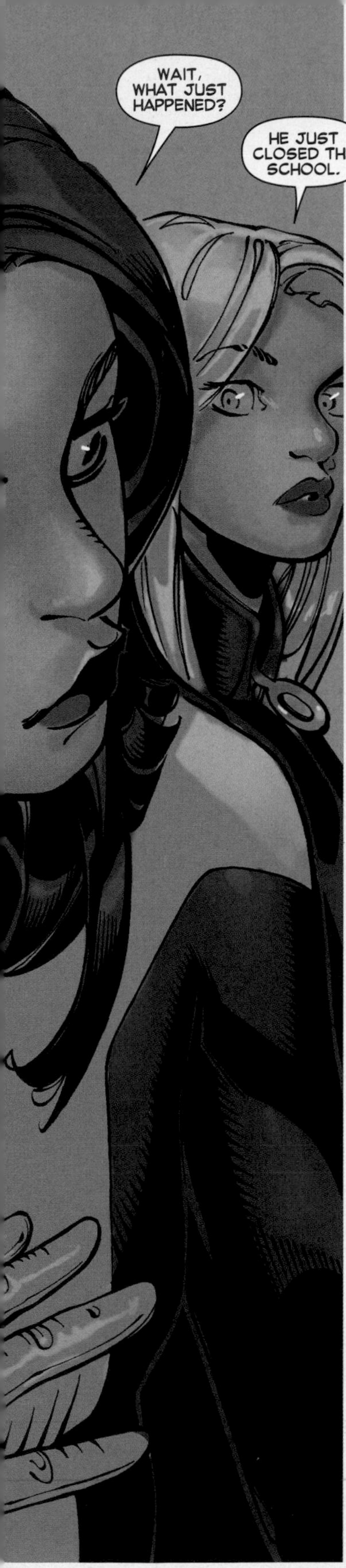
WAIT, WHAT JUST HAPPENED?
HE JUST CLOSED THE SCHOOL.

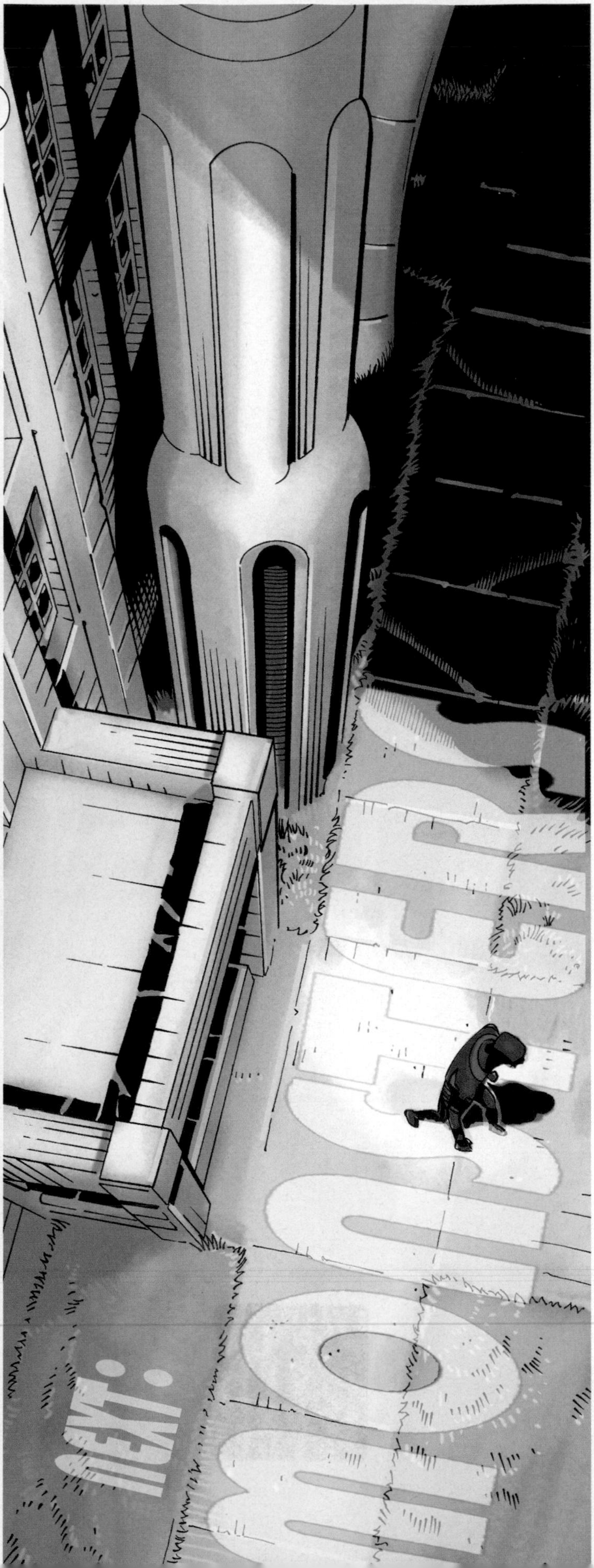
NEXT: MONSTERS

"Hold on to your hat because this is one heck of an X-Men book." – *IGN.com*

New York Times Best Seller!

"Bendis is off to a great start." — ComicList.com

REVOLUTION

BENDIS  **MARVEL NOW!**  BACHALO IRVING

AR

**UNCANNY X-MEN VOL. 1: REVOLUTION**
978-0-7851-6702-0 • DEC130777

"The setup and payoff will rock your socks, so hold on to them too." – *IGN.co*

© 2013 MARVEL

## TO REDEEM YOUR CODE
## FOR A FREE DIGITAL COPY:

1. GO TO MARVEL.COM/REDEEM.
   OFFER EXPIRES ON 3/25/17.

2. FOLLOW THE ON-SCREEN INSTRUCTIONS
   TO REDEEM YOUR DIGITAL COPY.

3. LAUNCH THE MARVEL COMICS APP TO
   READ YOUR COMIC NOW!

4. YOUR DIGITAL COPY WILL BE FOUND
   UNDER THE *MY COMICS* TAB.

5. READ & ENJOY!

YOUR FREE DIGITAL COPY WILL BE AVAILABLE (

TMAELPLDZ87V

MARVEL COMICS APP
FOR APPLE® IOS DEVICES

MARVEL COMICS APP
FOR ANDROID™ DEVICES

Digital copy requires purchase of a print copy. Download code valid for
use only. Digital copy available on the date print copy is available. Availa
ity time of the digital copy may vary on the date of release. TM & © Ma
& Subs. Apple is a trademark of Apple Inc., registered in the U.S. and ot
countries. Android is a trademark of Google Inc.

3  1901  05267  4522